THE Fashion ENCYCLOPEDIA

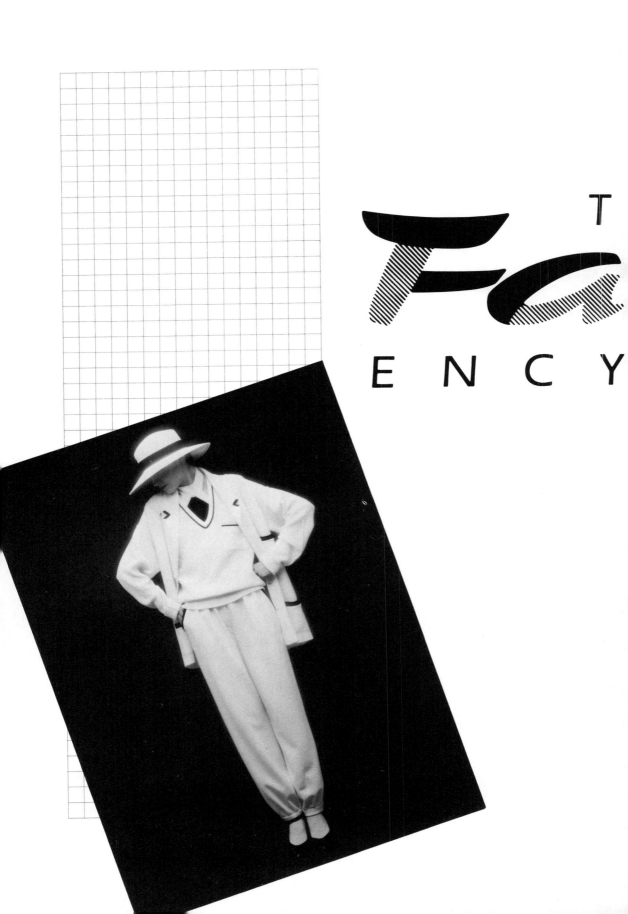

An Essential Guide to Everything
You Need to Know About Clothes

HE
shion
CLOPEDIA

Catherine
Houck

St. Martin's Press
New York

For information, write: St. Martin's Press
175 Fifth Avenue, New York, N.Y. 10010
Manufactured in the United States of America

Library of Congress Cataloging in Publication Data

Houck, Catherine.
The fashion encyclopedia.

1. Fashion—Dictionaries. 2. Clothing and dress
—Dictionaries.   I. Title.
TT503.H68   646'.34   81-21494
ISBN 0-312-28400-4   AACR2
ISBN 0-312-28401-2 (pbk.)

Design by Deborah Daly and Kingsley Parker

10   9   8   7   6

First Edition

The *Silk* entry first appeared as an article in *Cosmopolitan* Magazine.

Many of the illustrations were drawn by Laura Kagel.

INTRODUCTION

Some women just seem naturally to know all about clothes. They *understand* the language in fashion ads, aren't at all slowed down by words such as charmeuse or Moygashel or intarsia sweater. They know what Sant'Angelo does best, and the difference between a good and a less-than-good cashmere sweater. When a blob of ketchup lands with a splat on a silk blouse, they don't faint—the spot is dispatched in seconds. They know what makes a pair of gloves warm enough to wear when bicycling in 20-degree weather, what to wear to a black-tie dinner party at someone's house, and not only what Top-Siders are, but where to find them. Even more enviably, these savvy women seem to spend less on their clothes than anybody else. They pull Sonia Rykiel sweaters out of thrift-shop bins, know exactly when minks are on sale, and aren't the least bit afraid of buying $60 sweaters (reduced from $200) smeared with lipstick.

This book gathers together all those elusive tidbits of information about clothes that up to now have been the province of "people who know." The research done here is *not* one person's opinion on how you should dress but is the result of hundreds of interviews with manufacturers, designers, store buyers, trade associations, and other women. I've tried to clarify all those French words, dressmaker terms, fabric names, and care instructions that we hear and see constantly but which fashion magazines or newspaper ads seldom pause to explain. I've tracked down the most knowledgeable people in the industry to find out the definitive answers on whether or not silks, cashmeres, mohair can be washed. I've gotten the inside stuff about fabrics, such as what's so wonderful about Irish linen and why everybody is buying Gore-Tex raincoats. You'll learn why certain products have devoted cult followings, as most of us are supposed to know (but don't) what's so special about a Frye boot, a Chanel suit, a Coach bag. And you'll have fingertip information on all the important designers. I've included designers because talking about clothes without mentioning designers makes about as much sense as talking about art without mentioning artists. I don't expect most readers want to spend $500 for a Chloé skirt, but when you can tell the names of the best designers from those of sell-and-run manufacturers, you can often recognize terrific bargains on sale racks and in thrift shops.

The sages have always said that knowledge is power. And this truth certainly applies to dealing with clothes.

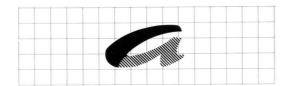

Acetate

A fiber made from wood pulp, acetate is the silky fabric most used in linings. Because it moves sensuously with the body, you'll also see it in taffeta and crêpe disco clothes, a trend that's more pretty than comfortable. Like most man-made fibers, acetate doesn't absorb perspiration and allow it to evaporate; if you perspire, you'll feel clammy. On the plus side, acetate is inexpensive, mildew-resistant, and lovely to touch.

Trade Names

In addition to their generic names, such as "polyester" or "acrylic," synthetic fibers are given trade names by individual manufacturers. Most common names for acetate are: Du Pont's "Acele," Celanese's "Arnel," Eastman Kodak's "Estron."

Care

Clothes with acetate linings should be dry cleaned. With all-acetate garments, dry cleaning is preferred not because acetate won't wash nicely but because ironing is such a pain. You should press while still damp, on the wrong side, with a cool iron; if the fabric dries, you'll have to wet it and start all over again to get out all the wrinkles. *Never spray acetate with perfume*, much of which contains a chemical called acetone that dissolves acetate. Spray yourself *before* getting dressed.

Acrylic

All those luscious sweaters you could swear were wool are instead made from acrylic, as are athletic socks, jogging suits, and the fleecy stuff inside gloves and bedroom slippers. In spite of the chilly sound of its ingredients—coal, air, water, petroleum, and limestone—acrylic is the warmest synthetic.

Should You Buy Acrylic Clothes?

Yes, if you're allergic to wool, don't like the scratchiness of inexpensive wool, or find that acrylic sweaters and knee-highs don't absorb as much moisture from the skin, thus being less drying for the skin. Yes, if the price difference between acrylic and natural fibers makes a difference. No, if you'll be running three miles or perspiring in an overheated office building. Like most synthetics, acrylic causes clamminess because it doesn't absorb perspiration and then allow it to evaporate. Other undesirable qualities: perspiration odors stick to synthetics more tenaciously than to natural fibers. So does dirt; light-colored cuffs get dingy fast, and a white acrylic sweater will take on a grayish hue long before a wool one does. On the other hand, colored acrylics don't show dirt, can be beautiful, don't mildew, and are mothproof, wrinkleproof, and often machine washable. Look especially for Marisa Christina's stylish handwoven acrylics for $40 to $60.

Trade Names

Monsanto's "Acrilan," American Cyanamid's "Creslan," Dow's "Zefran," Du Pont's "Orlon." Orlon, introduced in 1952, is the oldest acrylic; by 1956, more than seventy million Orlon sweaters had been sold.

Care

Unless machine laundering is okayed on label, acrylic sweaters should be washed by hand in warm water. They must be dried flat or else they'll stretch. You can also dry clean. Never put white or light acrylic out to dry in bright sunshine—brighteners applied during manufacturing tend to yellow in as little as thirty minutes, and never be white again. Fuzzballs are harder to remove on acrylics than on wools. Try a clothes brush first, then a dry sponge; as a last resort, shave them off with an electric shaver.

Adolpho

Nancy Reagan's favorite suit designer, Adolpho is an aristocratic Cuban who's lived in New York since 1949, and is known as an American designer. He made his first splash in the mid-1960s designing hats—huge fur berets, romantic Cossack hats, Panama straws—but soon became best known for his Chanel-inspired suits, which have now become a favorite lunching uniform of the international socialite set. Jackets are usually cardiganlike heavy knits with braiding around the edges; skirts, neither terribly full nor pencil-thin, are cut in a style becoming to the mature figure. You can find his suits and his equally coveted black rayon velvet evening skirts in the designer section of Saks Fifth Avenue and other department stores, or make an appointment to visit his 538 Madison Avenue boutique in New York (212 688-4410), where clothes are fitted on you in the fabric of your choice. Suits start at $500.

Adri

(Adrienne Steckling) believes that clothes should be soft, rounded, and supple to relieve the angularity and hard edges of modern life. Her moderately expensive evening separates inspired by athletic gear sell well, as do her roomy sweaters and blouses stitched with gold thread. This up-and-coming New York designer is originally from St. Joseph, Missouri.

After-Dinner Shoes

are evening shoes sold in the lingerie section of department stores for half the price you'll find evening shoes elsewhere. You can find silver and gold sandals, satin pumps with bows, and metallic or satin mules for under $30. Many of these shoes are made of polyurethane as unyielding as a table top, but others are made of kid leather. Though perhaps not formal enough to wear with a ballgown, they can be worn to black-tie parties and dinners with evening separates (see BLACK TIE) and certainly at home with a dressy hostess gown.

Alpaca

A member of the South American camel family, this nimble animal lives high in the Andes Mountains of Peru, where Indians have domesticated it for its fleece. Alpaca hair, which is shorn by hand every spring, grows as long as thirty inches and makes a lustrous, water-repellent wool. Attempts to breed alpacas in America and Australia have failed dismally, and the world's entire supply of fleece still comes exclusively from Peru, just as it has since alpacas were first discovered there by Europeans in 1836.

You're most likely to find alpaca blended with regular wool, or with the hair of llamas, in expensive, lightweight coats and jackets. A pure alpaca coat will cost around $300 in department stores. Gorgeous handwoven alpaca ponchos can be found in South American handicraft shops or import shops for $50 or $60, a real bargain in terms of the amount of luxurious fabric. Such import shops seem to abound around college campuses.

Amber

is fossilized resin from trees dating back fifty million years, to a time when horses the size of house cats and birds almost as big as airplanes populated the earth. Ancient Greeks thought this translucent, yellow-brown stone to be pieces of solidified sunshine, broken off from the sun as it sank into the earth. True amber comes only from the Baltic countries and the Dominican Republic. Baltic amber is considered the most beautiful, but the Dominican variety is also lovely. Much "amber" advertised by dealers today is not amber at all but copal, which is the resin of living trees currently grown in African orchards. When you're looking at milky-colored balls called simply "amber," not "Baltic amber" or "Dominican amber," it's probably copal. Baltic amber is not a common substance in contemporary jewelry; you'll find it mostly in antiques, and can expect to pay $100 or more for a necklace. Amber in which you can see fossilized insects is most prized of all.

Care
Wash in warm water with Lux, wipe with mineral oil or baby oil, and remove excess with tissue.

Angora
we owe to an incredibly cuddly rabbit originally from the Madeira Islands, now raised mostly in France and China. You'll find angora fleece most often blended in sweaters in a combination of 70 percent lambswool, 20 percent angora, and 10 percent nylon, though pure angora is available also. One-hundred-percent angora sweaters are softer than cashmere but not as sturdy; you can find them in a $60 price range, though designers such as Joan Vass and Missoni ask hundreds. Angora's fluffiness makes it irresistibly touchable on anyone young-looking and thin; on large women angora adds bulk.

Care
Pure angora as well as blends should hand-wash nicely if washed in warm, not hot, water and laid flat to dry. However, not all angora is properly pre-shrunk, which means some sweaters emerge from hand-washing or dry cleaning a size smaller. Buy pure angora only from a reputable store, one which will refund your money if the sweater shrinks. If label says Dry Clean Only, dry clean the first time it needs laundering so if anything goes wrong, you can't be accused of not following instructions.

Shedding
The blends don't shed, but pure angora leaves a trail of silky little hairs behind. If you're buying a white pure angora sweater, wear with a white wool skirt; ditto black with black, and so on.

Annie Hall Look
When Diane Keaton starred in Woody Allen's Academy Award-winning movie in 1977, she changed fashion. Before Annie Hall, we had loosened up enough to forget about wearing matching shoes and handbags, but still wore an Indian peasant blouse with an Indian skirt, a St. Laurent sweater with St. Laurent pants. Besides launching baggy pants, layered skirts, blouses, sweaters and vests, and challis skirts and shawls, Annie Hall launched eclectic dressing. Now, a silk blouse and pearl earrings are more chic with jeans than is a cowboy shirt. *Nobody* wears St. Laurent with St. Laurent, and you're likely to find your hostess wearing the tattersall cowboy shirt she no longer wears with jeans belted over a floor-length skirt of velvet.

Anthony, John

An American designer, in his early forties, whose suits and coats are bought for their fine tailoring, simple lines, and subdued coloring—for which he's been called "the minimalist of Seventh Avenue." You can find Anthonys in the $200–$300 price range (less on sale), or pay up to four figures for one of his beaded evening dresses. His beige, navy, or mauve silk suits, worn with a blouse a shade lighter in color, are favorite ensembles of executive women.

Antique Clothes

More and more people are catching on to the charm of clothes from other eras. "For years, nobody understood old clothes," says dealer Pam Coglan of Rutherford, New Jersey, who sells her wares at antique fairs. "They were associated with hand-me-downs and poverty. People wanted sparkling new things."

That attitude has changed drastically. Today "vintage clothing" is worn by Ali McGraw, Barbra Streisand, and Bette Midler. Brooke Shields wore an antique Victorian dress to the 1980 Academy Awards, Erica Jong goes to autograph parties in a 1930s silk dress, and Jill Clayburgh wears as many antique clothes as new ones in the film *It's My Turn*. With glamorous actresses now appearing in old clothes, women who never noticed them before are prowling through antique clothing stores, flea markets, and rummage sales, grubbing through attics and old cedar chests, and often they find that clothes from past decades are more finely made than today's. Says New York's Meredith Fiel of Best of Everything, "I sell silk crêpe de Chine blouses from the forties for thirty-five dollars, and they usually have shoulder pads, fagoting, embroidery, beads, or hand-carved buttons."

Some people prefer to shop at stores such as New York's Jezebel, where clothes are in mint condition but prices are sky-high; others prefer flea markets and antique fairs. All dealers complain that supplies are "drying up," but here, at present, is what's being sold.

For Summer Victorian (pre-1900) and Edwardian (pre-World War I) whites, with biggest demand for high-necked blouses with lots of lace ($60 up). Buttons are usually mother-of-pearl, not plastic, as in department-store imitations. Victorian dresses ($100 way up) aren't easy to sell because they have waists the size of drainpipes. Bigger sizes are often bought by brides, as they make the most romantic of wedding dresses, and—unlike conventional wedding gowns of satin and with chantilly lace trains—can be worn afterwards as party dresses.

Bias-cut cotton and rayon dresses from the 1930s and 1940s, with their shoulder pads and slinky skirts ($40–$60), are also much in demand, as are soft white cotton batiste blouses ($15–$35) from the same period. Gaily colored Hawaiian blouses with banana plants, orchids, and palm trees ($35) from the 1950s have inspired a whole generation of imitations, and for at-home wear, look at the 1940s chintz housecoats ($40–$60). Clingy, glamorous rayon or silk damask peignoirs with plunging necklines and shoulder pads ($40–$60) are sensuous and romantic, as are silk or rayon tap pants, camisoles, and slips ($15–$30) from the 1940s.

Snowy white cotton petticoats ($30–$50) often have drawstring waists, good for antique dealers because they'll fit a wide range of women, and also good for women who are chronic dieters and never know what size they'll be from one month to the next. You can wear one as a skirt in summer, or peeking out a few inches from under a skirt. Also look for white cotton nightgowns—belt them, hem a bit, and wear as dresses—safari jackets, pure silk shirts and blouses to wear with the sleeves rolled up, and old shawls to wear on cool evenings.

In Winter Petticoats can also be worn in winter, peeking out from under winter skirts. For summer, they were made of cotton or light muslin; in winter, from warm flannel or quilted cotton.

Nineteen-forties wool coats trimmed in fur go for around $80; silver fox boas, glass-eyed head and tail intact, go for $60 and are worn over Joan Crawford suits ($60 up) from the 1940s. (Dealers often have "never-worn" suits from this era.) "Tailoring was more important then," says Pam Coglan. "They used beautiful wool gabardine or rayon, and lined them meticulously." Also look for soft wool reindeer sweaters from the 1950s, and sweaters with beautiful geometric patterns.

Another fast-selling item is antique velvet. In the 1920s, silk velvet, now rare, was used; in the 1930s and 1940s, designers used rayon velvet, which drapes beautifully and has a luster seldom found in today's

"Antique clothes are most interesting when worn with contrasting textures," says Angela Fonda of Fonda's in New York. Here, she's put a white Victorian petticoat with boots and suede. She also likes to wear a lace vest over a sweater with jeans, 1940s hats with contemporary suits, antique kimonos over evening clothes. (Photo: Alan J. Copia © 1980)

velvets. Colors were rich blacks, wines, and greens, made into coats with puffy sleeves, hoods, and white satin linings ($80–$100). These coats were worn by sorority girls to their proms.

The best bargains of all are probably accessories. Victorian hats with gay plumes go for $30, as do men's derbys and top hats. Forties pillboxes with veils are $15 and under. Pointed T-strap shoes from the 1940s, never worn, go for under $20, Victorian lace-up shoes with mushroom heels for $40. Celluloid pins from the 1930s and 1940s can be found in flea markets everywhere from $1 to $12. Celluloid was the first plastic, and it has an entirely different consistency from plastic today. It can look like ivory, amber, or jade, and is more translucent. Most popular celluloid items: carved bracelets that look like ivory, Scottie-dog pins, anchors, horse heads, Ice Follies pins of ice skaters. Many of the pins are kinetic—they *move:* a baton twirler will twirl her baton or a dog's tail will wag.

Care

Far from being fragile, many old clothes are still around because they're tough and well made. They've already been washed or dry cleaned countless times; this does not mean, however, that you can toss antique clothes in the washer and spin them a few thousand times. Washing machines and detergents are meant for dealing with sheets and towels, not delicate laces and rayons; they must be washed by hand and ironed at just the right degree of dampness. Here are a few specifics for the most commonly sold antique clothes:

White cottons Look for ancient metal snaps or hooks that might rust during washing, and remove them. If the garment is stained, boil it (yes, that's the treatment to which old cottons are accustomed—our grandmothers boiled all white cottons and linens outdoors in large black pots). Pour one of the powdered enzyme bleaches such as Clorox 2 or Biz into a saucepan, along with tap water; swish around until you have suds; immerse the garment, and boil until it's snowy white—usually about fifteen minutes. Poke it occasionally with the handle of a wooden spoon, and lift out every few minutes to see how the stains are doing. Rinse, squeeze gently dry, and hang to dry, preferably outside in the sun. Watch carefully, and iron just before it begins to dry; otherwise you'll never be able to get the little wrinkles out. After the first rigorous bleaching you'll probably be able to get by with handwashing in a mild detergent, with an occasional soaking of an hour or so in enzyme bleach. *Never wash white garments with clothes of other colors—it dulls and yellows them.* (For any new stains, see STAINS.)

Colored cottons Wash cautiously in tepid water. Put a little vinegar in next-to-last rinse water to counteract alkaline effect of soap and brighten colors.

Old silk or rayon velvets For stains, take to a good dry cleaner. To get out wrinkles and weblike crushed lines, steam with a Wrinkles Away, both front and back (see p. 40). Steam agrees with this fabric, fluffing it out beautifully. If you don't have a Wrinkles Away, take the garment to the cleaners and have it steam pressed. Ironing doesn't do much good. If you want to give it a try, however, iron from the back only.

Old lace Wash in Woolite in tepid water. Never bleach, either with enzyme bleaches or Clorox, because you'll lose the lovely ecru patina that is the whole point of old lace. To stiffen a bit, pour a little sugar into the final rinse water. (See LACE.)

Silk or chiffon If the silk is a solid color, wash it in Ivory Snow in tepid water, and iron while damp. *If there's embroidery or a print, colors may smear during washing.* Ask your salesperson her opinion, as she may have already washed it before putting it out for sale. Otherwise, dry clean.

Linen Old linen is a joy to launder—it thrives on washing. Boil white linens just as you do white cottons, and iron while damp. (For specific stains, see LINEN, Care.)

Beaded garments Usually, antique beaded clothes were made with cut-glass bugle beads, which means the beads are both handwashable and dry-cleanable. Handwash sweaters in cold water, don't wring, and be sure to dry flat. Try not to clean bead-embroidered silks, rayons, and chiffons at all, but if you must, have them professionally dry cleaned, because if you wash them, you won't be able to iron between the beads. (See BEADED CLOTHES.)

Wools Handwash sweaters; dry clean suits. (See WOOL, Care.)

Where to Find

Nearly every large city in the U.S. has wonderful antique-clothing stores with items going back at least to the 1930s or 1940s. Don't bother looking under *antique clothing* in the phone book, however. Except for Manhattan, which does have such a listing, you'll usually find nothing. Most cities list antique clothes stores under *Clothing, Bought and Sold* or *Clothing, Secondhand;* once you find *that,* it's easy

to tell from the listings which stores carry antique clothes and which carry mere out-of-style castoffs from a few years back. Also watch ads in college newspapers or small weekly papers such as *The Village Voice* and *Soho Weekly News* in New York. Here are some particularly worthwhile antique shops around the country:

NEW YORK, N.Y.
 Fonda's
 168 Lexington (at 30th)
 685-4035

 Jezebel (expensive)
 265 Columbus Avenue (at 72nd Street)
 787-5486

 40's Wink
 1331 Third Avenue (at 76th Street)
 737-9372

 Harriet Love (expensive)
 412 West Broadway
 966-2280

 Best of Everything
 242 E. 77th
 (between Second and Third Avenues)
 734-2492

WASHINGTON, D.C.
 Geraldine's
 4105 Wisconsin Avenue, NW
 686-5050

 Deja Vu Antiques
 1675 Wisconsin Avenue, NW
 965-1988

CHICAGO, ILL.
 Follies Antique Apparel
 6981 North Sheridan
 761-3020

NEW ORLEANS, LA.
 Second Hand Rose
 3110 Magazine
 899-2098

Mathilda (wonderful Mardi Gras
costumes in addition to usual
stuff from the 1940s and back)
1222 Decatur
524-7027

DALLAS, TEX.
Faded Rose Antique Clothes
2720 North Henderson
826-7450

DENVER, COLO.
Ritz
415 Larimer
572-9072

BOULDER, COLO.
Ritz (mostly 1950s)
959 Walnut
443-2850

Bertha's Rudely Decadent
1388 South Broadway
733-9440

DETROIT, MICH.
Fabulous Second Hands
1437 Randolph
963-3657

SAN FRANCISCO, CAL.
Secondhand Rose
3326 23rd Street
285-6077

Matinee
1124 Polk
673-6145

Old Gold
2304 Market
552-2560

LOS ANGELES, CAL.
Auntie Mame
1102 South La Cienega Boulevard
652-8430

PORTLAND, ORE.
Shady Lady
823 NW 23rd
248-0518

SEATTLE, WASH.
Dreamland
1406 NE 42nd
634-2405

Shopping
Saturdays and peak hours can be more re-
laxed, because with other customers in the
store, you won't feel pressured. Warning:
If you're discovering antique clothes for
the first time, you'll be so charmed you'll
think everything you see is unique and
wonderful. While most things are one of a
kind, keep in mind that a competing store
down the street may have a similar item
for even less money.

Antron
Du Pont's trade name for one of its nylons,
made, as are all nylons, from petroleum,
air, and water. In price, Antron is somewhere between Qiana, Du Pont's most expensive nylon, and basic Du Pont nylon.
Antron is often used to make blouses and
running shorts, seldom for slips or skirts
because it has so much electrical static,
and skirts will ride up in front. Like all nylons, it resists wrinkles and mildew, has little absorbency, and may feel clammy in hot
weather.

Care
Dries magically fast, making nylon lingerie a blessing on trips. Can usually be machine washed in warm water and tumble
dried, though if it's not removed promptly
from the dryer, wrinkles will be set in by
the heat. Antron should be washed only
with clothes of similar colors, as nylon
picks up colors from other fabrics.

Antron III

A more luxurious nylon than plain Antron, Antron III is anti-cling and won't ride up. It's Du Pont's finest nylon, and is used to make slips and nightgowns by the biggest names in lingerie design.

Care
Same as for Antron.

Appliqué

(ap-lee-kay´) is the French word for *applied*. In fashion an appliqué is a piece of fabric cut out and applied to another fabric, such as your jeans, by gluing or sewing. Obviously, those sewed on are going to adhere better than those glued, which tend to curl around the edges.

Argyle

A knitting pattern of multicolored diamonds used in socks, sweaters, and mufflers. It originated in Scotland, where Argyll is the name of the clan whose tartan is used for this pattern. Today's most prestigious argyles are cashmere sweaters, still made in Scotland by Pringle of Scotland. Most common argyles are stockings. If you buy argyle knee-highs, get very muted colors; otherwise you attract too much attention to your legs.

Armani, Giorgio

Italian designer, often called the world's master tailor. Armani first made his reputation in menswear. His unconstructed, ever-so-slightly rumpled look (worn constantly by Richard Gere in *American Gigolo*) changed the look of men's haberdashery in the 1970s. He applied his tailoring skills to women's clothes in 1975, and soon women too were wearing his droopy masculine blazers and pant suits.

Diane Keaton wore one to collect her Oscar for *Annie Hall* in 1978, and today an Armani is the status blazer to own.

Armani's fondness for giant herringbone patterns and bold diagonal stripes, with asymmetrical lapels or buttonings on the side, sometimes overpowers small women. The cost of an Armani blazer is equally overpowering: up to $800. Since paying duty adds 10 or 20 percent to the cost of imported clothes, you can save money by buying Armani in Italy. He directs his $40-million-a-year empire from a Renaissance *palazzo* in Milan.

Army-Navy Clothes

When the world's number one designer, Yves St. Laurent, first visited New York, red carpets were rolled out for him at every haute couture store in the city. But what famous American institution did he choose to visit first—and loiter in longest? New York's army-navy surplus stores.

By now, everyone who is the least adventuresome in shopping forays has discovered the cavernous charms of a good army-navy store, with its rows and rows of jeans, pea jackets, khaki field jackets, olive-green Fidel Castro-like fatigues, bomber jackets, overalls, and clumpy boots, all at prices so reasonable that even the college students swarming about the place can afford them. Of course the majority of customers are men—all types, from Hell's Angels to corporate lawyers—and you may have to try on your selections in a rustic little cubicle hung with a dusty curtain that doesn't quite close.

Good surplus stores seem to stock a mixture of old and new: their sources for their $5 chambray work shirts from the 1950s or telephone-lineman windbreakers, only slightly used, are as secret as C.I.A. code names. New gear—"made for U.S. Navy" pea jackets or wool socks—*are* made by manufacturers for the U.S. Navy, but they also sell the exact same items to regular commercial markets, too. They discovered long ago that lots of folks appreciate the sturdy, pure, but inexpensive wools and cottons that go into sensibly designed military gear. (The old stuff is more likely to be pure natural fiber than is the new, as the military has discovered the convenience of synthetic-blend wash and wear.)

What do women buy most of in surplus stores? "We sell more pea coats than anything else," says a spokesman for I. Buss, one of New York's largest "roughwear" stores. "Authentic American Navy pea jackets are the most popular in the world. They're all in men's sizes, but a thirty-two or thirty-four is small enough to fit women." Price: $25 to $50 depending on condition of the coat.

For summer, women buy more military-style cotton twill shorts than anything else—English, French, Italian. Other items for women you might find at surplus stores: French Navy pea coats for $40–$60; thermal wool and cotton undershirts for $10; down parkas at $50 or $60; plaid cotton flannel shirts for $10–$15; blue British Royal Air Force coats for women, $50–$60. Don't overlook the rugged footgear, either: waterproof goosedown booties, for campsite or padding around at home, $20; Timberland and Herman Survivor hiking boots for $65–$70; Palladium canvas hiking sneakers with a sole so gripping you can almost walk up the side of a building, $35.

Finding Army-Navy Stores

It's simple: in the Yellow Pages, look under *Army and Navy Stores* or *Military Goods* or *Camping Equipment.* Here are some good ones around the country:

NEW YORK, N.Y.
  Unique Clothing Warehouse
  718 Broadway
  674-1767
  (A giant store—also has antique clothes of all descriptions.)

  Hudson's Camping Supplies
  105 Third Avenue (at 12th)
  GR 5-9568
  (Another cavernous giant—a New York institution that oozes authenticity.)

  I. Buss
  738 Broadway (off 8th Street & Astor Place)
  242-3338

CHICAGO, ILL.
  Uncle Dan's Ltd. (free catalogue)
  2440 N. Lincoln Avenue
  477-1918
  or:
  3350 W. Bryn Mawr
  588-9190

ATLANTA, GA.
  Old Sarge Army Navy Surplus Store
  5316 Buford Hwy Drive
  451-6031

NEW ORLEANS, LA.
  Westside Army Surplus
  522 Lafayette Gretna
  361-1215

SAN FRANCISCO, CAL.
  California Surplus Sales
  1393 Haight
  861-0404
  or:
  1107 Mission
  861-1083

  Lorber's Surplus Store
  1024 Mission
  621-4547

LOS ANGELES, CAL.
  Army Navy Store
  131 E. 6th (opposite Greyhound Bus
  depot)
  623-3142

  Camp Beverly Hills
  9640 Santa Monica Blvd
  274-8317

  Doughboys Surplus
  8334 Garvey Avenue Rsmd.
  283-5645

SEATTLE, WASH.
  Blocks
  1st & Pike
  622-7722

  Lighthouse Uniform Co.
  1532 15th W
  282-5600

AND on 1st, within a few blocks
of each other, a surplus row:

Federal Army & Navy Surplus
1013 1st;

Harry's Army & Navy Store
1310 1st;

Northwest Army & Navy Surplus
1115 1st;

Seattle Surplus
2400 1st

Art Sweater

Handknit, one-of-a-kind sweater. For the
last few decades, most sweaters have been
machine-knitted. In the last two years or
so, the market has been saturated with assembly-line handknit sweaters. Knitters in
Korea or South America knit parts of
sweaters—one woman whizzes through
backs, another does arms, and a third knits
all the parts together to make a sweater.

An "art sweater" is one designed and knitted altogether by one person, as no two
truly handknit sweaters are ever exactly
alike. Barbara Hokanson, Joan Vass, Caro-
lyn Eve are big names in art sweaters;
cost: $100 on up, though you can often buy
them on sale at season's end.

The Ascot: Tie the scarf around your neck once; loop one
end over and spread open the gathers. Either leave the
ends loose or tuck them into an open neckline for a more
tailored look. (Courtesy of Echo Scarfs®)

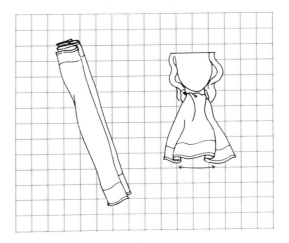

Ascot

A rectangular scarf with wide square
ends, looped high on the neck in a way in
which the knot is hidden. Traditionally
made of heavy silk and pinned, the ascot tie
was first worn in Victorian England by
gentlemen attending the Ascot Heath
horse races, and was later taken up here by
F. Scott Fitzgerald and his set in the 1920s.
Ascots are flattering to long necks, not so
becoming on shorter, wider ones.

Ashley, Laura

is a name synonymous with romantic, Vic-
torian-look cottons strewn with fields of
tiny daisies. Her high-necked blouses ($60)
and patch-pocketed smockdresses ($100)
have just the right amount of ruffles, and

her fabric designs are successfully imbued with the poetry of another era—most of them are transposed from antique china or the flyleaves of old books. Laura Ashleys can be worn in place of jeans, or dressed up with jewelry and heels. Somehow, it's hard to resist cutting off the plastic buttons and sewing on antique ones.

A Welsh designer with no formal training (she once worked as a Telex operator), Ashley sells her wares in eighty boutiques, found all over the world. U.S. boutiques are in San Francisco, Costa Mesa, Boston, Washington, D.C., Chicago, Ardmore, Pennsylvania, Westport, Connecticut, and Manhattan.

Laura Ashley does romantic Victorian blouses strewn with daisies.

Care

Though labels say machine wash, don't launder lustrous Ashley cottons with others at first—they sometimes run. Wash in lukewarm water. Vinegar in the next-to-last rinse water helps keep all those Dusty Rose and Old Lavender tones bright.

Assatly, Richard

An American designer in his thirties from Brooklyn, New York, Assatly isn't yet one of the big names in fashion but is carving out a niche for himself in the $200 price range. He's best known for his dignified cocktail and dinner dresses in beautiful fabrics; trendy, yet simple enough for any respectable suburban matron to wear. In addition to his own clothes, he designs for Simplicity Patterns.

Attaché Case

Although these were formerly seen mostly in the possession of men in gray flannel suits riding commuter trains, today any woman who is an executive, or wants to *look* like an executive, carries either an attaché or a portfolio case (see PORTFOLIO CASE). The attaché, with its solid frame and hard sides, is the biggest seller to business women, and its hard sides make it the perfect lap-desk on commuter trains or in airport waiting rooms.

All serious attaché cases are tan or brown leather, and go for $150 up, a hefty price until you consider that, with care, the patina of leather gets lovelier as it ages and you're therefore making a lifetime investment. The lining of one's case should also be of leather, or possibly suede or linen—never vinyl or synthetic—and it should match the exterior with a subdued color.

Attaché cases for women are lighter and not quite as wide as men's (two and a half to three inches wide as opposed to three or four inches for men with biceps). Usually, the case's interior will contain two or three compartments for organizing papers. John T. Molloy advises in *Dress for Success*, his handbook for the corporate woman on the way up, that one should never carry both an attaché case and a handbag. Most women, however, ignore this advice, having found that items such as a coin purse, wallet, lipstick, perfume, blusher, comb, checkbook, pen, keys, vitamin pills, or To Do lists get lost in the attaché case.

Good labels in attaché cases are: Mark Cross, Michael Scott, Schlesinger Brothers, Trussard.

Care

Rub it down from time to time with Lexol (see LEXOL). Unlike portfolios, which get easily bent out of shape if you leave them sitting around for awhile, the hard sides of an attaché case give it a built-in shape—one less worry there.

Avant-Garde

Originally, a French word referring to the leading part of an army; in fashion, it designates clothes breaking new ground. Last year, Perry Ellis's long gathered culottes and Norma Kamali's wildly cut swimsuits were considered avant-garde.

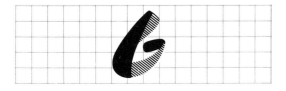

Babushka

A large triangular headscarf, or a square folded into a triangle, tied under the chin. Peasant women have worn them for centuries.

Bagheera

A wrinkle-resistant, crush-resistant velvet.

Balenciaga, Cristobal

(bal-lawn-see-ah´-gah) Along with Chanel and Vionnet, Balenciaga is considered one of the pioneers of modern fashion design. He was a Spaniard who worked in France, a master in tailoring for older women, and a designer of the grand tradition: his customers were nobody but the *crème de la crème*. He died in 1972.

Balmacaan

(bal-may´-can) A full, unbelted, loose-fitting overcoat with raglan sleeves, always of wool tweed. Named after Balmacaan, Scotland, a town near Inverness located in an area know for its tweeds.

Bandanna

A staple clothing item from the Old West, a bandanna is a piece of cotton about two

The Babushka: Use a large square folded into a triangle. Pull the front of the scarf over the forehead and knot the ends over the point of the triangle. Then pull the excess from above the knot to achieve a fuller look. (Courtesy of Echo Scarfs®)

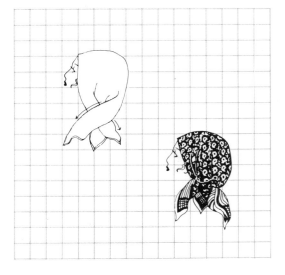

feet square, hemmed on all sides and printed in brightly colored geometric patterns.
Cowboys used them for neckerchiefs that
they could pull up over their noses either to
(1) protect themselves from the dust of cattle stampedes or (2) disguise their faces
when they robbed banks. A bandanna
could also be used as a washcloth, when
you camped beside a stream; a tourniquet,
in case of a rattlesnake bite; a handkerchief, in the days before Kleenex. Today,
the best, thickest bandannas are found in
sporting goods stores for a dollar, and not
only are they still good for all those practical uses, they *look* terrific. A red bandanna
with a white blouse and slacks is a knock-
out, especially on black women, or someone with a deep tan.

Bandeau

In French, it means "a band." In American
fashion, it has come to mean clothes cut
with a straight horizontal band over the
bust—can be a gown falling softly from a
band of lace with tiny spaghetti straps, or
could be a strapless jumpsuit. In swimwear, a bandeau can be either a one-piece
suit or a bikini, but is strapless. Bandeaus
are the biggest swimsuit sellers because
your tan isn't marred by strap marks.

An elasticized strapless bandeau top
looks terrific under a summer blazer on almost anyone except the flat-chested. Nor is
a bandeau flattering on women with very
wide shoulders—the band draws a horizontal line right underneath the shoulders,
emphasizing their width.

Bandolier

An American Indian shoulder bag, usually
a pouch made from buckskin and embroidered with beads. They were carried by
women of the Great Plains Indian tribes,
who kept combs, herbal cosmetics, and

sewing things—for quick mends of the
family's clothes—in them. Much copied today, bandoliers can be found for $10 or $15
in any boutique selling Indian artifacts,
such as Tepee Town in New York.

Ban-Lon

Originally the trademark of Joseph Ban-
croft & Sons for a process that used heat to
add crimp and stretch to synthetic knits.
You'd find Ban-Lon in socks, sweaters, and
knitted dresses worn by many Americans
during the 1960s, and often sneered at by
hippies and clothes snobs. Today the trademark is a symbol of the Banlon Marketing
Corp., which is a private testing laborato-
ry. The black-and-red Ban-Lon label means
items have been pretested for such characteristics as colorfastness, shrinkage, and
accurate laundering instructions.

Basile

(bah-sil´-lee) The name of a manufacturing
corporation in Milan, Italy, known for giving free rein to creative designers. Basile
clothes have little *touches*. Blazers, for example, might be designed with the most
conservative possible lines—but you'll find
blue and red silk threads woven into the
tweed. In American department stores,
you'll find Basile cocktails-and-dinner
dresses in vibrantly colored printed or embroidered silks, cottons, and linens for
around $400; tweedy separates run $800 or
more for slacks and jacket.

Bass Weejuns

In almost all matters of fashion, whether
handbags, hats, or slacks, the French and
Italians have traditionally occupied themselves with turning out luxurious, delicate
items, while America has specialized in
sturdy, sensible wear. In shoes, especially,
the fashion world has fawned over Italy's

A steady seller since 1936, Bass Weejuns® were the first loafers.

buttery soft, needley heeled, impractical footwear, ignoring America's wonderfully comfortable but clunky contributions such as Old Maine Trotters, Naturalizers, and Lighthouse boots. In 1980, however, just as Americans were buying record numbers of European shoes, Europeans developed a taste for U.S. footwear, and certain American shoes promise to be nearly as popular as jeans in the 1980s. The hottest American shoe manufacturer is Bass, and their hottest shoe is the Bass Weejun, made on the same last—on the same shaped wooden form—since 1936. "We noticed how popular a slipper-type moccasin was in Norway and decided to develop a similar one," says Joe Peach of Bass. "The new product was called a Weejun, from Norwegian-Injun." The G. H. Bass Company was founded in Wilton, Maine, in 1876, the year of Custer's last stand, and thrived by making a hand-pegged farmer's boot called the "National Plow Shoe." During World War I the company was called upon to develop a shoe warm enough to keep pilots' toes from getting frostbitten in their unheated cockpits and the Bass Flying Boot was worn all dur-

ing the war, later by Charles Lindbergh on his famous flight from New York to Paris in 1927. Today, besides the Weejun, Bass makes leathery sandals (Sunjuns), saddles, and bucks, few selling for over $50. Find them in local department stores or boutiques, or write G. H. Bass and Co., Wilton, Maine 04294 to find the store nearest you.

Batik

(bah-teek´) A method of dyeing fabric that originated on Bali and other Indonesian islands. Wax is spread on the fabric to be dyed, and color applied to the unwaxed areas. The covered places stay their original color, while the uncovered spots are dyed. On a really fine piece of work, several dyeing procedures are applied to get the final pattern. The lovely veined effect on hand-dyed batiks happens because the wax usually cracks during dyeing. Most batik is machine-printed today, but you can find hand-dyed caftans and tunics in import stores.

Batiste

(bah-teest´) The finest, softest, lightest-weight grade of a fabric—can be linen, cotton, synthetic, or wool. Think of white baby clothes, the expensive kind given as presents at baby showers. For adults, the most common use is expensive embroidery-trimmed lingerie, most often a polyester/cotton blend, but lately 100 percent cotton.

Beaded Clothes

are back. For the past decade, nobody wore glitter except country-music singers and circus acrobats. Now, you can pay $3,000 for Ralph Lauren's bugle-beaded jacket or $4,000 for a Halston chiffon embroidered with silver and gold-plated sequins. You can also buy gorgeous beaded wool sweaters from the 1950s for $35 and sumptuous beaded rayon jackets from the 1930s for under $100. For prices between these two extremes many manufacturers are turning out opulent machine-beaded clothes. The difficult question is, how do you care for them? Here are a few facts from Brooks-Van Horn Costumes, the company that provides both Seventh Avenue designers and Ringling Bros. Circus performers with beads and bangles. Beads you're most likely to see on clothes are:

Bugle beads The best-selling beads for clothes. Cylindrical, made of glass, can be any color, though bronze-colored ones have outsold all others. Most beaded antique sweaters and jackets are sewn with bugle beads. *Care:* All glass beads are both handwashable and dry-cleanable. However, beaded clothes can't easily be ironed, so for those that wrinkle count on dry cleaning. You might consider having beaded clothes spot-cleaned only.

Sequins Small, sparkling discs, pierced in the center for thread, made from plastic sheeting. Proceed with caution: the Ringling Bros. variety is washable and dry cleanable, but other, cheaper versions melt in dry-cleaning chemicals, or colors run. Buy sequined clothes in dark colors, and wash or clean them only if you must.

Paillettes Large sequins; also called spangles.

Rhinestones Diamondlike beads made from cut glass. Care as for bugle beads.

Bean, L. L.
See L. L. BEAN.

Beene, Geoffrey

One of the giants of American fashion, Beene was among the earliest to feel that designer clothes shouldn't be only for a privileged few; after a decade of designing haute couture for the world's richest women, and after making Lynda Bird Johnson's White House wedding dress, he turned much of his energy toward designing inexpensive clothes for his new Beene Bag line. Always praised for his fabrics, he began using interesting but distinctly non-haute couture fabrics such as mattress ticking to make low-cost sportswear.

Beene clothes are always loose and soft. "If you're afraid to roll clothes up and put them in a tote bag, they're not right for modern life," he says. Whether you're buying an inexpensive Beene Bag shoe, one of the $400–$3,000 couture Beene outfits preferred by Faye Dunaway and Jacqueline Kennedy Onassis, or Beene Bag sportswear for under $200, you're unlikely to see the blazers and man-tailored suits that Beene thinks are too stiff. An airy Beene cotton suit for summer is considered a must by fans from Germany to Japan, England, and Italy, where he's America's most popular designer. Beene, a short Southerner in his fifties (from Haynesville, Louisiana), made the Coty Fashion Hall of Fame in 1974.

Bellbottoms

Trousers flaring at the bottom, worn for centuries by sailors of all nations because they were roomy enough for acrobatic leaps and climbs among the riggings. You can still get the authentic Navy bellbottoms, with buttons in front instead of a zipper, at army-navy stores for $10 or $15.

Geoffrey Beene is known for loose, soft clothes in beautiful fabrics. Beene summer suits, such as this one of sheer wool gauze and white floral-printed linen, are especially coveted.

Belts

What's most important about belts is that, more than any other accessory, they can add or subtract inches, both horizontally and lengthwise. Here are the four basic laws of wearing belts.

1. The overweight, and especially overweight and short, should wear narrow belts of the same color or material as the outfit. Nothing is more disastrous for a short person with no waistline than a large, cheerful horizontal strip right across the middle. A narrow matching belt won't interrupt the lovely, height-adding vertical lines of a one-tone outfit.

2. The thin, and especially thin and long-waisted, should revel in large belts in contrasting colors. Wide belts will add the horizontal lines you need to stave off that emaciated look, and draw attention to your small, neat waist. If you're also somewhat too small both above and below the waist, add softening fullness by belting a loose blouson top and full skirt with some sort of wild dramatic belt such as one of Turkish

or Moroccan silver, one of the new dayglo-colored rubber belts, or a pewter mesh belt with an Art Deco buckle.

3. If you're shortwaisted, but tall and thin enough to afford the horizontal line of a belt, match your belt to your blouse color rather than your skirt or pant color—it will elongate your waist.

4. If you're longwaisted, belts (preferably wide) should be matched to skirt or pants.

In general, buckle belts look better on dresses than do tied belts, because when you knot a tie, the two ends fall down in front, looking from the side as though you have a pot belly.

Most respected names in belts: Gucci, Hermès, Fendi, Morris Moskowitz, Kieselstein-Cord.

Benares Cloth

(beh-nar´-eez) Indian fabric, used a lot in Indian clothes, usually cotton or rayon, woven with metallic threads. Wash in Ivory Snow, dry flat, and iron on a low setting while damp, or you can dry clean.

Bermuda Shorts

Long shorts, ending just above the knee. During the 1930s and 1940s, Bermuda was the same popular vacation spot it is today, and the government enforced a strict regulation against women appearing in public in short shorts. Bermuda-length was a compromise. The length, chopping across lower thighs, is unflattering to almost everybody except girls with beautiful legs.

Bias Cut

clothes are slinky, clingy, fluid. Think Jean Harlow in her bias-cut slipdress, think the elegant, doomed women of 1930s Germany in the film *The Damned.* Think every dress or skirt you've ever had that seemed magically graceful, even if you were twenty pounds overweight. French designer Vionnet invented the bias cut back in the early 1920s, and anybody interested in making sophisticated but sexy clothes has used it ever since. Today Halston is a particularly fine master. You can expect to pay handsomely for a bias cut, though you don't have to buy super-expensive designer clothes to get one.

Bias-cut works this way: next time you're in a dry-goods store, take a bolt of fabric and pull it from end to end, or one side to the other. You'll notice the fabric doesn't "give" at all. Grab the corners and pull the material *diagonally,* however, and you'll be amazed to see that it stretches and "gives" like mad. When patterns are laid diagonally across the bolt, a lot of material is wasted in the cutting, but the ensuing garment will be deliciously fluid and supple. It will also be a luxury item, because not only does cutting on the bias take more material than cutting straight, but somebody has to know how to sew. Bias-cut seams have a way of rippling, puckering, and pulling unless they're sewn *exactly* right.

You'll find clothes cut on the bias mostly in soft, fluid materials such as jersey and satin (the satin bias-cut slipdress first worn by Jean Harlow is one of the sexiest dresses ever made; see p. 128). Trousers, blazers, tailored clothes are never bias-cut. Sometimes labels or advertisements will tell you an outfit is bias cut; other times they seem to expect you to know you're trying on something special.

Care

For everyday upkeep, follow label directions. What's tricky about bias-cut skirts is that they're hard to re-hem, should skirt lengths change—stitches tend to pucker. You'd better count on paying a professional, and even then the skirt may not look 100 percent right.

Bikini

A two-piece swimsuit of minimum coverage, consisting of a tiny bra with strings, and a tiny bottom cut as low as possible. The name comes from Bikini Atoll, in the Marshall Islands southwest of Hawaii, first testing site for atomic bombs in 1946. The shock the blast caused inspired the swimsuit name, as it was thought it would cause a similar reaction. American soldiers returning from Europe after World War II did indeed shock people by telling of the new swimsuit, and though every chic Frenchwoman had one by 1954, few dared wear them in America until approximately 1965, when Brigitte Bardot made them an international fashion.

Bikinis with a shirred bra are the swimsuit of choice for thin women; heavy women do better in one-piece swimsuits. (See SWIMSUITS.)

Bis, Dorothée

See DOROTHÉE BIS. (There is no real Dorothée Bis—it's the name of a company.)

Black Tie

You spend your life in pants and sweaters, but the invitation says black tie. What to wear? If you possibly can, confer with those hosting the gala night, or with a socialite friend to whom dressing up is as natural as wearing jeans. What people wear where differs so radically from region to region, and with age, that giving general advice borders on the futile. However, here are a few guidelines of the most basic sort.

Dinner at a private home This is the occasion for evening pyjamas, perhaps silk pants, camisole, and a flowing jacket, or velvet pants and top with a ruffly blouse. You can also wear a short cocktail dress, or possibly a long evening skirt and blouse.

For a big dinner dance You're dealing with the most formal of all social fêtes. A dinner dance calls for a long beautiful dress, floaty, bare, clingy, devastating. In other words, pull out all the stops and dress to kill—wear your mother's diamonds, your best friend's mink, bare, strappy high-heeled evening slippers with ultrasheer stockings. Though short dresses are also fine, the mainstream *mode d'attire* will be long, full skirts for dancing.

An opening, reception, benefit, or dinner in a posh restaurant Here, local rituals are so important that it is difficult to prescribe a formula. Openings and receptions tend to draw a hobglob of every sort of evening attire possible. Safest is a short cocktail dress or evening separates in a stunning fabric, but on the covered-up side. For an opening in an art museum you might wear more imaginative clothes; for a D.A.R. reception, something simple but elegant.

If the invitation says *black tie optional,* that too calls for a short party dress or evening separates, as does *semiformal.*

Wraps

Nearly as big a challenge as what outfit to wear, is what to wear on top. In winter, almost any fur, except rabbit-trimmed bomber jackets and tattered antique raccoons, will do, no matter what length. (A great investment is a fur sling cape from the 1940s, going for $60 to $90 in second-hand-fur stores.) If you can't get your hands on a fur, wear the dressiest coat you have, zip it off immediately inside the door, and don't worry. Unlike medieval Japan, where you could be beheaded for wearing the wrong thing, nobody will notice—or care. In summer, a mantilla—a lacy Spanish shawl—is a nice wrap, as are old hand-crocheted shawls (find them at flea markets for $15 to $25). For fall and early spring, you'd feel perfect in a black velvet coat, or cape (see ANTIQUE CLOTHES). Brocade coolie jackets with lots of embroidery are favorites of those who can afford them, as are heavy antique damask kimonos.

Blass, Bill

One of America's most well-distributed designers, Bill Blass does *not* aim his collection at a small group of rich, *outré* New Yorkers. Many times a year, Blass is on the road to the heartland, appearing at benefits and mixing happily with his customers at country clubs and receptions. If personal popularity were a criteria for success as a designer, Bill Blass would win hands down. Indeed, on almost any criteria for success Blass does win hands down: he did a $200 million business in 1980; twice elected to the Coty Hall of Fame, he's been the recipient of every award worth winning in fashion; and both his dress and Blassport sportswear lines are recognized as superbly well made. His detractors say that his sportswear is too boxy and suburban, his evening dresses too fanciful, but he continues to design by his philosophy: women want simple tweedy separates for day, no-holds-barred femininity at night. He's perhaps most celebrated for his unapologetically glamorous eveningwear, the velvets, taffetas, crêpes on which he lavishes ruffles, lace, feathers, glitter. You can buy his Collection III evening clothes in the $200-to-$400 price range.

Blazer

A blazer is defined as a lightweight, loose-fitting, tailored jacket. First worn by Cambridge University cricket players in the late nineteenth century, these jackets were called blazers because they were made of loud-colored fabrics with bright stripes or plaids. When women began wearing them in the 1930s, they were detested by men who thought they were mannish and unfeminine.

Blazers are also the uniform of the preppy college girl, always a staple of horsey, upper-middle-class suburban life, and they now seem to be as natural a uniform in America as Mao jackets in China. It does seem unthinkable not to have a brown tweedy blazer, preferably by Ralph Lauren, Calvin Klein, or Anne Klein, to wear over brown tweedy skirts, blue jeans, and fall dresses. Evening blazers in white cashmere or wool gabardine will get you nicely through chilly spring evenings, and for summer, one must have a nubby silk or linen blazer to wear over a tube top.

Fit

Classic blazers come just to the bottom of the buttocks. A blazer that's longer than that will shorten your legs and make you look dumpy. If you're overweight or short, tone your blazer to match your skirt, so your body won't look broken up in the middle by a horizontal line. Single-breasted blazers are more flattering to heavy women, double-breasted to thin. Boxy blazers are more slimming than fitted ones.

Shopping

Look for blazers that are supple; if it's stiff as a board, you'll look stiff too. Lining should be the same color as outside fabric. Avoid buying a strangely colored blazer at a "final" sale—it's too easy to think, in your enthusiasm, that the great bargain

Bill Blass has always thought that evening clothes should be unapologetically romantic, and has been putting cascades of ruffles in his collections for years.

will go with everything when in reality that faintly greenish shade of tan will go with nothing.

In your perusal of sale racks, you'll undoubtedly come across the perfect blazer except that one of the lapels is funny-looking—half the size of the other. This flaw is nearly always a matter of faulty pressing—the dry cleaner can easily set it right. Other sale items will have quaint-looking lapels because styles have changed. Though advertising copywriters push blazers as being the sort of classic you can wear forever, actually, shapes change about every five years, effectively making current styles obsolete.

Care
Always button a blazer when it's hanging in the closet; otherwise lapels get funny, and deep creases develop down the middle of each side.

Bleeding
The running or dissolving of dyes during washing. When you want the dye to dissolve, as with Indian madras, the process is called "bleeding." When you *don't* want to see your washwater turning bright blue or purple, it's called "running." Thanks to modern technology, running is not the problem it once was, but even now you should never trust bright reds, purples, and greens. Wash clothes in such colors separately the first few times.

Bloomers
Very loose pants gathered around the knee. The name comes from a nineteenth-century feminist, Amelia Bloomer, who thought it foolish for women to wear skirts in athletics, and suggested bloomers.

Bloomingdale's
is at 59th Street and Third Avenue in New York and has branches in Boston and suburban areas. It has a reputation for being the most trend-setting store in the world. As one writer commented, "Bloomingdale's isn't so much a department store as a social phenomenon, it sells not merchandise so much as awareness." Every chic tourist in Manhattan pays a visit to the store for the same reason every New York designer and fashion model habitually sallies through its swinging doors: to see what's new. Bloomie's is not the world's largest store (that's Macy's on 34th Street), nor the most expensive (Dallas' Neiman-Marcus, with its mink-lined bathrobes), nor is there a claim to carrying on a grand old tradition, as have such historic stores as Atlanta's Rich's, Detroit's J.L. Hudson, or Bullocks in Los Angeles. Bloomingdale's is, however, the most successful retail store in history, with sales per square foot four times the national average. Never mind that a *Time* magazine writer called it the "adult Disneyland." For the latest, most sumptuous merchandise from every foreign country in the world, from India to the Australian outback, you have to go to Bloomingdale's.

For clothes, most Bloomingdale's stores break down something like this: first floor and street level, accessories. Second floor: trendy younger-type clothes, with disco music. Third floor: here you'll find the latest Paris fashion rages in ready-to-wear from Kenzo, St. Laurent, Cacharel, and Sonia Rykiel, along with all the top American designers such as Halston, Anne Klein, Ralph Lauren, Calvin Klein, and Perry Ellis. The stock answer to the question "Where do you find the most beautiful women in New York?" is "Bloomingdale's, third floor."

Don't

shop in Bloomingdale's on Saturday. Shop after noon. Go near the ladies' hosiery counter. Wear a fur coat—coat checkers won't take them. Expect to *buy* shoes in the shoe department—salesmen have been seen there, but to connect with one, you'll need the tactics of a Green Bay Packers linebacker.

Do

shop on rainy Monday or Thursday evenings. Look carefully through sale racks—sometimes the latest merchandise doesn't sell as anticipated, meaning you can get exotic, lovely things at half price, or the same price you'd pay for mediocre stuff in a shopping center in Des Moines.

Blouses

For women pleasingly endowed in the bosom, and with nicely shaped arms and shoulders, nothing beats a clingy, revealing sweater. Women who don't have perfect bodies, and who like to be feminine and businesslike at once, prefer blouses. Here's how to wear blouses to camouflage flaws:

Short, shortwaisted, or overweight Blouse and skirt should be of the same tone; otherwise the horizontal line formed where the two meet will accent the formlessness of your middle. Never roll long sleeves to elbow length, because that too adds horizontal lines around the middle. Your blouses should be tailored and simple.

Small-busted, thin, or round-shouldered Forget simple tailored blouses and buy blouses with tucks, shirring, pleats, and gathers galore in front. These are called dressmaker details, and they're never borderline tacky as polyester lace or too many ruffles can be. In summer, roll long sleeves up to just above the elbows.

Swaybacked Wear your blouse outside skirt and belt.

Narrow of shoulder Avoid sleeveless blouses at all cost; buy cap or elbow length for summer, roll up long sleeves to elbow.

Broad of shoulder, round-faced, or short-necked Buy blouses with as plunging a "V" neckline as you can get away with for the vertical lines. Traditionally, blouses are left open to the third button.

Shopping

Most versatile blouse color is cream. Most versatile shape is classic open-collar—bows have a way of being there when you later wish they'd disappear. Blouses should be long enough to wear belted over skirts and pants, or as a jacket over another blouse. Never buy blouses that are skimpy. If what you want is a shirt, buy a preppy-looking shirt with button-down collar, but a blouse, even a simple one, should have *grace*. When you try on a blouse, lift arms over your head—the blouse shouldn't tug across the back or threaten to rip at the armholes; neither should it pull out at the waist.

Blouses and the seasons Unlike sweaters, blouses can be worn year-round. Roll up sleeves in summer; in winter, wear a light thermal vest underneath. (See THERMAL UNDERWEAR.)

Blouson

The term once meant a loose, blouse-type jacket with a drawstring, but has come to mean a loose blouse with bottom gathered at the waist by the skirt waistband. If you're wearing a loosely cut blouse and raise your arms and then lower them, the pulled-out blouse has become a blouson. Looks good on nearly everybody—if you're chubby, extra flesh is hidden, and if you're thin, it's disguised by the fall of fabric.

Boa

A long round tippet of fur wonderful for keeping necks warm. Will impart a romantic look to suits and cloth coats, and looks especially good with a full-length sweater coat. Natural lamb boas can be found new for $25, silver fox for several hundred. You can buy adorable 1940s boas for $60 in antique shops, but be prepared for the reactions that the glassy stare of the deceased animal can bring out of people.

Boatneck

("bateau-neck" in French) A long horizontal neckline, used mostly on pullover sweaters. Not becoming to the broad-shouldered.

Bodice

The part of a dress between shoulders and waist.

Body Clothes

Also called stretch dressing. The advent of the man-made elastic fiber called spandex, which has the stretch of rubber but is lighter in weight, has set a lot of people yearning for the new comfort of stretch clothes not just at their dancing classes but all the time. Designers such as Betsey Johnson, Norma Kamali, Maya, and Giorgio Sant'Angelo feel that stretch clothes will be the clothing of the future, and are working to develop blends of spandex with such comfortable fabrics as cotton, wool, silk, cashmere, and even lace. "We all feel better in clothes that move with rather

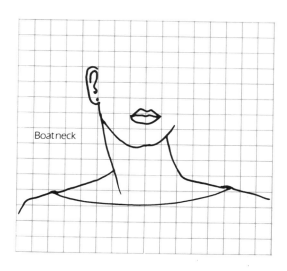

Boatneck

than against the body," says Norma Kamali. "People are tiring of stiff, revamped styles from earlier decades." Find body clothes in the leotard section of department stores, and in small, futuristic boutiques. (See HIGH-TECH CLOTHES.)

Body Stocking

Leotardlike undergarment, usually flesh-colored, worn under transparent clothes. Takes the place of bra, panties, and stockings. Find in the leotard department.

Bolero

A short, waist-length jacket with rounded corners, worn open. Originated by male Spanish dancers and bullfighters.

Boots

are the most macho shoes in the world. What's fun about boots isn't how they look and certainly not how they feel, it's what they're saying, namely, "I'm tough and sexy and dangerous." Boots have been the shoe of choice for all violent men of the past millennium. Military men have always worn them; pirates such as Bluebeard and Captain Kidd wore them and tucked their cutlasses into the tops; Russian Cossacks wore theirs to bed. Cowboys in the Old West wore them because, they said, the heels kept their feet from slipping through stirrups.

"Boots are the most symbolically savage of all footwear," says Dr. William Rossi in *The Sex Life of the Foot and Shoe.* "For the macho, it isn't enough merely to *be* masculine, they must stomp this impression into the minds of others." So possessive have men been of this privilege that one of the criminal charges brought against Joan of Arc was that she dared wear boots. Obviously, women took so enthusiastically to boots just as women's liberation became a force because we, too, want props that make us threatening and tough!

When Buying Boots

Unlined leather "breathes" and is most comfortable. A tricate lining, part cotton and part synthetic, is also reasonably absorbent and comfortable, but vinyl or nylon will trap moisture and cause your feet to feel clammy and claustrophobic. All vinyl boots are uncomfortable and crack easily. Imitation rubber, sealed, molded vinyl/polyurethane rain boots, on the other hand, are the only boots that really keep feet dry in wet weather, and are a necessity. Timberland makes a low hiking boot with a nonslip sole that's fabulous for snow or ice.

Care

Clean your boots with saddle soap. Never let mud or dirt accumulate on boots—moisture will be drawn from the leather, leading to drying and cracking. Get rid of scuff marks with same-color Meltonian polish, buff, then apply a coating of Lexol (see LEXOL), a leather food. Buff to a mellow low-glow luster.

If your boots have gotten drenched in a rainstorm, rub in some Lexol *immediately;* then let them dry naturally, away from heat—don't put near a stove, fireplace or radiator, for this will cause them to stiffen and crack. If you have shoe trees, put them in the boots while they're drying, or stuff temporarily with crumpled newspapers.

To get rid of salt stains, rub leather gently with a solution of half white vinegar and half water. Wipe well with water, treat with Lexol. The stains will disappear, but if the leather's gotten shriveled, as usually happens with salt, that will be a permanent blight.

For suede boots, use a protective silicone spray from the beginning. Every few months, spray on a couple of coats: the silicone keeps dirt on the surface where it can be easily brushed off. To get spots or salt off, rub gently with fine sandpaper or flint.

Bottega Veneta

Even if you can't afford $200–$300 for a buttery Italian handbag, visit these New York, Beverly Hills, or Neiman-Marcus boutiques to see what many connoisseurs consider the world's most beautiful leather. Bottega Veneta never puts initials on its bags, and brass or metal hardware is virtually nonexistent. Thrifty customers wait for the yearly sale around the first week in June. If you happen to be in Venice, you can escape import duties by buying at their home store on the Calle Vallaresso.

Bouclé

In French, the verb *boucler* means to curl into ringlets. In fashion, it means fabric with a loopy, curly surface. Bouclé yarn can be either acrylic, wool, or a blend, is usually made into jackets, sweaters, or blazers, and is expensive or not, depending on the designer using it. Not a rugged fabric—the loops are susceptible to snagging, and once unlooped, cannot, like Humpty Dumpty, be put right again.

Boutique

French word for a small, chic shop in a fashionable district. All women who love clothes spend a lot of time in boutiques, because it's here that you find the clothes of talented designers not yet famous or high-priced: handpainted silks, unusual knitted sweaters, jewelry, natural-fiber lingerie, clothes made from antique fabrics, the kind of swingy, slightly-below-midcalf winter cotton skirt that looks so terrific with boots, *arty* clothes. Sales in boutiques, incidentally, tend to start a month later than those in department stores.

Boys' Departments

Since retailers are convinced that women care more about clothes than boys do, and will therefore pay more, sportswear for boys costs 25 to 50 percent less than the same items in the women's department. You can find no-iron cotton shirts, large selections of cotton or wool crew-neck sweaters, vests, pants, blazers, trenchcoats, belts in boys' departments. No need to feel self-conscious, either—more and more savvy women are buying there, at least if they're not big-busted, overweight, or exceptionally tall. Boys' shirts and sweaters are understandably skimpy in the bust, and pants are slim-hipped. However, alterations are free. Sizes run as follows:

Boys'	is equivalent	
size 20	to our size	12
18	to	10
16	to	8
14	to	6
(and so on)		

Bras

The 1960s question of "to bra or not to bra" has been answered affirmatively. A woman who wears an A cup or a small B doesn't need a bra, but everyone else does. "Wearing a bra prevents the stretching induced by gravity and maintains the shape of the breast," says Dr. Richard Ellenbogen, a plastic and reconstructive surgeon in Los Angeles, California. He likes to point out to dissenters that the barebreasted braless young women shown in *National Geographic* photos usually show excessive premature sagging. Here are a few pointers to help with bras:

Size

For numerical size, measure rib cage just under the breasts, and add five inches to this figure; if you measure an odd number, such as 33, go on to the next number, 34. For cup size, measure directly over the breasts. If breast measurement is an inch bigger than rib cage size plus the five inches, you're an A cup. Two inches, a B; three inches a C; four inches a D.

Fit

A well-fitting bra should fit without your having to tighten straps—tightening straps doesn't lift the breasts, it merely lifts the back of the bra. Perform the strap test: drop one strap—if support is lost on that side, the bra doesn't fit.

Wrinkles in the cups could mean a bra is either too small or too large. If too small, the breasts are pushed to the sides rather than outward, filling out the cup.

To get a good fit, call your favorite department store or lingerie shop and make an appointment with the fitter. They're professionals at seeing that you get the bra that's most comfortable and flattering, and their services are free.

Types of Bras

Gone are the days when you wore one simple pointy bra with everything. Today you need different bras for different clothes. Here are some of the most common types available:

Stretch bra   Made of a stretch fabric, this variety offers least support but gives a smooth, clinging "no bra" look. The one-size-fits-all size is designed for women with small-to-average, firm breasts—an A, B, or small C. Two of the most popular stretch bras: Formfit Rogers' "Naked" and Lily of France's "Glossies."

Natural Bra   Not quite as smooth a look as a stretch bra, but the soft, natural-looking cups provide better support. Probably the biggest-selling type of bra. Examples: Vanity Fair's "Underglows," Vassarette's "Frankly Feminine." Buy either a natural or stretch bra in flesh tones and you can wear it under semitransparent linens and cotton voiles without the bra being noticeable.

Underwire bra   Definitely the bra for large-breasted women, this bra is an engineering marvel designed to provide support and lift without straps gouging holes in your shoulders. Maidenform's "Sweet Nothing" comes with matching bikini, as do Lily of France's "Glossies."

Minimizer   A bra constructed to press breasts toward the sides rather than lifting them outward, so that an overly large bust looks about one size smaller. These bras come only in sizes C, D, and DD. Try Warner's "No Exaggeration" or Carnival's "Diminish."

Maximizer   Finally someone has designed a bra to make the most of small-breasted women without padding. Before, A-cup bras were simply scaled-down versions of 34B, the average national size, and nearly always wrinkled in the cups; now Flexnit's A-OK line is specifically for AA and A sizes. You can also buy bras with a whispery-thin layer of Fiberfill, a far cry from falsies of the 1950s. Body heat is transmitted through them, for one thing, so that if you're dancing with a man your breasts will feel as warm as the rest of you. Still other bras, such as Olga's "Young Secret," make you look larger by pushing you up from underneath with a combination of miniwire and liner.

Sports bra   Another new development has been the bra especially designed for running and tennis, to minimize tissue-destroying bounce and keep breasts comfortable, even when hormonal cycles have made them sore. Also, some doctors believe that running without a proper bra contributes to nonmalignant cysts in the breasts. Sports bras should have wide elastic straps and no-seam cups (elimination of seams prevents nipple irritation), and should either slip over your head, thus eliminating fasteners, or have fasteners padded to prevent abrasion. Since nothing could be more uncomfortable than running in a tight band of clammy synthetic fiber, sports bras are made of absorbent, washable cotton fabric. Probably the biggest-selling sports bra is Formfit Rogers' "Running Bra," which has plush-lined straps.

Bras for Summer

Have you noticed that your bra always feels more uncomfortable on hot days, and may leave angry red lines when you take it off? That's because bodies expand in hot weather. Keep at least one absorbent cotton bra in a larger size around for really steamy days.

Care

Never put a good bra in the dryer—heat destroys elasticity. Buy bras in nude colors rather than white—they don't start looking as dingy as fast; to get rid of dinginess, soak for an hour or so every few weeks in one of the gentle enzyme bleaches such as Clorox 2 or Biz. Don't hang a white bra made from synthetic fibers such as nylon in direct sun—it will yellow.

British Warmer

An all-weather coat with zip-out lining. Usually means a man's coat, but the term is sometimes used for women's.

Brocade

A heavy, luxurious silken fabric with a raised design woven into the fabric on a special loom. Used occasionally for expensive evening skirts or jackets. China has been exporting lovely silk and rayon brocade robes lately, more subdued than the former loud and lustrous fare. Find them in the loungewear section of department stores.

Brooks Brothers

was America's first store to sell ready-made clothes, and has changed little since 1818, when it was opened in lower Manhattan to "make and deal only in merchandise of the best quality, to sell it at a fair profit only, and to deal only with people who sought and were capable of appreciating such merchandise." Theodore Roosevelt and Woodrow Wilson were both sworn in as President in Brooks suits, Ulysses Grant fought his Civil War battles in a Brooks military uniform, and Abraham Lincoln was wearing a Brooks frock coat when he was assassinated at the theater. The store was sacked during the Draft Riots of 1863 and moved uptown, finally set-

Some people find the Brooks Brothers® look dowdy. Others revel in its understatement. The wool flannel skirt and button-down, cotton gingham shirt is "assuredly Brooks Brothers."

tling at Madison and 44th. Today, Brooks Brothers has twenty-one stores around the U.S. and one in Tokyo, all bastions of subdued tastefulness with mellowed wood-paneled walls and nineteenth-century prints of fox-hunting scenes.

Despite Brooks' turn-of-the-century men's club atmosphere, the women's line, initiated five years ago, is doing so well it accounted for 10 percent of total sales last year. The store's specialty is, of course, classics, mostly in natural fibers and most more finely cut versions of the men's clothes that have been selling steadily for several decades. At Brooks Brothers you can find an A-line skirt no matter what the current style. You can also count on Harris tweeds, cashmere, madras, seersucker, Chesterfield coats. Brooks now makes a gray flannel suit for women ($250) every bit as reassuringly conservative as the men's. Look for the pure cotton oxford button-down shirt to wear with it. The store's best-selling item to women at $23.50, it comes in candy stripes or in traditionally muted shades of blue, pink, cream, and white. Khaki slacks are straight and tailored—no "wacky pants," bellbottoms, or harem belly-dance pants at Brooks. Be sure to try on the famous red plaid robe in Brooksflannel, a washable, soft wool-and-cotton blend ($100), and don't overlook the silky cotton turtlenecks, made in England, for $21.50.

For a catalogue, write Brooks Brothers, 346 Madison Avenue, New York, New York 10017. Getting the catalogue, with its odd little sheep logo, in the mail every few months is like hearing from your college alumni group.

Buckskin

An inexpensive leather of deerskin, and a sartorial staple of the Old West. Since Indians had no woven cloth, they became skill-ful in tanning buckskin until it was as soft as the most expensive French leather today. The men wore fringed leggings and shirts, women dresses and leggings. Fringed deerskin jackets are still going strong and can be found for $60 or under.

Care
See LEATHER.

Burberry Coat

The unisex status-symbol trenchcoat of all time. For $450 you can own a Burberry, and from the way this English import is selling off the racks at Burberrys on 57th Street in New York and in expensive department stores around the world, a lot of people consider that a reasonable price.

"What better way to quietly show you're wealthy?" asks one Burberry owner. "Not everyone recognizes Burberrys—only other Burberry owners and people of discernment know." Says another, "When you consider that you can wear the coat fall, winter, and spring, fair or rainy weather, four hundred and fifty dollars for one terrific coat makes more sense than one hundred and fifty each for three mediocre coats." At any rate, one of the first pleasant errands of the newly successful is to buy a Burberry, as Dustin Hoffman was doing in his first scene in *Kramer vs. Kramer*. Then you can wear it with the insouciance of Humphrey Bogart in the fog of the Casablanca airport.

So, what's so special about a Burberry besides the price? The coat is very light, due to a special blend of Dacron polyester and German cotton, and the distinctive plaid zip-out lining (not included in the $450) is of the finest wool. However, what really makes a Burberry are the English tailoring touches that haven't changed in sixty years. The handstitching, which you'll find on collar, buttons, buttonholes,

The Burberry® is the best-selling trenchcoat of all time. Since the coat costs $450, a lot of people buy the Burberry plaid scarf instead.

and pleats. The "bluff" hem, in which hemmed lining is stitched to hemmed coat. "D rings" on the belt for one's map case and sword, Burberrys having been first issued to British officers headed for French trenches in 1914. "During the war I crashed in the Channel when wearing a Burberry trenchcoat and had to discard it," one World War I fighter pilot wrote Burberry. "The coat was returned to me a week later, having been in the sea for five days. I have worn it ever since and it is still going strong."

Burberry trenchcoats for women are virtually the same as men's. However, the coat doesn't always look as dashing on women as it does on most men. If you're short and overweight, a double-breasted coat will make you look like a box (you can buy a single-breasted Burberry, which would be more flattering, but *that's* not the authentic trenchcoat). Also, the same beige that gives the coat its delicious feeling of anonymity draws color out of certain skin tones.

To find out where Burberry is sold nearest you, write:

Burberrys International, Ltd.
1290 Avenue of the Americas
New York, New York 10104

Button-Down Shirt

A simple tailored shirt, usually cotton, with collar buttoned to shirt in front. The president of Brooks Brothers, who introduced the shirt to America in 1900, first dubbed it the "polo collar" because English polo players buttoned down their collars to prevent them from flapping in their faces as they rode. Classic button-down shirts for women are $23.50 at Brooks Brothers today; some designers, such as Ralph Lauren, charge twice that amount.

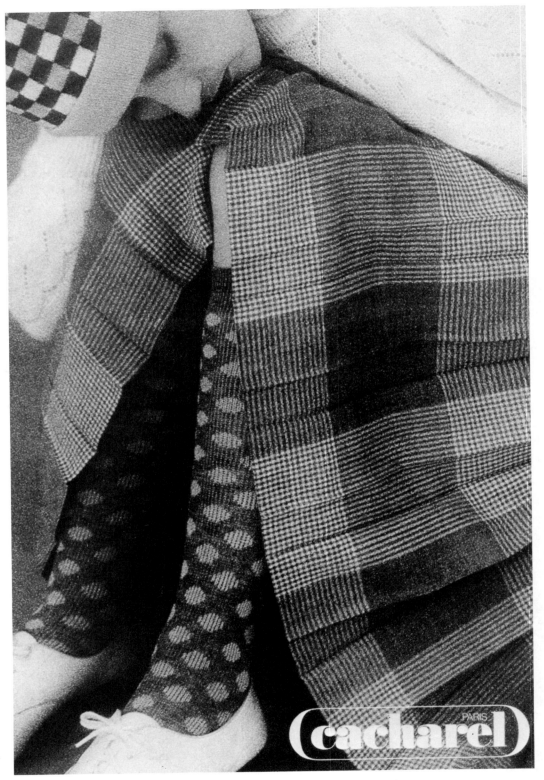

Cacharel® clothes are known for gorgeous textures and prints.

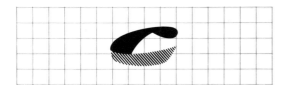

Cacharel

(ka-sha-rel´) One of the first French clothes manufacturers to turn out high-quality ready-to-wear clothes was Jean Cacharel, a tailor and shirt manufacturer from Nîmes. Working with designer Emmanuelle Khanh, he began the unheard-of business of making designer clothes in a medium price range, and by the mid-1960s, his soft, classic separates, particularly his flowered cotton blouses, had become world-wide status symbols. His clothes, now designed by Corinne Sarut, sell in forty-nine countries. Cacharel clothes are known for their sometimes vivid, sometimes subdued colors and prints—where everyone else's blazers will be unrelievedly brown, Cacharel is likely to have one in a rich shade of red. Where other designers' silk blouses will be discreet beige, Cacharel's are likely to have finely etched prints in many colors, as are his famous, tailored Liberty of London cotton blouses with their delicate florals. A Cacharel blazer costs around $150, a cotton blouse $60.

Caftan

A loose, long-sleeved robe of great comfort, worn since ancient times. Turks covered theirs in Islamic embroidery, North Africans' were made of printed cotton, Hebrew men left them unseamed at the sides and wore them as a type of overcoat. Around 1967 Halston, the Black Muslims, and hippies all rediscovered caftans, making it possible for everyone to go everywhere from the beach to black-tie parties in the kind of airy, biblical robes not seen for centuries. Short, heavy women probably should not wear caftans—you'll look like a mound of fabric. On the tall and/or overweight, they're great. Most people should have one around for a housedress—not being chafing or constricting, they're more comfortable than jeans, especially on hot days.

Shopping

Try Indian import stores, also resale shops. Resale stores, which put their highest prices on standard officewear, sometimes sell hand-embroidered ethnic clothes for as little as $15.

Calfskin

is used mostly for high-quality shoe leathers. Some of the most expensive shoes are made of calfskin, but so are moderately priced ones. When shined regularly, calfskin takes on a burnished look.

Calico

Cotton cloth printed in sharply etched, small print designs, much used for patchwork. The name comes from Calicut, India, where cottons were first printed with designs and mass-produced in the mid-nineteenth century. American manufacturers copied the process, and a homemade dress of calico invariably clothed the pioneer woman heading west in a covered wagon train. (See PRAIRIE DRESS.)

Camel's Hair

clothes are a terrific investment. In good department stores, you can find blazers for around $200 and coats for under $300. They're softer than wool and naturally water-repellent, and camel's hair never wrinkles. When researching his book for the upwardly mobile, *Dress for Success*, John Molloy found the camel wraparound coat tested best of all coats at giving women both authority and appeal. Also a color term, "camel" is used to describe a yellowish tan. A "camel coat" usually means a wool coat that's camel-colored. "Camel's hair" has to mean, by law, real camel's hair, though camel's-hair-and-wool blends are often advertised as camel hair. If it's pure camel's hair, you'll often see a label with a camel on it.

Camel's hair comes only from the two-humped camel, native of the Chinese and Mongolian deserts. The harsh desert climate caused this ancient animal to evolve a thick coat of insulating hair to keep it cool by day and warm at night. In spring, this hair is shed naturally, gathered, and sold.

Drawbacks Camel's hair isn't as sturdy as wool. It pills and frays more easily, so it wouldn't be the best choice for a mother of three to wear day in and day out. Camel's-hair-and-wool blends are sturdier, though less soft, than pure camel's-hair clothes.

Cameo

A ubiquitous item of jewelry at antique flea markets. Some cameos cost only a few dollars, others hundreds—yet at first glance they all look the same. The difference: good cameos are carved out of shell, onyx, or agate, with the tiny design stained a different color from the background. The back of a shell or mineral cameo is dull. Plastic cameos, with the relief pattern moulded and glued on, are the cheapies and are shiny on back. Also, frames make a difference in price, silver or gold costing more than a tin or brass alloy.

Camisole

The top half of a slip without the bottom. Camisoles have been used for years as lingerie, today are among the most versatile of tops. A plain, solid-color silk camisole is a can't-lose investment: in summer wear it under unbuttoned shirts, under unzipped jumpsuits, and under nubbly silk or linen blazers (texture contrast is stunning). Or pack a weightless little camisole in your attaché case and take it to the office; if you have an early dinner date, you can exchange your workaday blouse for it—a little jewelry, and you'll be dressed up. A beautiful winter look: a camisole top with evening skirt or pyjama bottoms, worn under a satin blazer of contrasting color. In winter you can also wear it as lingerie—silk is one of the best insulating materials ever devised by nature. Almost everybody looks good in camisole tops except very broad-shouldered women—the straps draw the eye outward. However, a scoop-necked camisole instead of a straight horizontal bandeau style would be fine on the broad-shouldered.

Canned Chic

There is such a thing as appearing too perfect, also known as the "interior decorator" look. People whose shoes match their handbags, whose coat matches their skirt with a hat to match that, who dress assiduously in the look of one fashion designer, who try to look exactly like pictures of fashion models, are all trying too hard. "In the good old days of the slick magazines, there was always someone who followed their advice to a 'T,' " says Gloria Vanderbilt in her book *Woman to Woman*. "No one looks more ill-at-ease than someone who's been prepackaged."

The idea today is to look like your own person, not like a mindless dupe of the fashion industry. (Of course, you don't want to be so far outside the mainstream that you look bizarre—that's even worse. The trick is to have style *and* be dressed appropriately for the occasion.) Never before could you choose from so many modes of fashion. You can mix one designer's clothes with another's or with a pair of trousers from L. L. Bean; you can throw in some westernwear, antique clothes, hand-wovens, ethnic things. Whereas twenty-five years ago the well-dressed woman would appear in Mainbocher or McCardell, with all the appropriate accessories, today she'd look more chic in, say, a $100 Anne Klein skirt matched with a $20 Indian blouse, belted with a $1 thrift-shop belt, a $200 Fendi leather bag, and a pair of $35 Bass walking shoes.

Cap Sleeves

Very short sleeves with no seam at the armhole. Since they stand out from the arms like little caps, they're a disaster to anyone with too-wide shoulders. Wonderful on narrow, thin shoulders.

Capes

No matter how romantic, capes look good only on tall, dramatic people, such as Count Dracula. Cloaks (see CLOAKS) are floor length, capes shorter. What's good about capes: for 3,000 years people have found them unconstricting and comfortable. What's bad: adjusting them to the modern handbag. "Your shoulderbag doesn't work at all," says one cape owner. "If you carry a large handbag underneath, it bulges; if you carry the bag outside, your arms get cold." Most women carry clutch handbags, sometimes out, other times inside. Top-of-the-line cape: Designer Pauline Trigère, who has been famous for a decade for her beautiful capes, has never stopped wearing them herself. A Trigère wool cape is around $900.

Capezio Shoes

If you like the slender, aristocratic look of ballet slippers in all makes from lizard to

Cap sleeves

pink satin, Capezio is your most authentic brand. The company was founded in 1887 to make ballet slippers, and in the 1940s was discovered by the fashion world. While continuing to make professional dance slippers, Capezio also began selling inexpensive ballet shoes, which have sold steadily ever since.

Cardigan Sweater

The sweater cut down the front like a jacket, which has no collar. A cardigan worn open over a contrasting-color blouse is a great look for the top-heavy woman—the sweater provides two slimming vertical lines from hip to shoulder. A cardigan is a practical, comfortable way to layer and keep warm. It gets its name from the British Earl of Cardigan, who wore one during the Crimean War of 1855.

Cardin, Pierre

French designer, who became a big name as fashion revived after World War II. He was the first French designer to sell both ready-to-wear and custom-made couture clothes on the same premises, first to introduce the miniskirt and, recently, the first designer to be appointed exclusive consultant to China's brand-new fashion industry. Though clothes he likes to show on the runway at haute couture openings lean toward plastic hula-hoop dresses and space-age jumpsuits, the ready-to-wear Cardin clothes you'll find in America are a masterly blend of conservatism and femininity at reasonable prices. A black rayon dinner dress with white collar and cuffs is $160, his suits around $200.

Care

What baffles and most frustrates people about caring for clothes is the guessing game over whether to dry clean or risk washing at home. Since 1972, a Federal Trade Commission ruling has required that all clothes, both domestic and imported, be labeled with care instructions. However, if a garment is washable as well as dry-cleanable, the manufacturer need specify only one method. "The only time manufacturers put both options on their care labels is on cruise clothes," says a spokesman for the American Apparel Manufacturers Association. "They reason that whereas a woman would usually dry clean, she may not be anywhere near a dry cleaner and will want to know, when making her purchase, if the garment can also be washed." Consumer groups claim that manufacturers automatically put "dry clean only" on all clothes to protect themselves, as home launderers are more apt to botch the job, reappearing at the store as irate customers; few manufacturers have denied they practice "defensive labeling."

The truth is, many "dry clean only"-labeled clothes can be handwashed at home by anyone willing to take the time. Of course, home ironing will seldom approach the professional perfection of a good dry cleaner with all his steam gadgetry. On the other hand, unless you're doing business with a dry cleaner who keeps his solvent super clean, white linens and white cottons will begin to turn gray after a few cleanings. Probably the most idiotic abuse of care labeling is to put a "dry clean only" label on white linens and cottons—they should be washed, as they have been for centuries. Many people feel also that cashmere sweaters respond badly to dry-cleaning chemicals and take on a nicer softness and luster by being handwashed. Look under specific fabric entry for details on care, but generally, you can clean clothes as follows:

Machine washing (gentle cycle only) and drying okay, in warm, not hot water, *or* dry clean.	Acrylic, modacrylic, nylon, polyester, rayon, cotton (except white cottons which turn gray from repeated dry cleanings and brightly colored cottons which may run while laundered). *Never* put a "dry clean only" item in the washing machine or dryer.
Handwash in lukewarm water *or* dry clean.	Wool, cashmere, angora, mohair, silk, brightly colored cottons, linen (except white linen, which shouldn't be repeatedly dry cleaned).

| Dry clean only. | Tailored clothes with linings, brightly colored silks, acetate; anything with a nasty stain (see STAINS), anything expensive or ornate with a "dry clean only" label. |

Now, whether you decide to launder or dry clean, you want the best possible results. Here's what you should know about each method:

Dry Cleaning

Nothing is more frustrating than to pay a lot of money and have clothes come back out of shape, faded, or dingy. Yet, when this happens, statistics show that the fault belongs to the cleaner very seldom. Most dry cleaners belong to a regional cleaners' association, which maintains a lab acting as an arbitrator in disputes; in about 65 percent of all cases the fault is the manufacturer's; the rest of the time, blame is divided about equally between customer and cleaner.

One common manufacturing mess-up is cheap fusing. Interfacing is the stiffening material added to collars, button bands, waistbands; on high-quality clothes, the interfacing is sewn in. In more and more mass-produced clothes, especially suits and raincoats, it's glued in, a process called fusing. When fusing hits dry-cleaning solvent, the fabric puckers, bubbles, or buckles. Another problem is poor dye, especially on vividly colored silks. Pleats that aren't permanent, sequins and glitter that dissolve, imitation leather in which the polyurethane element separates from its backing, are other common headaches. According to William Seitz, president of the Neighborhood Cleaners Association, how much you pay for a garment has little to do with how safely it dry cleans—expensive designer clothes turn up in their arbitration lab as often as shopping-center specials. "Generally speaking, high fashion is concerned only with creating something ravishing. The designers couldn't care less about how it's going to wear," Mr. Seitz told a *New York Times* reporter. Replied a spokesman for Ralph Lauren, a designer whose clothes Seitz says turn up regularly at the arbitration lab, "No designer or manufacturer can send every fabric out to be tested. As a fashion leader, Ralph is always looking for new fabrics and to the best of our ability we try to ferret out any that won't meet our standards. We buy from reputable mills, but there's no one-hundred-percent guarantee about anything." And said Allen Tucker, president of the Calvin Klein menswear division, "We're trying to correct whatever problems we had, like finding the right fusing for Calvin's soft look. It just takes a while to obtain perfection." At any rate, once the lab has determined the manufacturer is at fault, you can march back into the store with your report and probably get a refund.

When the fault is yours, what happens is usually this: you spill a drink, or a grapefruit squirts on your skirt—spots which, to your relief, disappear immediately. Then, a few weeks later, the skirt comes back from the cleaners with a subtle stain. Outrage! But you had an invisible stain, which emerged in all its glory only during the heat of cleaning.

When the cleaners mess up, the most

common complaint is gray and dingy clothes. When dry-cleaning solvent isn't kept clean enough, it redeposits dirt and dye back on your clothes. (Hint: Dirty solvent leaves a detectable smell of cleaning fluid on clothes; clothes cleaned in a properly maintained solvent come back to you odorless.) Don't hesitate to take unsatisfactory work back and complain.

Another problem is that the spotter overestimated the toughness of your fabric, and used too strong a spot remover—goodbye to color along with stain. *Always take anything with a stain to the cleaners immediately*, because once it oxidizes and sets, the situation calls for more aggressive spotting. Result: a damaged or weakened fabric. Always clean clothes at the end of a season, not the beginning. You probably figure they'll just get wrinkled when you pack them away, but a few wrinkles are better than body acids and invisible stains setting in over an entire summer.

Home Laundering

Some women enjoy caring for their clothes as much as possible on their own, and find washing and ironing lovely fabrics a sensual experience. When care labels say "machine wash," you can just throw the garment in the washing machine and dryer without much fuss. Handwashing, though, does call for extra care. Here's a look at the tools you'll need.

Soap When handwashing fine clothes, it's best not to use a common laundry detergent. Most are designed for use in the family washing machine, to deal with heavy grease and dirt. Such aggressive sudsing might dull the finish or weaken fine silks, wools, linens.

The two soaps most recommended by manufacturers of delicate fabrics are Woolite and Ivory Snow. Woolite is a detergent, but designed with a solvent system gentler than the others. "Woolite won't strip the oils and natural lanolin from wools," says a spokeswoman for the company. The other favored soap, Ivory Snow, is the only pure soap. "It's made just as it was in 1879, of lye and fat," says Patrick Hayes of Procter & Gamble. "Ivory Snow is a granulated version of the soap." Ivory Snow and synthetic detergents clean equally well and in the same way, by reducing surface tension, loosening and dispersing the soil and holding it in suspension so that it isn't deposited back on clothes. In areas with hard water, however, soap leaves a scum on clothes if they're not well rinsed, and a ring forms around the tub. Though this happens only in hard water, it was enough to bring about the mass use of detergents, which require no extra rinses in any water.

Besides being gentler products, Woolite and soap are preferred by many people because these products are biodegradable, meaning they're able to be broken down by bacteria after use and again become part of the natural environment.

Whether you use soap or detergent, be sure to use enough, and to swish the clothes around plenty of times. (Never rub delicate fabrics vigorously.) Water temperature is also important. "Cold water washing doesn't do a thing for clothes except remove perspiration," says Dr. Fred Fortess of the Philadelphia College of Textiles and Science. "The colder the water, the less likely your detergent will go completely into solution and emulsify soil. Don't be afraid to use lukewarm water . . . it's only hot water that causes the problems with running dyes and shrinkage." To get lukewarm water, "always dissolve soap flakes first in hot, then add cold."

Deodorant soaps also have a use in home laundry. Synthetic fibers such as polyester and acrylic tend to pick up perspiration odors easily; any garment can develop odors on hot days when you're exerting yourself. Work up a lather under the arms with a good strong deodorant soap such as Dial or Zest, swish the entire garment in your regular detergent a few times, and rinse.

Bleaches When laundry is especially dingy and stained, or you're washing white clothes, you need extra cleaning power. Most effective are chlorine bleaches such as Clorox, but these are also most likely to damage fabrics. Never use chlorine on delicate fabrics such as silks or nylons, on vivid colors, or on elastic underwear containing spandex. Not as effective but much safer are the all-fabric bleaches, which use oxygen-containing compounds rather than chlorine. *Consumer Reports* ran tests on these bleaches, and found A&P All Fabric Bleach, White King, Safeway's White Magic, and Clorox 2 most effective. Less effective as bleaches were Poly Tex, Biz, Woolite, Miracle White, Snowy Liquid, and bleach substitutes such as Axion, Borateem Plus, and Miracle White Super Cleaner. All bleaches worked better when problem clothes were soaked in the recommended bleach/water/soap solution overnight than when they were soaked for only half an hour or put directly in the machine. All-fabric bleaches can be used safely on most clothes except those of colored acetate, silks, and wool; they are particularly good at brightening antique clothes.

Wrinkle removers Next to soap and water, your most important home laundry tool is your iron. If you've been ironing with the same iron for years and years, you might do yourself a favor by shopping for a new one. The American iron, the first

successful home appliance and one electrical item the Japanese *don't* do better, is still a big bargain in terms of cost ($20–$30) and has been improved so much in the past few years that a ten-year-old model is about as *au courant* as a Model A Ford. Today's plastic-topped irons are a full pound lighter than standard irons of a few years ago. They have cool-touch shells so that you don't get burned, and they heat up and cool down in half their former time. Self-cleaning flushes out particles of fabric that get into steam vents, and cleans sediments from tap water itself; you no longer have to use distilled water. Gone are the fabric-insulated electrical cords, which frayed—irons now have standard electrical cords. A clean plastic water window tells you how much water you have left. Here are a few hints on getting the best performance from your iron.

- Don't use the iron until it preheats for the recommended time. If the iron is not sufficiently preheated, water will not be changed to steam—instead it will drip from the vents and spot the garment being ironed.

- Don't store the iron on heel rest with steam left on "On"—water may drip from tank into steam chamber, causing spitting and possible water-spotting next time the iron is used. It's a good idea to empty all water from an iron after use to prevent possible corrosion, should the iron be accidently knocked over, causing remaining water to seep through steam vents.

- To clean an aluminum soleplate (bottom of the iron), make a paste of mild scouring powder and a little water. Apply and remove with a damp cloth, wiping thoroughly. Turn on steam and iron over an old towel for a couple of minutes to remove any remaining residue from the steam vents. For scratches on an aluminum soleplate, smooth with very fine sandpaper or the finest steel wool. Slight scratches on a nonstick soleplate make no difference.

Almost as important a gadget as your iron is a steamer, the best of which is Wrinkles Away.

Wrinkles Away is the size of a large flashlight, weighs less than a pound, uses ordinary tap water to operate, and needs no ironing board or pressing cloth. You simply hang wrinkled clothes on a hanger, add water to the steamer, and give it three minutes to heat up; point it at wrinkles and watch them magically disappear.

You wouldn't use a steamer to press just-washed clothes—an iron is better—but for clothes you've been wearing, or that were packed in a suitcase or got a little beat up hanging in the closet, Wrinkles Away is terrific. For wools and silks, which shouldn't be ironed dry, steaming is a necessity. For wool, steaming not only takes out wrinkles, it fluffs the fiber up again. Of course, you can hang wrinkled clothes in the bathroom and take a long, hot shower, but this clumsy procedure wastes water and doesn't always work.

The regular model is $18. A dual-voltage model, which will work in any hotel in any

This electric hand steamer is the most useful invention since the iron in the eternal battle against wrinkles; it's indispensable with wools. (Wrinkles-Away ® by Franzus Company, Inc.)

country (and save you a fortune in pressing bills, even on heavy suits), costs $25. You can find Wrinkles Away in the Housewares section of department stores, or you can write or call the company to order, and find out where it's sold near you. Their address:

Franzus Company, Inc.
352 Park Avenue South
New York, New York 10010
212 889-5850

Care Labels

Most important for taking care of clothes is reading the manufacturer's care labels. However, you can be only so specific on a label a half-inch wide. Here, the American Apparel Manufacturers Association explains exactly what those terse instructions mean.

	WHEN LABEL READS:	IT MEANS:
NON-MACHINE WASHING	Hand wash	Launder only by hand in luke warm (hand comfortable) water. May be bleached. May be dry cleaned
	Hand wash only	Same as above, but do not dry clean
	Hand wash separately	Hand wash alone or with like colors
	No bleach	Do not use bleach
	Damp wipe	Surface clean with damp cloth or sponge

(Courtesy of The American Apparel Manufacturers Association, Inc.)

	WHEN LABEL READS:	IT MEANS:
MACHINE WASHABLE	Machine wash	Wash, bleach, dry and press by any customary method including commercial laundering and dry cleaning
	Home launder only	Same as above but do not use commercial laundering and dry cleaning
	No Chlorine Bleach	Do not use chlorine bleach. Oxygen bleach may be used
	No bleach	Do not use any type of bleach
	Cold wash Cold rinse	Use cold water from tap or cold washing machine setting
	Warm wash Warm rinse	Use warm water or warm washing machine setting
	Hot wash	Use hot water or hot washing machine setting
	No spin	Remove wash load before final machine spin cycle
	Delicate cycle	Use appropriate machine setting; otherwise wash by hand
	Durable press cycle Permanent press cycle	Use appropriate machine setting; otherwise use warm wash, cold rinse and short spin cycle
	Wash separately	Wash alone or with like colors
HOME DRYING	Tumble dry	Dry in tumble dryer at specified setting—high, medium, low no heat
	Tumble dry Remove promptly	Same as above, but in absence of cool-down cycle remove at once when tumbling stops
	Drip dry	Hang wet and allow to dry with hand shaping only
	Line dry	Hang damp and allow to dry
	No wring No twist	Hang dry, drip dry to dry flat only. Handle to prevent wrinkles and distortion
	Dry flat	Lay garment on flat surface
	Block to dry	Maintain original size and shape while drying
IRONING OR PRESSING	Cool iron	Set iron at lowest setting
	Warm iron	Set iron at medium setting
	Hot iron	Set iron at hot setting
	Do not iron	Do not iron or press with heat
	Steam iron	Iron or press with steam
	Iron damp	Dampen garment before ironing
MISCELLANEOUS	Dry clean only	Garment should be dry cleaned only, including self-service
	Professionally dry clean only	Do not use self-service dry cleaning
	No dry clean	Use recommended care instruction. No dry cleaning materials to be used.

Cartier Rolling Ring

(also called the puzzle ring) One of the great jewelry classics, this ring was designed by Louis Cartier in 1924 and has been selling steadily ever since. It's made from three interlocking bands of pink, yellow, and white 18-karat gold, and costs $260 in any of Cartier's sixty boutiques around the world.

Cashin, Bonnie

American designer known since the 1940s for her loose-fitting sportswear. While other designers often go in for tight skirts and tailored blazers with shoulder pads, Bonnie has never swerved from her belief that clothes should be worn loose, in functional layers.

She was the first important designer to make ponchos for women, and has always specialized in tweeds, knits, canvas, and leather. Her leather jerkins and fur-trimmed poplin raincoats ($345) are especially collected. She grosses over $25 million a year, but unlike most major designers such as Blass, Halston, and the Kleins, she never licenses her name for perfumes or sheets.

During the 1940s, she lived in Hollywood and designed clothes for films, two of the most famous being *Laura* and *Anna and the King of Siam*. Cashin was elected to the Coty Hall of Fame in 1972.

Cashmere

Unintelligent, unfriendly, and mountain-dwelling Kashmir goats are raised only in remote parts of China, the Soviet Union's Outer Mongolia, Iran, and Afghanistan. Attempts have been made to reestablish this high-strung Himalayan creature everywhere in the west from the Alps to Texas, but the animal refuses to grow usable fleece anywhere but in its original habitat. Even there, the amount of fleece each goat produces a year is only four ounces, and to get to this fleece, the goats must be combed by hand by nomadic tribesmen each spring. Combed fleece is then brought down mountain trails in bags carried on human backs, and on by camel to city merchants. The amount of cashmere available is less than four million pounds annually, as compared with more than 24 billion pounds of man-made fibers.

A cashmere sweater or coat is one of the blue-chip investments to be made in clothes. Fiber is so fine that, ounce for ounce, cashmere has more insulation power than any other cloth. Besides being the warmest of fabrics for the weight, it doesn't wrinkle, it breathes, and it's soft and pliant. A cashmere sweater is more comfortable than blazers, blouses, or dresses to travel in because it doesn't pull at your arms, and a well-made sweater lasts ten to twenty years, or more. According to Pringle of Scotland, the world's largest manufacturer of cashmere knitwear, customers often return their sweaters to the factory after fifteen or twenty years to be reshaped. "Cashmere is not easily destructible," says William McEwan, Pringle's managing director.

Shopping for Cashmere

A sweater is the best value in cashmere, followed closely by a coat. Cashmere coats don't attract lint, even the dark coats. After a few years they may begin to fray around cuffs or neckline (wearing a scarf helps prevent this). Cashmere scarves are easily lost, skirts eventually show abrasion around the seat. Cashmere ski underwear, sold at Saks and in ski shops, is a luxury but terrific. It costs more than wool or synthetic thermal underwear, but is warmer, lighter, and never itchy. Cashmere nightgowns, the latest thing, are probably no more comfortable than a thick flannel.

Look for thick cashmere—not only is a sweater of substance more luxurious, but thin cheapies are the sweaters that pull apart at seams. "One-ply" on the label means it's made of the finest, most closely knit of cashmere yarn. Look for $60 sweaters, and coats for under $300, during Columbus Day sales; watch newspaper ads, buy off-season. Learn to recognize cashmere, and you can pick up sweaters in good thrift shops *sans* labels, for $5. They're also a good buy for $20–$30 in resale shops. Best labels: Pringle of Scotland, Ballantyne, Braemar, Jaeger, Brooks Brothers.

Care

Dry clean or handwash. To launder, use Ivory Snow or Woolite, dissolving the soap first in hot water, then adding cold to make lukewarm water. For white or pale sweaters, you can occasionally add a capful of ammonia to the water to eliminate grayness. Soak for a few minutes to allow soap to work. Never rub hard (if sweater has spots, dry clean). For next-to-last rinse, add a quarter of a cup of white distilled vinegar to a few inches of water, swish, and rinse again until vinegar odor is gone. Pat dry in a towel, and then lay flat to dry.

Challis

(shal´-ee) A soft, lightweight fabric printed with floral patterns against a dark background, made of cotton, wool, or synthetic fibers. Liberty of London's wool challis fabric is considered among the world's finest. Skirts are more commonly made of challis than are blouses. Dresses are also common, especially for winter.

Care

Follow label directions. Colors sometimes run if handwashed.

Chambray

(sham´-bray) The chambray industry got a huge boost when Gloria Steinem abandoned her cashmeres and silks for jeans and chambray workshirt, the uniform of early women's movement demonstrations. Also much worn by generations of grubby college students of both sexes. Chambray is a plainly woven fabric, usually cotton, similar to denim but lighter in weight. It's usually a solid color, with white filling threads giving it a pastel appearance. Though chambray is not a fabric with an interesting texture, it's soft and heavenly to wear, as workingmen have known for a century.

Care

Machine wash.

Chamois

(sham´-ee) Originally a super-soft, pliable leather from the skin of the chamois antelope of Europe, today the term is used in reference to any soft skin, usually from sheep, goats, or deer, usually a pale yellow color. Chamois running shorts cost $125, a wild extravagance but considered the softest shorts in existence.

Care

Pale, unlined chamois leather can easily be washed. If you see a skirt or top drastically marked down merely because it's gotten dingy, grab it. Handwash in lukewarm water; if it dries stiff, knead a few minutes.

Chanel, Coco

(1883–1971) French designer. What a life she had, and what a life the legendary Chanel suit has had, being worn exactly the same, give or take a few inches in hem length, for fifty years. Still considered *the* suit investment, one can be bought for

The fabled Chanel suit still sells almost exactly as Coco designed it in 1930. (Photo: François Lamy)

$1,500 and up, in any of the twenty-one Chanel boutiques found in stores such as I. Magnin, Garfinckel's, Neiman-Marcus, and Saks. You don't need a private appointment, just go in and look around. To find the boutique nearest you, write or call Chanel, 9 West 57th Street, New York, NY .10019 (212 688-5055). The Chanel suit has a collarless, boxy jacket worn with a straight skirt. Sewn into the bottom edge of jackets, to help them keep their shape and hang properly, are the famous metal-link weighted chains.

Chanel herself was an orphan. Her mother died when she was six; her father left her with her grandmother and then vanished, and the beautiful Chanel was sent to a convent. While visiting an aunt in a nearby country garrison town, she met a handsome, aristocratic officer, and went to Paris with him as his mistress. With his financial backing, she opened a millinery shop with dazzling success, and soon not only her hats but her clothes and style were seen everyplace chic in Paris. Women from barmaids to marquesses took up her passion for suntanning, and her soft tailored suits and knits helped free women from corsets and high stiff collars. In 1914 she introduced wool jersey, and in 1915, rayon; by 1924, everyone was wearing the first perfume created by a designer, Chanel No. 5.

The toast of Paris until the Germans took over the city, she finally closed shop and fled Paris in 1939. Unfortunately, she soon returned with a handsome German officer, and spent the rest of the war comfortably in the Ritz Hotel under his protection, a liaison which caused so much enmity that her fashion career was shattered. Not until 1954, at the age of seventy-one, did she dare reopen her business, at which time she again became a great success.

Charmeuse

A soft, clinging satin, lustrous on one side and dull on the other. It's the name of a type of weave rather than a fabric, and can be made of rayon, silk, acetate, nylon, polyester, or blends of any of these. Silk charmeuse is a fabric of such luxury it's hardly used anymore except by couture houses, though those of us with limited funds can still find silk charmeuse dresses from the 1920s and 1930s in antique shops for around $100. Of the man-made fibers, rayon is considered most comfortable, since it breathes; Qiana nylon and acetate are most lustrous. Always a fragile fabric, it must be dry cleaned.

Chatelaine

Silver perfume bottle from the 1890s, usually richly patterned, worn hanging from a long silver chain around the neck. New York models seem to most love wearing theirs with silk blouses, blue jeans, and wildly expensive French boots. Some are oval and have tiny holes in them; these were worn by their original owners with tiny perfume-soaked sponges inside. Most are gracefully oblong or round, with tops that screw on tightly so you can carry your favorite scent in them. The most sought-after chatelaines have the Gorham sterling silver mark on bottom and can still be found in flea markets and small antique stores for $100. Silver-plated ones cost half that. (See SILVER, Care.)

Chemise

A straight-lined, unbelted dress. (Also called a chemisier.) The chemise was the dress worn by flappers of the 1920s, along with their headache bands and raccoon coats, and reappeared in 1957 as the despised sack dress, inspiring the hit rock 'n' roll record "No Chemise Please." Men have never liked the shapelessness of the chemise, but the style is a favorite among women who like to dress for health. "The chemise is the most comfortable dress for women today," says designer Mollie Parnis. "It's easy to move around in and entirely non-constricting."

Buy any chemise only in soft, floating fabrics; a stiff fabric doesn't move with the body, isn't at all sexy, and is the sack dress all over again. Chemises are particularly nice for the swaybacked, but not so flattering to large-breasted women, who look bulky in them.

Chenille

(shah-neel´) The French word for fuzzy caterpillar, chenille is a velvetlike cord of yarn with fibers of cotton, acrylic, or wool protruding from it like the tufts on a caterpillar's back. When made of cotton, this soft, super-fluffy yarn is very absorbent and has traditionally been woven into bathrobes. (Tuftees has been selling the same thirsty little 100-percent cotton chenille bathrobe since the 1940s—still only $26!) Chenille bedspreads are another classic item. Right now, gloriously colored cotton chenille sweaters by such knitters as Carolyn Eve of Boulder, Colorado, are collectibles. Handknit cotton chenilles cost $100 or more, but machine-made acrylics costing as little as $12.90 do a respectable job of imitating the look.

Cheongsam

(chung-sam) A long tight skirt slit thigh-high on one side, or knee-high on two sides. Favorite gear of exotic Oriental beauties out to seduce males in adventure movies.

Chesterfield

A straight, tailored double- or single-breasted coat with a velvet collar. The style originated in England in the early 1950s and was named after the eighteenth-century Lord Chesterfield. A standard "preppy-look" item, you'll always find a Chesterfield coat at Brooks Brothers, where this season's charcoal gray herringbone tweed model sells for $285. Top-of-the-line Chesterfield is usually Yves St. Laurent's, priced at $1,320.

Cheviot Wool

(shev´-ee-ot) A type of tweed with a surface so rough it's almost prickly. Now mostly made by machine, cheviot tweed was originally a rough homespun, named for sheep from the Cheviot Hills along the English-Scottish border. It's used for coats and jackets.

Chiffon

The most floaty of fabrics, chiffon can be woven from silk, polyester, or nylon. The most common chiffon is of polyester; most expensive and filmy is of silk. The Empress Josephine, Napoleon's wife, could pull her silk chiffon dresses through a wedding band. Obviously, so gossamer a fabric is going to move with the body and be titillating, so chiffons are always for eveningwear.

Care

Because chiffon is so light, manufacturers often add special starches to the fabric to make it less cobwebby; these additives are what cause water rings to appear when liquid is spilled on it. Short of contacting the manufacturer, you won't know whether your chiffon will waterspot or not, so try not to let drops from a misting water glass fall on it. However, a good dry cleaner can remove water spots—if one fails, try a better one. Light-colored chiffon should be handwashable in cool water with Ivory Snow.

A Chinese slipper is the world's widest, most comfortable shoe to wear on any surface but cement. (Photo: Herb Dorfman)

Chinese Slippers

The national shoe of China is a wide Mary Jane with one strap across the top. They're made of sturdy cotton with rubber soles, and to find a more comfortable $6 shoe would be impossible. They're roomy enough to accommodate the most broad foot, yet the strap somehow keeps them anchored securely even on a narrow foot. They don't rub, pinch, or feel clammy, are a balm for toes with corns, and can be worn alone in summer or with wool knee-highs in winter. Waitresses love them. Some people find the rubber soles aren't heavy enough to keep their bones from jarring when walking on city cement. Find them in Oriental import stores everywhere.

Chino

(cheen´-o) Tan-colored twilled cotton fabric, fabulous for inexpensive sturdy pants because it will take indefinite washings. Chino is the same fabric used by British troops in nineteenth-century India, when they dyed their white uniforms with coffee and curry powder and called them by the Hindu term for dust-color—khaki. It got its name during World War I when it was brought from China and worn by soldiers in the Philippines.

Classic front-pleated chino slacks can be worn any season, as can denims. Sasson is known for nice chino slacks; "wilderness stores" such as L. L. Bean, and Kreeger and Sons in New York, sell flannel-lined ones for winter.

Chinon

The world's only fabric made from milk, Chinon is a Japanese product made with casein, the principle ingredient in cheese. Chinon is described as "silkier than silk" by the Toyobo Co., Ltd., its producer; it has little static electricity, meaning that it, like natural fibers, doesn't attract dirt easily, is mothproof, and doesn't wrinkle. The fabric is used for eveningwear, blouses, and lingerie.

Care

Should you iron it with a steam iron or a too-hot iron the fabric will pucker nastily. Follow label directions.

Chintz

A cotton fabric with a slight gloss, usually printed with brightly colored designs of flowers, but can be plain. Adorable chintz housecoats from the 1940s, with shoulder pads and puffed, elbow-length sleeves, one of the most popular summer items in antique shops right now, go for $40 or $50 in mint condition. Chintz is usually hand-washable.

Chloé

(klo´-ee) A super-expensive French ready-to-wear firm, at the helm of which is a brilliant designer named Karl Lagerfeld. (See LAGERFELD.)

Circle skirts are thus called because they literally form a circle with a hole in the middle for the waist. (Fashion by Donna Karan and Louis Dell'Olio for Anne Klein & Company)

Circle Skirt

Literally, a circle of material with a hole cut in the center for the waist. A swingy, graceful skirt, slender at the top where nobody wants bulk, more voluminous toward the bottom.

Ciré

(sear´-ray) A glossy, slippery wax applied to a fabric, giving it a finish somewhat like patent leather. You'll see ciré finishes mostly on nylon parkas for rain or mildly cool days. Ciré doesn't breathe and isn't comfortable to wear for long periods of time.

Care

Never leave a ciré jacket folded or twisted in the same position for months on end—white streaks will develop along fold lines. Otherwise, follow label directions. If they say don't dry clean, it's because the wax will dissolve in dry-cleaning solvent.

Claiborne, Liz

American designer. Her company has grown in four years from a $250,000 venture to an $80-million-a-year operation. Not interested in breaking new ground in fashion, Claiborne wants to make sensible clothes for the working woman. Neither is she a natural-fiber snob. "I use wearable, not fragile, fabrics that can pack well," she says. "Polyester crêpe de Chine not only costs less money than silk, it doesn't wrinkle. Plus, it looks exactly like silk." Her clothes are relatively inexpensive: blouses cost $30 or $40, handknit sweaters as little as $60.

Classics

In literature, art, and music, works characterized by restraint, formality, and simplicity are said to be in the tradition of classicism, as opposed to works of passion and flamboyance, which are considered romantic. Also, a classic is a creative work of such excellence that it outlives its own day and attains a certain timelessness. By this definition, any article of clothing that's been in style for more than three or four years could be considered a classic: in addition to the much-touted blazer, classics include such long-lasting and diverse items as A-line skirts, Chanel suits, polo coats, turtleneck sweaters, jumpsuits, and even blue jeans.

What's nice about classics is that you can buy them on sale at season's end, and be reasonably sure they won't be obsolete by the beginning of the new season.

Cloaks

Capes are short; cloaks are voluminous, full-length, and more graceful and romantic. For formal wear, you can find black velvet ones in antique shops for around $120. For times when you want to look dramatic and romantic but not formal, you might hire a seamstress to make you up an Irish Kinsale cloak, a beautiful wrap still worn in west County Cork. The cloak

Floor-length cloaks are the most elegant possible evening wraps, and are easy to make yourself.

49

should be made from handwoven tweed gathered under a wide collar, fastened with a large hook and eye, and falling to the ground in unpressed pleats. For the pattern, write Folkwear Patterns, Box 98, Forestville, California 95436.

Cloche

(klosh) A close-fitting, bell-shaped hat, first worn by the 1920s flappers. Antique shops sometimes sell darling ones for under $10. They're actually quite practical, because they keep ears warm and covered.

Clog

This clunky, wooden-soled shoe has rested in nearly everybody's closet at some time, and usually isn't thrown out until such shabbiness has set in that they become a health hazard. "When you first buy a pair of clogs, it's because you like the anti-fashion look," says one long-time clog owner. "Then, you're dismayed, because it feels like you're walking on stilts. You can only wear them a little at a time at first, or you get blisters. Then . . . I don't know . . . you gradually get used to them, and they make

This Olofdaughters clog has been a best-seller in Sweden for hundreds of years and was the first clog to arrive in America, about twenty years ago.

all your other shoes feel flimsy. You learn to love the roominess, the clomping sound they make, the secure feeling of a wooden sole." They're good for walking in the rain because of their height, not so good for driving.

Clogs are a derivation of the Dutch wooden shoe, and have been worn in Scandinavia and Holland for centuries, where they are considered good for posture of the back and spine. Olof Daughters of Sweden introduced the first clog in the U.S. seventeen years ago, and these Swedish-made shoes have been selling steadily ever since.

Clotheshangers

Thin wire hangers that are free from the cleaners are bad news; plush satin hangers, which cost $12 for five, are good news. Fortunately, you now can buy five nicely shaped plastic hangers for a dollar that are also good news, as are wooden ones.

Thin wire hangers were designed only to get your cleaned clothes from store to home. Nothing should hang on them for more than a few days, and never for an entire season, as they'll cause clothes to lose their shape, will leave indentation marks at the top of the shoulder, and sometimes, in damp climates, will leave rust marks. Never hang wet clothes on them to dry.

Coach Bag

The best European handbags are admired for their aristocratic delicacy of appearance. American handbags tend to be sturdy-looking styles that remind you somehow of western saddles (no accident—both are made from cowhide). Most famous of these handbags, and the only American-made bag to have a boutique in Paris, at 23 rue Jacob, is Coach.

Few Coach bags cost over $110. The two

Coach® bags are made from cowhide and are admired for the natural markings of the leather. This style has been an American classic for over fifteen years.

biggest sellers—the basic clutch with detachable shoulder straps and solid brass industrial zipper, and the crescent shoulderbag with brass stirrup buckles—cost only $66 and $82 respectively. All bags are made of tanned cowhide, and leather is left completely "naked," to show off natural markings; no two Coach bags are exactly alike. No handbags in the world look better with sportswear.

You can find Coach in department stores all over the country. Or write to Coach Leatherware, 516 West 34th Street, New York, New York 10001, to find the store nearest you.

Coats

Several different surveys, from one conducted by the *National Enquirer* to John Molloy's survey for *Dress for Success*, have found that what men notice first about a woman is not the size of her bosom or color of her eyes, but her socioeconomic level. Since in winter a coat is the only garment that shows, more men judged the class of a woman by her coat than anything

else about her. Moral: when planning your clothing budget, allot more proportionately to a good coat than anything else.

Two salient facts to remember when buying a coat:

- If you're short or heavy, stick to the long vertical lines of a full-length coat. Avoid hip-length coats, with a horizontal line to widen you at just the wrong spot; in fall and spring, wear trenchcoats or sweater coats instead of jackets. Also avoid tentlike coats such as balmacaans, and stick to tailored, single-breasted coats with long simple lines—polos, Chesterfields.

- Biggest coat sale at season's beginning is Columbus Day, October 12. After that coats begin to go on sale in November, are reduced even more after Christmas, and are closest to give-away prices in April.

Color

You can have the thinnest figure and closets of clothes, but if you opt for unappetizing color combinations, it will all be futile. No book can show you what colors look good together, but here's a handful of basic observations about color and clothes:

- The lighter a color (the more white in it), the more attention it attracts; thus, if you're wide-beamed on bottom, you'd wear a somber or dark skirt with a light top, never a dark top with a light skirt. If you're topheavy but slender on bottom, you'd go in for darker colors on top, lighter colors on bottom.

- Light colors reflect heat and light away from the body, thus helping you stay cool in summer; dark absorbs heat and light, warming you up.

- The law of areas used in interior decorating also works with clothes: use strong colors in small doses, restful colors in large amounts. Thus, single-tone dressing will usually be more elegant in beige or cream, with a purple belt, than *all* flaming purple with a beige belt. Of course, some people look fabulous clad entirely in fire-engine red and deep purple.

- A few classic color combinations with which you can't lose are:

  Navy blue suit with a cream blouse

  Burgundy-colored suit with a gray blouse or sweater

  Single-tone dressing in any tasteful color

  Dressing all in browns and creams

  Beige sweater with a red sweater tied around the shoulders or a red belt

  A solid-color skirt with a patterned blouse picking up the skirt's color, or vice versa

  In summer, blue and white or red and white.

FASHION COPY COLORS DEMYSTIFIED

Amethyst	clear pale violet	Coral	a reddish orange
Aquamarine	blue-green, the color of sea water; in Spanish, *aqua* means water	Curry	a rich yellow-brown; mustard-colored, like the spice
Aubergine	dark burgundy, like an eggplant (French word for eggplant)	Forest green	deep, dark green, the color of evergreen trees
Azure	deep blue-green, from Côte d'Azur	Fuchsia	reddish purple
		Ginger	pale brown, the color of ginger root
Bisque	light grayish brown—color of unglazed ceramic ware	Heather gray	mauvey gray, a muted purple
Cadet gray	straightforward battleship gray	Heliotrope	pinkish purple, as are the heliotrope flowers which turn toward the sun
Celadon (cell´-ah-don)	a pale gray-green, derives from the pale green glaze you see on Chinese porcelains		
		Hyacinth blue	deep purplish blue
		Hyacinth red	grayish red-orange
Cerise	cherry red; moderate to deep red	Ice blue	a cold light blue, with no red in it
Cerulean	dark blue	Jade	dull green
Chinese red	dazzling bright red	Lilac	pale pink purple
Claret	wine-colored; color of French Bordeaux	Loden green	a dull, opaque green, similar to Khaki

FASHION COPY COLORS DEMYSTIFIED

	green, only darker; a favorite wintry English color	Primrose	pink, a color made famous by Mamie Eisenhower, who was a pink freak
Maize	yellow, color of ripe corn	Putty	light grayish brown
Mango	reddish orange, like the fruit	Royal	dark blue, but not as dark as navy blue
Marigold	strong orange yellow	Russet	rust-colored; terracotta
Mocha (mo-ca)	deep rich brown, like coffee with chocolate	Sepia	a reddish-brown pigment originally extracted from the ink of cuttlefish
Nile green	opaque, earth-colored green, found in ancient Egyptian art		
Palomino	bone, with slightly yellowish hue; color of vanilla ice cream	Slate blue	gray blue
		Taupe (tope)	dark brownish gray
Parchment	grayish yellow, as in the skin of a sheep or goat that was used for paper in ancient times	Teal	dark greenish blue, named after the small, short-necked river duck
		Ultramarine blue	deep purplish blue
Peacock blue	blue with a greenish hue	Vermillion (ver-mil´-yen)	brilliant orange red
Platinum	yellow		

Corduroy

Velvets, velveteens, and corduroys are pile fabrics, which means they have a surface much like a well-kept lawn—tiny threads sprout from the foundation cloth just as grass grows from the ground. Of these three, corduroy is the one that is ribbed, with ribs (called "wales") running lengthwise down the fabric. These wales may vary in width from a fine "pinwale," with as many as twenty-one ribs to the inch, to "wide-wale" with only two or three. The silkiest, most lustrous corduroys are 100 percent combed cotton.

Corduroy was given its name in the mid-1700s, by a French importer. Bringing in the new fabric from England, he was one of history's first merchants with demonstrable P.R. savvy—he decided to promote the fabric by associating it with royalty, calling it "Corde du Roi, Cloth of the King." The first American mill to make corduroy is the 170-year-old Crompton Company, in Crompton, Rhode Island, which first added corduroy to its line in 1885; Crompton corduroys, velvets, and velveteens are still considered prestige fabrics the world over. Two American manufacturers known for particularly nice corduroy clothes are Luba, which makes a beautiful $150 coat, and Evan-Picone, with its corduroy blazers, skirts, and pants.

Care

Dry clean, or wash according to label instructions. If you wash, remove the inevitable lint with a clothes brush *while still damp* after washing.

Corselet Belt

A wide belt laced and tied in front. First worn by the bare-bosomed women of ancient Crete in 1400 B.C., most lately seen in the Russian peasant costumes of St. Laurent. As with any wide belt, it looks adorable on the small-waisted, but abominable on a thick waist.

Cotton

Opening a newspaper or magazine lately, you're likely to run into one of the spate of articles on "The Return of King Cotton." "Cotton, the one-time monarch and chief provider of the Old South's agriculture, is moving back onto its throne," reports *The New York Times*. Exports are at their highest level in nearly fifty years and the 1981 crop has been the largest in several decades. Designers from Perry Ellis to Christian Dior are working with cotton, and, reports *U.S. News and World Report*, "Cotton goods are in heavy demand everywhere from chic New York boutiques to J.C. Penney." Why does everyone suddenly want their blouses and skirts and sweaters and socks and even handbags to have been grown in cotton fields? Here are a few reasons:

- *Comfort.* Cotton *breathes*, meaning it absorbs moisture from the body, transmits it through the fabric, and allows it to evaporate; if moisture is trapped by a nonbreathing fabric, you'll feel clammy. With normal activity, the average person's body gives off three pints of water daily, and if you're jogging or playing tennis, much more. Because each tiny fiber of cotton is a network of micro-chambers with a hollow center, cotton absorbs this moisture like a sponge. Says one physician, "Because cotton helps moisture to evaporate, a good case can be made that you'll be more comfortable exercising in a cotton shirt than without a shirt." Cotton is also comfortable because it's soft, never sticky or scratchy, and causes few allergies. In summer it can be woven loosely for coolness, in winter thick and tight for warmth.

- *No static electricity,* which means clothes won't cling annoyingly or attract dirt as readily as synthetics. With an all-cotton blouse, you won't have the "ring-around-the-collar" or graying cuffs that you'll have with polyester or a blend, and no synthetic will stay as snowy white.

- *Washability.* Because wet cotton fiber expands and gets stronger, you can wash it with water as hot as you like; unless the care label says not to, it can be bleached, even boiled. Cotton is the most reasonable of fabrics for a sweltering, steamy August day because you don't have to worry about ruining it by sweating all over it. A cotton blouse won't pick up body odor like synthetics, won't fade or get perspiration stains as will silk. Of course, unlike drip-dry synthetics, cotton does usually have to be ironed. A chemical procedure has been developed to make wash-and-wear cotton, which has been available in men's shirts since 1979 (Lady Arrow and a few other manufacturers make these shirts for women also), but this no-iron fabric has not won universal acceptance. Bloomingdale's so far doesn't carry these shirts, according to a salesman, "because they don't feel right." Macy's and Gimbel's do carry them and sell thousands. The U.S. Department of Agriculture, National Cotton Council, and Cotton, Inc., who worked together to perfect the Norwegian procedure giving cotton no-iron qualities, maintain that this chemical pretreatment in no way interferes with comfort or feel of natural cotton. When you talk to people who bought these shirts, some think the shirts are great, but others report they're not as comfortable as regular cotton, and bemoan the increasing scarcity of pure untreated cotton clothes. The final verdict is not in.

- *Ecology.* Cotton takes about one-fourth as much energy to produce as do petroleum-derived synthetics, and modern agricultural know-how has enabled American farmers to grow some fifteen million bales a year on one-third the acreage needed fifty years ago to produce the same amount. The fiber, furthermore, doesn't compete with food for land—since cottonseed oil is widely used in cooking, a cotton crop is both food and fiber.

12,000 Years of Cotton Dresses

Before getting into how to give your cottons loving care, it might be interesting to take a quick look at the colorful past of this staple natural fiber, the world's oldest woven cloth: Carbon-14 tests show that cotton has been cultivated in India and China as far back as 10,000 B.C. and in the Americas as early as 2,500 B.C., in Peru.

Indian prints were first imported to Europe in the seventeenth century, where, since supplies were so limited, cotton became more prized than silk and was worn only by the rich. Meanwhile, seed was brought from the West Indies for planting in the American South, beginning in Virginia in 1607. From then until 1792, a few hundred bales of cotton were grown and shipped to Europe each year. By 1810, that figure had jumped to 160,000 bales. What launched the South's cotton boom was, of course, Eli Whitney's cotton gin, a machine that separated cotton from seed. In order to gin that much cotton, somebody had to pick it first, which is why there were more than a million slaves in the South by 1810.

Today 75 percent of American cotton is grown in Arizona, California, and New Mexico, 25 percent in Dixie—in Louisiana, Mississippi, Virginia, Arkansas. The growing itself goes like this: after sowing, plants take about two months to reach their full height of three or four feet. Blossoms form, with petals turning from creamy white to yellow to dark red within three days, withering, and falling off, leaving a pod called a cotton boll. This fluffy white boll is a tempting dinner to unvanquished boll weevils, fleahoppers, tobacco budworms, banded wing whiteflies, and pink bollworms, and for every five bales of cotton making it to market, one is lost to these hordes.

So much for cotton in its natural habitat. What should you know about cotton in the stores? Here's a small glossary of explanatory terms:

Brushed cotton The fabric surface is literally brushed, making it softer and warmer by creating insulating air cells.

Combed cotton When cotton fiber is turned into yarn, it is first carded, which means the fibers are disentangled and shaped into a thin web, and then may or may not be combed as well. In this process, shorter, coarser fibers are combed out from longer ones, resulting in a finer, softer, and stronger cotton yarn.

Cord-Set A process allowing you to safely wash and tumble dry 100 percent cotton with no shrinkage.

Egyptian cotton is considered the finest cotton grown in the world. First introduced to Egypt by Alexander's armies, the plant has thrived ever since in fertile Nile valley soil. Egypt, however, doesn't manufacture good fabric, so a big-name designer would probably buy his raw cotton in Egypt, and then ship it to Italy or the Orient to be made into cloth.

Indian cotton Distinguished by being the purest cotton fabric, grown, manufactured, and printed in India by ancient methods making little use of modern chemicals. Though often coarser than other cottons, Indian cotton is loved most for its authenticity. (See INDIAN CLOTHES.)

Italian cotton The term "Italian cotton" refers to cotton from the U.S., Egypt, China, and elsewhere that's shipped to Italy to be made into fabric. Italian prints are considered the world's most beautiful, and the fabric itself is often so light and airy that a breeze from a window will dry it.

Mercerized cotton has had a finish applied to it imparting a silky luster lasting as long as the fabric lasts, and which also makes the cloth stronger and more resistant to mildew. Manufacturers love mercerization, which was invented in 1844 by a calico dyer named John Mercer, because much less dye is needed to dye mercerized cotton.

Pima cotton is a cross between American Pima cotton, which was the native cotton planted by southwestern Indians, and Egyptian cotton. Because of its silkiness and extra strength, it's considered to be the finest cotton grown in America today, mostly in California and Arizona.

Sanfor-Set The process making cottons drip-dry. It treats the fabric by running it through an icy, liquid ammonia bath, changing the molecular structure of the fibers and virtually eliminating wrinkling.

Sea Island cotton Another fine, lustrous cotton, grown mostly in the West Indies, also on islands off Georgia, South Carolina, Texas, and Florida.

Care

A great advantage of cotton is that the more it's worn and washed, the softer the fabric gets.

White cottons often get dingy if you have them dry cleaned too often, but most cottons can be either washed or dry cleaned. If white cottons have no elastic on them, you can soak them overnight in Clorox, guaranteed to leave them sparkling white. You can also boil them in Lux and bleach. If you carefully handwash your whites and they seem to gradually be turning gray, perhaps you're not using enough detergent. Be generous. "When you're handwashing, you have to squeeze and knead to force soap through the fabric," says Dr. Fred Fortess of the Philadelphia College of Textiles and Science. "Cotton is full of little crevices where soil and soot can hide, whereas dirt on synthetics is all on the surface and can more easily be washed off." With colored cottons, a next-to-final rinse with a little vinegar will brighten the colors by getting rid of any leftover soap. Iron while still damp. Some cottons will need only a touch or two with the iron, others will wrinkle dreadfully.

Cotton mildews easily, mildew being a fungus that coats the surface and turns a nasty gray or yellow. To prevent it, never leave damp clothes wadded up—they can mildew within hours. A good dry cleaner can often remove mildew spots.

Unless the label indicates a garment has been Sanfor-Set, you can count on 100 percent cotton shrinking at least 3 percent in washing or dry cleaning, sometimes a little more.

Coty Awards

are to U.S. fashion what Oscars are to Hollywood. Coty cosmetics began sponsoring the annual event in 1942, in a successful attempt to raise the prestige of Coty cosmetics. Judging is done by a "jury" of 450 editors and newspaper people from all over the country, and an award trophy called the "Winnie" is awarded each year to an American fashion designer whose work has had the most significant effect on women's dress during the previous year. When a designer has received the Winnie or menswear trophy three different times, he's automatically in the Coty "Hall of Fame." Living Hall of Fame winners are: Galanos, Bill Blass, Geoffrey Beene, Bonnie Cashin, Oscar de la Renta, Halston, Calvin Klein, Kasper, Ralph Lauren, Mary McFadden, Pauline Trigère.

Courrèges, André

(coor-rej) Leading French designer of the 1960s, who did lots of appliquéd minidresses with clear plastic cutouts, worn with his signature white plastic boots. He has a chic boutique selling high-priced sportswear on East 57th Street in New York.

Couture

The made-to-order lines of famous designers, their latest fashions done in their most expensive fabrics and with no details of workmanship spared.

Covert Cloth

A durable, closely woven heavyweight twill with a diagonal rib; the best covert cloth is of wool, but it can be made from synthetics. Used for suits and coats, especially heavier-style trenchcoats. Calvin Klein does a luxury trench in wool covert cloth, with removable wool lining, for $500.

Cowboy Boots

Everybody from Prince Charles to Catherine Deneuve is clomping around in them these days, not necessarily because they're comfortable ("Dallas" star Larry Hagman complains constantly about his feet) but possibly because they give male and female alike what has come to be called a "bad-ass gait" (see BOOTS). The cowboy boot happens to have the most colorful past of any shoe in America, beginning around 1850, with the great cattle empires and dusty trail drives across the prairie to Dodge City, Kansas. Cowpunchers wanted their boots high-heeled so heels wouldn't

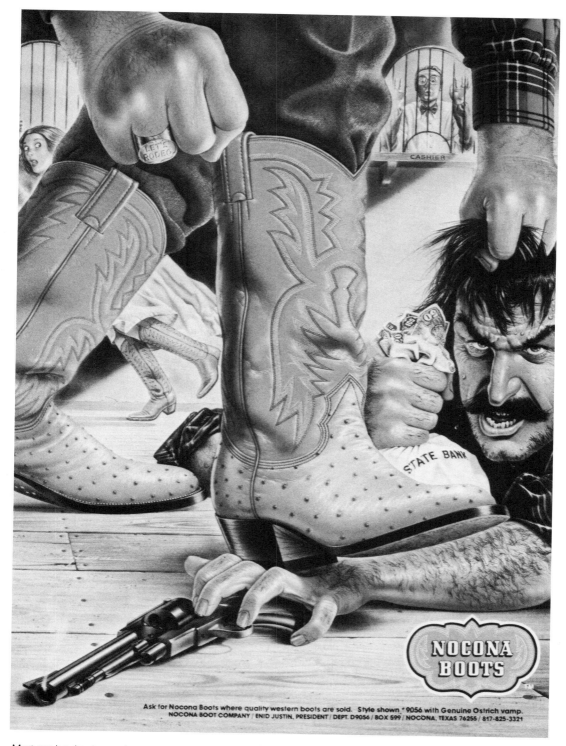

Most cowboy boot manufacturers are aware of the appealing macho quality of their wares. The most macho ad of all is run by Nocona, whose president is no shoot-'em-up gunslinger but an eighty-six-year-old woman, Miss Enid Justin. She's been in the business since 1925. "At first, making boots was pretty rough going," she says. "The cowboys just didn't want to buy from a woman."

slip through stirrups, and so they could be dug into the sod to pull against a rope. Pointed toes slipped into stirrups easier than round ones, and thin soles gave the feel of the stirrup. Hand-tooling and stitch-work on the sides were to keep the boots from wrinkling too much at the ankles; this artistry was also—no doubt about it—to give the cowboy a little dash and glamor to set him aside from flatfooted farmers and townsmen. "Any cowhand who wore cheap boots was considered without pride," says Andrew L. Von Louth in *If the Shoe Fits*. "The cowboy might give a month's pay for his boots, but he owned only one pair and kept them on from sun-up until he rolled into his bunk for the night." The frontier cemetery was called boot hill because most occupants died with their boots on. The term "bootlegger" also derived from cowboy boots; scoundrels who sold liquor to Indians in spite of laws forbidding this trade would smuggle pint bottles onto reservations in the tops of their boots.

When looking for your own pair of boots, here's what to keep in mind:

- If you're going to buy a pair of cowboy boots, they might as well be the real McCoy—*Texas* boots. The most snobbish name in boots from the Lone Star state is Lucchese of San Antonio. Handmade boots start at $200 and go to $3,000. Oldest and biggest names—the "big three" of Texas bootmakers—are Tony Lama of El Paso, Nocona of Nocona, and Justin of Fort Worth; their boots will run from $90 to $150. Pay less, and you'll have to settle for boots so poorly tanned they're hard and stiff. Heels would probably be plastic, soles cemented rather than sewn on.

- Calfskin, cowhide, and horsehide are the most authentic leathers. Skins such as lizard, python, and shark cost more because they're rare, not because they're more comfortable, and using the skins of exotic animals for shoes is an ecological disaster. None of these animals are farmed; they must all be culled from the ranks of dwindling wildlife.

- Cowboy boots don't fit like other footwear. With a cowboy boot, your heel *should* slip up and down a little; no slippage means the heel is too tight. Likewise, if you can easily pull the boot on while sitting down, it's probably too big. Good boots have pull straps, and the idea is to ease the foot in while standing and tugging (get a salesman to show you how). If you have a high instep, *no* cowboy boot is going to be entirely comfortable, especially when driving.

If you don't have access to a good selection of boots, you might consider ordering by mail. Many boot companies have devised quite a sophisticated order form, in which you take a dozen different measurements of your feet, and make a tracing of each foot. Some people think this method is even more efficient than buying from some bored salesperson who knows nothing. Two companies with free catalogues are:

Lucchese
1226 E. Houston Street
San Antonio, Texas 78205

Tony Lama
Box 9518
El Paso, Texas 79985

Care
See BOOTS.

Cowl-Necked

An authentic cowl is the hood attached to a monk's robe. In fashion, you'll sometimes see a softer version of the monk's cowl draped down the back of a chiffon evening dress; most often you'll see it in sweaters draped in a soft fold around the neck in front. Because they're bulky, cowl-necked sweaters look better on thin, long-faced women than short, thick-chested ones. (See SWEATERS.)

Crêpe

A dull fabric with a crinkly surface produced by twisting during the weaving process. It can be made out of silk, or synthetics such as polyester or acetate, though lately many middle-price designers have been working in rayon. Albert Nipon's dresses in black rayon crêpe, for around $200, are a huge success. Crêpe is the classic material for loose, flowing evening pants, worn all year around with various blouses and a gold belt.

Care

Follow label directions. Crêpe is usually washable, but ironing can be tricky. Never press crêpe on the right side because even synthetic crêpes will develop an unpleasant shine. Press with the grain, using no steam—pressing against the grain can distort shape. If you use a steamer to take out wrinkles between cleanings, turn the dress inside-out first.

Crêpe de Chine

(crep-duh-sheen) A lightweight crêpe, usually handwashable. Clothes of crêpe de Chine should be flowing and loose, because too tight a fit will pull this delicate fabric apart at the seams. If you're broad-shouldered, buy a blouse that fits the shoulders, and then have it taken in elsewhere. Everyone should have a cream-colored, tailored, crêpe de Chine blouse, and it's best to pay a little more and buy silk crêpe de Chine fabric. Because of static electricity, synthetics get dirty at cuffs and collar in a day, while silk can be worn several days; both are washable.

Care
See SILK.

Crew-Neck Sweater

The great look of the Eisenhower years, this simple pullover with its ribbed neckline, fitting around the bottom of the neck, has become a sportswear classic. You can buy them in fine Shetland wool in the boys' department of Saks for $15, to be worn over a crisp boy's cotton shirt (Pierre Cardin, at Saks, $20). They look splendid with jeans, and also with a knee-length A-line skirt, brown tweedy stockings, and loafers. And of course, no more classic look is possible than that of a crew neck worn over a blouse with a Peter Pan collar, along with straight tailored pants and a blazer.

Since you'll often be wearing crew necks with a blazer, try them in the store *with* a blazer—if the sweater is a little too big around the neck, it will bulge in front where the blazer opens.

If you have large hips, never wear a crew neck of a different color from your pants or skirt—you'll have a horizontal line directly across the hips, exactly where you don't need it.

Crochet

A loop is made with a strand of yarn and a hook, and another loop is pulled through this one, until a chain is produced. Sometimes you can find lovely hand-crocheted vests and sweaters in handcraft stores. Best bargain: flea markets sell crocheted collars from the 1940s for $4 or $5.

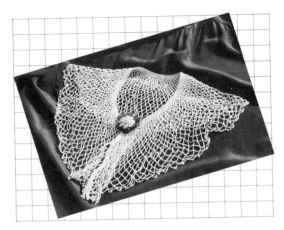

Hand-crocheted collars from the 1940s can be found in antique flea markets for a few dollars.

Crocking

means that dye from the surface of one fabric has rubbed off onto the skin or onto other fabrics. Colored suedes are among the worst offenders.

Cross, Mark

See MARK CROSS.

Cuddleskin

One of the more irresistible synthetic fabrics, used by Barbizon for nightgowns and robes. Inside, it's soft and feels like flannel; outside is a polyester, nylon, and cotton blend that looks like satin.

Culottes

A skirt divided into pants; when you're standing, they look like a skirt. Culottes were first designed in the 1930s for bicycling in Bermuda, which had strict regulations against women wearing shorts.

Culottes tend to be more flattering to overweight women than are trousers because they're more flowing around the thighs. Also, if your calves are large, midcalf culottes and boots hide them. Finity does $60 culottes flattering to nearly everyone.

For some inexplicable reason, the average male dislikes culottes on women.

Cummerbund

A wide, pleated sash worn around the waist, usually fastened with hooks. Used mostly with evening pyjamas. Looks terrific on anybody long-waisted.

Cupro

Trademark of Bemberg Industries for a silklike material of rayon and polyester. Used for linings in the most expensive designer clothes, such as St. Laurent's.

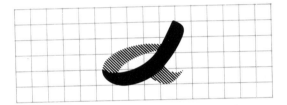

Dacron

Trademark of Du Pont for their polyester, the first polyester put on the market, in 1952. A terrific fiber to blend: Dacron and wool is one of the biggest-selling fabrics of all time. You have the beauty of wool, but with Dacron, it won't wrinkle, is not going to bag at the seat or knees, and won't stretch. Cotton and Dacron, 60/40, is also a workhorse blend.

According to *The New York Times*, 100-percent Dacron is the preferred material for clothes in China, where natural fibers are considered bourgeois because they require so much time to care for.

Care
Usually machine washable.

Damask

A rich-looking, one-color fabric, woven in floral patterns in which the patterns are

Lush, romantic Oscar de la Renta evening clothes are desired by all aspirants to the jet-set life.

more lustrous than the background. Your mother probably has a linen damask table-cloth in her cedar chest. Almost any fabric can be woven in damask, but the most beautiful are silk, linen, and cotton. Anne Klein's silk damask evening pyjamas and ruffled blouses are probably the most exciting work being done with damask in fashion, if you can afford $170 for a pair of evening pants. However, American manufacturers have recently come out with a perfectly beautiful cotton damask, domes-

tically grown and produced and therefore half the price of linen and silk.

Décolletage

(day-co-la-tage) The wearing of a daringly low-cut dress or nightgown.

De La Renta, Oscar

American designer, born in 1933 in the Dominican Republic. His Latin blood shows in the vividness and romance of his luscious evening clothes. No simple little black dresses worn with pearls for de la Renta. His rich-gypsy clothes abound in lush colors, spangles, dazzling embroidery, and trim. He does an inexpensive line ($150–$200) but these clothes are more conservative and without the exuberance of his regular ($1,000 up) line. He's been in the Coty Hall of Fame since 1973.

Delavé

(day-lah-vay), as in blue jeans *delavé*. American manufacturers persist in considering French words more sophisticated than English ones. *Delavé* simply means bleached, washed-out.

Démodé

(day-mo-day) Out of style, just missing it. Not up to date.

Denim

is probably the most popular fabric ever made, with over a billion square yards sold a year. Because the fabric is manufactured from a special strain of cotton which grows well only in America, the U.S. makes the world's best denim, one-third of the national cotton crop going for this purpose.

Authentic denim is a 100-percent cotton twill weave with white threads running in the crosswise direction and blue threads lengthwise. Unlike most fabric, which is woven first and then dipped in a dyebath, denim is yarn-dyed, meaning individual yarns are dyed *before* weaving. Natural denim is always a dark indigo blue; if it's light blue, it's been bleached or chemically faded. Brushed denim means the surface has been mechanically brushed to make the fabric softer. You can buy your denims in many different weights, ranging from 14-oz. for work clothes to 10-oz. for summer dungarees.

Care
See JEANS.

(Le) Dernier Cri

(dern-y-ay-cree') The very latest fashion

Design Community

If you run into a Design Community label, you're probably looking at something that's comfortable, because although the design may look completely *au courant*, it's likely to be based on designs thousands of years old, such as Japanese samurai pants or Hebraic coats. As were the originals, clothes are constructed without zippers or buttons, and are fastened with ties made of same material as the garment. A *Ms.* magazine writer said, "Once you've put them on in the morning, loose clothes have a polite way of staying out of your mind ... they don't insist on communing with you through odd little tugs, pulls and strains." This could also be the philosophy of Design Community. You can expect an earthy, tactile quality, because fabrics are handwoven whenever possible, and dyes come from plants and minerals. Biggest sellers are prewashed crêpe de Chine silks (you can wash for sure), a year-round blend of linen, cotton, and rayon, and handwoven cotton seersuckers.

You'll find Design Community clothes in boutiques only, never department stores, because "our clothes work *together* ... one blouse in a blouse department would be totally lost." Write Carol Kent, 128 West 23rd Street, New York, New York 10011 to find a store near you, or visit the two New York stores.

Diamante Top

(dye-ah-mont´-tee) Means fabric is covered with sparkly, glittery beads or stones. Dia-

mante is French for "made of diamonds."
Diamante clothes got their start in the
1960s when singers such as Janis Joplin
and Elvis Presley wore them on stage.

Di Camerino, Roberta

Italian designer/manufacturer, who is best
known for her *trompe l'oeil* ("trick the
eye") prints—collars, pockets, cuffs, all il-
lusion, are printed on. Most famous are her
trompe l'oeil handwoven velvet bags,
which cost into the four figures. She first
made her name in Venice in the 1940s designing handbags, and her oiled calfskin
with the initial R is one of the status handbags. There are thirty-eight European Di
Camerino stores; she's also carried in U.S.
department stores, and has a boutique at
645 Fifth Avenue at 51st Street, in New
York.

Dickey

A detachable blouse front or collar, such as
the neck of a turtleneck; gives the look of a
blouse or turtleneck, worn under a dress or
another blouse, without the bulk.

Dinner Dressing

From New Guinea headhunters who put
bones in their noses for feasts to the Ed-
wardians who always wore tails to dinner,
most people have enjoyed making a good
dinner something of a celebration. Today,
even though most of us don't often dress
black tie for dinner, to be so "laid back"
that you appear in the same mudhen attire
that you wore to work seems to be saying that you're above the little ceremonies
that delight the rest of us. It's abysmal
when someone spends hours cooking a
gourmet dinner, and guests show up in
their I ♡ NEW YORK T-shirts and dusty
Adidas—the implication is that your culi-
nary efforts are no big deal. When a guy

takes you to dinner, greeting him in the
same blazer you'd wear to work not only
says the occasion is nothing special, but
your appearance may *depress* him.

Most people are anxious about work.
When they're out socially, they want to
forget, to be festive, and any outfit that
looks like the office will drag them back.
Dress up, down, or ethnic, but even if
you're going to a pizza parlor you can wear
your embroidered rayon suit jacket from
the 1940s, or the Turkish silver belt with
the tassels, or your silk macramé vest with
your jeans. Not only men but other women
will appreciate the extra effort.

Another guideline: *Concentrate on
your neckline and hands.* If you were going disco dancing, you'd want something
flowing and clingy because your *body* is on
display. At dinner, what shows is throat
and hands. Whether you're in jeans or silk
chiffon, it's sexy to show some skin on top.
Those same women who agonize over
broad hips are usually bosomy and in their
element at dinner; they look better than
anyone thin in low, *low* V-necks, whether a
daring sweater or a blouse left unbuttoned. Overly thin women should probably
think along the lines of a dress with a beautiful collar, sensuous pearls, or antique
lace. Something soft. Since your hands are
seen so closely, the interesting rings and
bracelets that wouldn't be noticed at a party will have center stage at dinner.

Dinner Ring

Any ring so exotic you wouldn't wear it to
work. What jewelers mean by dinner rings
are oversized, massive rings with a contemporary design, usually inlaid with diamonds and colored stones.

Dior, Christian

(dee-ore´) French designer (1905–1957).
Dior dominated postwar French fashion

and became the first great commercial success in fashion. He had a line of everything from gloves to stockings, and in 1950 made more money than all the rest of French couture together. His A-line silhouette has become a classic, and he was first to use pirouetting, lively models in fashion shows instead of regal, expressionless ones. After he died, his assistant, Yves St. Laurent, became head designer for the House of Dior for three years, a position held today by Marc Bohan. Bohan is considered a leader of contemporary design and his clothes are much copied by mass manufacturers. The house is especially known for beaded evening dresses. Dior ready-to-wear price range: $110 for a silk blouse, $200 for a wool blazer.

Dirndl Skirt

A plain full skirt, gathered at the waist. Originally a German peasant costume. Today's modified version, only slightly gathered and falling in a narrow line rather than a voluminous one, has become a classic style because it looks graceful on plump and thin alike. J. G. Hook makes a wool bias-cut dirndl skirt that looks good on anyone, for $66.

Disco Dressing

changed the look of evening clothes in the 1970s. Instead of trying to look aristocratic and statuesque, everyone wanted swingy clothes that would move sensuously on the dance floor in high-wattage colors. "You want bright colors or metallics that can hold up under the lights," said designer Stephen Burrows, who still spends five or six nights a week in discos and made his name designing easy-moving disco dresses. "You want skirts short, because they keep your legs free."

In some discos, they might turn you

Dirndls are no longer voluminous peasant skirts worn by German milkmaids. Today's soft, gently gathered version is flattering to almost everyone. (Fashion by Bill Blass, Ltd.)

away if you don't shimmer and glitter a bit outrageously; at others, you'd wear what you wore to class that day. The only rules are: Avoid synthetic fabrics, which retain perspiration and easily pick up odors; rayon is *not* a synthetic, and rayon-and-metallic tunics and jumpsuits are terrific for disco. Avoid anything constricting—if you feel tugs at the armholes when you lift your arms, your outfit isn't for dancing. Wear light, cool clothes, blouses rather than sweaters, airy skirts or harem pants rather than tweed pants, and avoid heavy jewelry, which will roll around and drive you crazy.

Discount Stores

We've all been envious when we remark "What a lovely . . ." and the reply is, "Yes, isn't it? I got it for only $9.98 at . . ." You wonder how some people always seem to know the latest good discount stores. No mystery: you simply buy the latest paperback guides to your city, such as Barbara Patridge's *Bargain Hunting in L.A.* (Tarcher, $5.95) or Elaine Louie's *Manhattan Clothes Shopping Guide* (Macmillan, $5.95).

Discount outlet sales hit $2 billion in 1980, up from $750 million in 1975. Here's how these "pipe rack emporiums" can offer you the latest looks at 20 to 60 percent below department-store prices.

- *Overruns* Designers don't usually sew their clothes themselves—they send patterns out to contractors, who agree to make up a certain number of items. Often the minimum number of clothes a contractor will make is more than the designer can sell; these extras, or overruns, are then sold to discount stores. Or maybe a designer falls in love with a fabric and wants an exclusive on it, and the mill says fine, but you've got to order 3,000 yards. He buys, then gets orders for only half the goods. His misfortune is a discount house's good luck. Overrun clothes are often either more drab and dowdy than average or more adventurous than most people have the nerve to wear.

- *Seconds* Manufacturers usually have a system of inspection of their products, in which "firsts" are deemed perfect, "seconds" have slight flaws, often so minor as to be unnoticeable, and "thirds," or "rejects," are disasters. Seconds either are sold at a discount in their own factory outlets or go to discount stores; thirds are torn apart to be made into entirely new fabric.

- *Last season's clothes* Probably the majority of merchandise in most discount houses is from one to three years old, items nobody could sell.

- *Samples* If you can wear a size 8, you may feel like Cinderella slipping on the glass slipper. During the first and second weeks of August, and first and second weeks of February, discount houses often get a bundle of the very latest clothes, not even in the stores yet, because they're the sample 8's modeled for buyers in showrooms. This is mostly a New York phenomenon.

- *Low overhead* Discount stores are able to keep down prices on all this bargain merchandise because they pay little rent and skimp on amenities such as individual dressing rooms—one huge, drafty room does for all, and the store itself is almost never in a fashionable part of town.

A few of the country's most famous discount stores are:

- *Filene's of Boston's bargain basement,* famous for its system of time-tagging clothes, reducing the price on an item every few days until the price is at give-away levels. Gambling on whether a dress will still be there in three days, at half the price, can be as absorbing as betting the horses.

- *Loehmann's,* oldest and largest discount store in the country; the original Brooklyn, New York, store was opened in 1920 by Frieda Loehmann, notorious for prowling Seventh Avenue in a shabby bag-lady black dress. Today Loehmann's has outlets everywhere, most famous being the Bronx, New York, store with its 15,000 square feet of fluorescent-lit, wall-to-wall bargains. Stock is kept at 35,000 garments, with 2,400 new ones coming in daily, and merchandise turns over about thirteen times a year, twice as often as that of most department stores. Other branches are in Washington, D.C., which emphasizes evening clothes; San Francisco; Pompano Beach, Florida, and Los Angeles.

    Learn to recognize colors on label fragments. They're usually cut away rather than torn out entirely. Anne Klein is always burgundy and brown. Cacharel is a vivid blue and green.

- *Pillars of Eagle Rock,* near East Los Angeles (213 257-8166), which tries to keep its clothes at half price or below. Good for the California designers and manufacturers.

Djellaba

(jel´-uh-ba) A loose caftanlike garment of cotton or wool with wide sleeves and a hood, worn in northern Africa. From time to time designers become fascinated by djellabas; Geoffrey Beene, always con-

cerned with comfort, puts them in his line from time to time.

Doeskin

The soft inner side of sheep or lambskin, used mostly for gloves.

Dog-Collar Blouse

A high-necked blouse with a strip of material high around the neck, very Victorian. A similar effect can be achieved by buttoning all buttons on a cotton blouse, turning the collar up, and pinning the two edges together with a bar-shaped pin. Looks great with suits or vests on long-necked women.

Dolman Sleeve

A sleeve with the armhole cut halfway to the waist; tapers from a voluminous armhole to a narrow wrist. Looks good on women with narrow shoulders, but is a disaster for wide shoulders.

Dolman sleeve

Donegal Tweed

A tweed with thick, colored slubs, handwoven in cottages in the mountain ranges of Donegal County, Ireland. The fabric is warm and water repellent. Irish caps are traditionally made of this fabric, and L. L. Bean sells a Donegal tweed hat for women called a "Blue Stack" hat.

Dorothée Bis

(doh-roh-tay beece´) French designer/manufacturing operation. Bis has boutiques scattered over the world, each of which has, somewhere on the premises, a life-sized rag doll sitting languidly in a chair. Owned by manufacturer Elie Jacobson, with wife Jacqueline as the designer. Dorothée Bis turned out some of the most trend-setting clothes of the 1960s and 1970s, and in the 1980s their following is still young and funloving. Look for knits of all kinds in beautiful colors, often color-coordinated ensembles, with coats, ribbed wool stockings, and knitted caps all designed to work together. A pair of Bis wool walking shorts runs around $60, flannel midcalf pants $140.

Dotted Swiss

A sheer, stiff, nonlustrous white cotton with dots woven in.

Double-Breasted

describes any garment with a double row of buttons down the front of a coat or jacket, an elegant look on thin or average-sized figures. Not for wide-shouldered, top-heavy, or overweight women. Anne Klein is a master of aristocratic double-breasted tailoring.

Double Knits

are machine-knitted with a double set of needles and look exactly the same on the right and wrong sides. Double knits have a bad name in fashion, but actually a good double-knit wool is a terrific fabric. It stretches and conforms to body shape, which makes it comfortable to wear; and you can hang it on hangers—all other knits must be folded in drawers.

Down

is the soft, fluffy fur underneath the feathers of waterfowl, mostly from China and Northern Europe. It's a wonderfully ecologically correct substance since, unlike fur, it's a food by-product. Only ducks and geese have down; chickens and turkeys have only feathers. Down keeps the birds warm by trapping air, and does the same for us, creating a greater dead air space per unit weight than any other insulator. In other words, nothing else is so warm and light at once. "Vests take about eight ounces of down, coats one and a quarter pounds," says Howard Winslow of the Feather and Down Association. "In 1979, we imported four million coats, and produced over two million in the U.S." Probably everyone who doesn't already have a down coat is thinking about buying one, so here are a few guidelines:

- *The fatter the coat, the warmer* Coats come in different thicknesses, and you don't necessarily want the thickest unless you live in Alaska. Though a bulky coat of 100 percent down is warmer than a thin coat of 100 percent down, bulkier coats may also be bulkier because they have more feathers in proportion to down. Feathers are flat, don't trap air nearly as well as down, and don't hold up as long, though many manufacturers think a few feathers improve resilience. Best mixture is 12 percent feathers, the rest down, though due to a worldwide down shortage, you're most likely to find 20 percent feathers, which is okay too. More feathers than that, and the efficiency of the coat goes down with every feather.

- *Beware of leaking down coats* If you see a light fuzzy film anywhere, don't buy—stitching is loose somewhere, and stuffing is escaping. The situation will only get worse. Bill Blass down coats ($180) have gotten rave notices on their nonleaking construction.

- *Make sure your down coat is down* Stores sometimes advertise quilted fiberfill coats as down coats, so read the label.

- *Bad news* Unless you have your coat especially made water repellent, a service some dry cleaners offer for about $25, when it rains you'll freeze. Down loses its warmth when wet.

Care

According to the Feather and Down Association, laundering will actually improve down's fluffiness. Handwash with a mild soap, soak for twenty or thirty minutes, rinse until no suds are present. If the coat feels slippery, that means further rinsing is necessary to remove all soap. When taking the garment out of the washtub, support it carefully so that excess water weight won't push the down into clumps. (Don't panic if you do find temporary clumps—use your fingers to manipulate the down back into place.) Tumble dry, with machine set at "gentle," for about three hours, putting into the dryer a clean pair of tennis shoes or rubber shower shoes to prevent clumps, and two or three bath towels to absorb moisture. Hang on a hanger, with plenty of air circulating, to complete the drying, occasionally plumping up the down, as you would a pillow,

with your hands. If you find a quill has worked its way through the fabric, don't pull it out, as you'll probably pull out down along with the quill, but, working from the back, try to grasp the quill with your fingers and pull it back inside. If the fabric is wrinkled, use a Wrinkles Away to steam—never an iron.

You can also dry clean.—$14 seems to be the average price for a full-length coat.

Don't pack your coat tightly over the summer, or leave it in a plastic bag.

Dresses

Most advice on buying clothes says to put your money into separates, because two or three tops and a couple of skirts and pants which all interchange give you a wider variety of looks. However, most of this advice applies only to slender people, overlooking the way (a) skirts and tops of different colors chop short people in the middle, making them look six inches shorter, and (b) the horizontal line at the waist causes the eye to meander leisurely across just where, if you're overweight, you don't want any lingering glances. A dress, which is one unbroken line from top to bottom, is the most slimming garment made. A belt should, of course, be the same material as the dress.

In a sea of separates, only two American designers have made names for themselves in affordable day dresses: Albert Nipon and Diane Von Furstenberg. In England, Jean Muir is the best-known designer of this kind.

Dressmaker Details

are little extra touches adding grace and quality to clothes: tucks, pleats, topstitching, shirring, stitching detail around collars and cuffs.

Duck

A strong, plainly woven cotton, not quite as heavy as canvas. However, the terms duck, sailcloth, and canvas are often used interchangeably today. The name comes from the Dutch word *doek*, a heavy cotton cloth used for sailors' summer uniforms. L. L. Bean's duck chino pants (also called sailcloth pants) are especially nice.

Duffel Coat

A hooded coat, usually three-quarter length, with rod-shaped wooden buttons fastening through rope or leather thongs. Also called a toggle coat, the style originated with the Navy during World War II. The Duffer Division of J. G. Hook makes an authentic duffel coat for $120.

Dungaree

The word is derived from a heavy Indian cotton called dungaree. Today, nearly everyone refers to jeans as jeans, but for a long time the word "dungarees" was interchangeable with the word "jeans."

Ellen Tracy

is not a person but a privately owned American company about thirty years old. The company made its name in blouses, in which it still excels; it went on to become a junior sportswear line, and now makes clothes for "executive career women," i.e., they're good for the office. Ellen Tracy silk blouses, at $70 to $90, are particularly nicely made; their $50 polyester blouses are virtually indistinguishable from silks. Many prestigious department stores, such as Saks, have Ellen Tracy boutiques.

Ellis, Perry

American designer, a young Virginian who made a huge splash in only three years. Articles about him tend to have titles such as "Designs to a Different Drummer" or "An American Original." He goes against the current by doing exactly what everyone else isn't doing, yet instead of turning out eccentric, out-of-style clothes that don't sell, his innovations somehow look "right" and sell $10 million worth a year. If other designers are doing pants, he does skirts; if others are turning out silk blouses, he turns out bulky sweaters. "I'm driven to point out the alternatives," he told *Vogue*. "I just want to keep all the options open for everyone, so you can wear what you want." His consciously flawed handknit mohair capelet sweaters ($200) helped start the current sweater boom, his wide-leg pants ($88) were a season ahead of the culotte craze. He never makes silk blouses. "Cottons are easier . . . people seem to worry less about them," he says. He never designs formal evening clothes. (*"I'm* not formal. I don't go to those places or those parties and don't care about them.")

An Ellis outfit is so recognizable that women who care about their own individual style seldom wear his separates together. Other women like putting on a complete "look." "With Perry's clothes you don't need much else," says Nina Santisi, his press director. "I never wear jewelry."

Ellis has won Coty awards two out of the three years he's been designing.

Embroidery

Ornamental needlework.

Perry Ellis designs new-look sportswear in natural fabrics; his fans particularly love his handknit sweaters and wide-cut flannel pants. (Photo: Bonnie West)

Empire Dress

(ohm-peer´) A low-cut dress gathered under the bosom. The style dates from the period of the Napoleonic Empire, 1804–1814, and was worn by the Empress Josephine. You should be reasonably slender to wear this one; anybody with a large bust will look top-heavy.

Emporium

An old-fashioned word for department store.

Epaulet

(eh-paul-ette) A decorative shoulder strap, formerly on military uniforms, now on all sorts of coats and jackets. In French, it's *epaulette.*

Erté

American designer, famous for his super-glamorous clothes of the 1930s. His name is associated with an Art Deco look.

Espadrille

This proper, preppy shoe has a canvas top and straw bottom. Formerly a Basque folk shoe, it became an international classic when Yves St. Laurent embroidered flowers on the canvas in early 1960. The shoe seems to cry for an A-line skirt and Brooks Brothers oxford shirt. Quality name in espadrilles: Jacques Cohen. Price: About $25.

Estevez, Luis

A California designer, of Cuban birth, best known for reasonably priced short evening dresses with imaginatively cut-out necklines.

Eton Jacket

A short blazer ending squarely at the waist, first worn by Eton College boys in England early in the century.

Evan Picone

A large-volume American manufacturing firm, begun in the late 1940s by Charles Evans and Joseph Picone, an Italian Master Tailor. (Evans has since departed from the business.) The Evan Picone line is all separates, very conservative, tailored, neither fashionable nor unfashionable. In a word, *classics.* "You can wear an Evan Picone outfit for years," says one devotée. "It's not like designer stuff, where you can say, 'that's last year's Ralph Lauren.'"

Evan Picone is the largest "better sportswear" manufacturer in the U.S., and therefore gets first choice of many new fabrics. Particularly fine: their Viyella, the true English-made wool-cotton blend; their Shetlands; their Saxony wools with a touch of polyester so carefully blended that you can't feel it, but which keeps the suit from wrinkling. Joseph Picone himself still lives at the factory and runs it, insisting on European tailoring touches. "We press open all our seams, use only horn, pearl, or metal buttons. All of our zippers and pockets are functional, no gimmicks, and everything is fully lined, rare in our price range," says the firm's Elizabeth Jessen. (Blazers $115, skirts $60.)

Eyelet

Fabric with decorative pattern of small holes reinforced with buttonhole stitches. On the cheap stuff, stitches are too far apart, so that raw edge of fabric frays; lots of unwelcome little threads will sprout unattractively after every laundering.

Fagoting

A dressmaker's detail, fagoting joins two fabric edges together with an openwork criss-crossed embroidery stitch. A sort of open seam—looks as though there's a tiny bit of lace between the edges, which usually run in vertical rows up and down blouses or dresses. A great effect for top-heavy women because of all the vertical lines.

Faille

(fie) Light, soft silk or synthetic fabric with tiny ribs. Used for evening clothes. Most popular at the moment: evening pants of black rayon faille.

Fair Isle Sweater

Sweater with bands of beautifully colored geometrical designs woven into a neutral background, usually around the neck. Name comes from Fair Isle, one of the Scottish Shetland Isles, where the sweater originated. Between World Wars I and II, knitting Fair Isle sweaters from printed

Fair Isle sweaters are outdoorsy, wholesome, and preppy. (Photo: from Land's End catalogue)

patterns became a fashionable pastime in Britain and America.

Fake Furs

In his book *Man Kind?* (Dell), Cleveland Amory has a chapter entitled "Real People Wear Fake Furs," in which he eloquently describes the horrors of trapping wild animals. Few people who read the book ever feel the same about fur coats again, and take as much pride in wearing a handsome fake as other women do in their luxurious foxes and sables. The "fake fur" industry is thriving, with designers from Bonnie Cashin to Carol Horn turning their talents toward making beautiful coats, sometimes astonishingly close imitations of real furs, other times beautiful in their own right. Most are frankly fake, best sellers being grooved beaver, raccoon, and mink in colors of pink, wine, and emerald.

Best Fibers

According to the Good Housekeeping Textiles Institute, acrylic, modacrylic, polyester, or combinations of these three fibers are preferred; rayon doesn't hold up as well. Thickest and heaviest coats are also the warmest. Some reputable trade names are: Borg-Animal, Furtex, Tallyho, Malden.

Cost

Under $250, jackets for under $100.

Care

Modacrylic, the most common fake fur fiber, is "heat sensitive"—if you should fold your coat up against a radiator, the fibers soon get bent and mashed-looking. Most coats can be dry cleaned; if a coat says "clean by furrier method," that too means dry clean, but the process will be more expensive.

Fashion Designers

"Don't pay for a label," goes the bad press against designers. "It's all hype and nobody but a sucker buys." Recent books on fashion such as John Molloy's *Dress for Success* and Emily Cho's *Looking Terrific* are downright hostile to designers, advising readers never to buy labels for the security of the name, and the books never mention a single designer by name. Reading the sections on clothes in books on saving money, such as *How to Live Better and Spend 20% Less*, you'd never know fashion designers existed. Yet, trying to be knowledgeable about clothes without knowing anything about designers is like talking about art without mentioning artists. Not to have a single designer item in your wardrobe is as silly as having *all* designer things: after decades of designing only for the wealthy, designers are now putting most of their talents into turning out ready-to-wear. For the first time ever, designer fashion has become moderately priced, and most of us can buy at least one or two good things a year on sale.

Why buy designer names? Not for the fabric, though designers, much more than mass merchandisers, will search the world over to bring you the most lovely new fabrics. Still, fabric can only cost just so much, and sometimes designer clothes are made of simple white cotton. Workmanship? With labor so expensive these days, everyone including designers is trying to simplify, and you're as likely to find labor-saving cuts, such as buttons instead of zippers and elasticized waists instead of waistbands, on a designer dress as on a department-store special. Sometimes designer workmanship can be downright shoddy. What you *are* paying for is the designer's eye for style. Somehow that Calvin Klein or Gloria Sachs will seem, for reasons you can't even articulate, perfect for this year's look, while the $60 dresses are a maddening inch too short, or too wide in the shoulders, or decorated with too much lace.

The rule of thumb most women with common sense go by is that if you can get it for less, you do. A simple crew neck is much the same no matter who designs it; a ruffly evening dress needs a more talented hand.

According to *The New York Times,* top designing talents break down something as follows:

Designers most consistently coming up with new ideas   New York's Perry Ellis, Betsey Johnson, and Norma Kamali; Italy's Armani; Paris's Karl Lagerfeld, Claude Montana, Thierry Mugler, and Sonia Rykiel.

Designers creating the world's most spectacular eveningwear   America's Bill Blass, Mary McFadden, Galanos, Oscar de la Renta; Paris's Marc Bohan of Christian Dior; Rome's Valentino.

Designers providing high-caliber, poised styles that a woman knows are "right"   America's Calvin Klein, Ralph Lauren, Geoffrey Beene, Halston; Givenchy in Paris; Missoni in Italy.

World's foremost designer   Yves St. Laurent in Paris.

Fashion Magazines

In the U.S. only seven publications deal heavily with fashion. They are:

Vogue and Harper's Bazaar   Dubbed the fantasy press, and picketed from time to time by Woman Against Pornography, these magazines often use teen-aged girls as models, dredge them in makeup, put las-

civious expressions on their faces, and photograph them in $2,000 dresses. Copy tends to be rather breathless, such as "At Armani always, a total way of dressing done in a totally unexpected way." Though you won't learn much about how to blend new styles into your existing wardrobe, though such subjects as antique clothes or second-hand clothes are never known to have been mentioned in these magazines, and though the sixteen-year-old models wearing the clothes have, unlike the rest of us, a collective figure of total perfection, you *can* learn what's new from the top designers. Even though the clothes shown may cost in the four figures, department stores will quickly be selling inexpensive versions, and you can save more money by investing in a new look that will be around for a few years (most trends come in five-year cycles) than buying, through ignorance, a look that's peaked.

Look for: *shoes:* height of heels, toes rounded or pointed, stockings opaque or sheer; *skirts:* are they looser or slimmer, longer or shorter (no one slavishly follows hem lengths anymore, but the cut of a skirt may look better one length than another); *pants:* skinny, baggy, long, short; *belts:* wide or narrow, worn over blouses that are inside or outside; *jackets:* lapels wide or narrow, length of jackets compared to skirts, shoulders padded or soft; *necks:* v-necks or bows, Victorian or contemporary, cowls or turtles.

Glamour and Mademoiselle   These magazines, filled with luscious sweaters and plaids, are magic for anyone going off to college. Models aren't quite as unreal as in *Bazaar* and *Vogue,* and clothes advice is more practical. *Glamour* has a terrific little feature called "Fashion Workshop," which actually acknowledges that you may not want to throw out your entire last year's wardrobe and deals with how to update. Both magazines are aimed at a young audience, but any woman with a youthful figure can relate to the sportswear.

Women's Wear Daily Reports news of the fashion industry on a daily basis. Though women with a passionate interest in fashion often subscribe, main readership is fashion editors, retailers, clothing manufacturers.

W is a biweekly publication geared to a wealthy readership "who want to be plugged into the latest cultural trends," says managing editor Mort Sheinman. "As a fashion publication, *W*'s big advantage is its short lead time, we can turn on a dime . . . get the Paris collections to you in color in two weeks at longest. The magazines take two months." Only problem here: the superb fashion coverage is mixed in with socialite coverage and you'll learn more than you ever wanted to know about how Mr. and Mrs. Walter So-and-So entertain in their Caribbean resort home.

Big Beautiful Woman A breakthrough attempt to hook up fashion with reality, this new magazine aims at the twenty-five million women in the U.S. who are size 16 or larger. "We deal in each issue with the latest and truly flattering fashions for our fully dimensional woman," says the magazine's Statement of Policy. "This is where you stop feeling guilty about being a large size woman and concentrate on being the beautiful and attractive person that you are." Maintaining that the large woman has previously been a captive buyer of inferior, ill-designed, and ill-made merchandise, the magazine reports on attractive fashions modeled by women of the same ample proportion as their customers. To subscribe, write Big Beautiful Woman,

9237 West Third Street, Suite 1201, Beverly Hills, California 90210.

Fashion Signature

A certain touch a designer is famous for and makes over and over, such as Mary McFadden's braided belts, Pauline Trigère's scarfed coats. Anybody can have a fashion signature: Jacqueline Kennedy Onassis' famous oversize impenetrable dark glasses are a signature touch, as are Gloria Steinem's aviator glasses, Bianca Jagger's walking stick.

Fedora

A felt hat with a small to medium-sized brim and a creased crown. It has a man-tailored feeling. The most popular style of hat sold to women today, next to cowboy hats.

Felt

is one of the oldest fabrics, used by man before spinning and weaving were invented. Raw wool fibers were put into the bottoms of sandals to make them softer, and these fibers, pressed down by the heat, weight, and moisture of the foot, stuck together to form the matted fabric we call felt. Modern felt is made from wool and/or fur rolled and pressed by machine. There is no such thing as synthetic felt. Cheap felt is stiff, cardboardlike; good felt is soft and pliable to the touch.

Fendi

Newsweek called the five Fendi sisters of Rome, Italy, "the world's most exclusive furriers and leather artisans." They're known for their imaginative use of animal skins and pelts. They make suitcases out of donkey skins, as well as a fur jacket they called the "Noah's Ark" fur with a collage of pelts from baby rabbits, lambs, squirrel, and mole. Furs range from a few thousand to $100,000 in price and can be found in expensive department stores, such as Bergdorf Goodman's in New York.

Fisherman's Sweater

Not all clothes have charming or delightful reasons for coming into being. Fisherman's sweaters originated on the Aran Islands in the wild Atlantic, where for centuries fishermen have ventured out in tiny craft which don't always return. The families of these Irish fishermen developed their own individual knitting patterns so that the drowned bodies of their men could be recognized when they washed ashore weeks or months later—wool

The most authentic fisherman's sweaters are Irish, from the Aran Islands. They're handknit in cable-stitched patterns with unbleached wool, which is naturally water repellent. (Sweater by Galway Bay Products Ltd. Courtesy of the Irish Export Board).

doesn't disintegrate in the ocean as does flesh.

A genuine Irish fisherman's sweater is of thick cream-colored wool, and handknit in cable patterns. Wool is left unbleached and natural oils make them practically waterproof. You can buy them for around $140 at Irish import stores such as the Irish Pavilion in New York, or send 75 cents for a mail-order catalogue to Shannon Mail Order, Shannon International Airport, Ireland.

Fishnet T-Shirt

Everybody thinks these mesh shirts are to be worn in summer, over a blouse, perhaps, since you can see through all the holes. Actually a fishnet T-shirt is Norwegian thermal underwear; worn under a close-fitting sweater or shirt, the mesh construction traps warm body air while allowing moisture to evaporate.

Flange Shouldered

(flanj) A flange is a flat border on top of shoulders extending an inch or so beyond them.

Flannel

A downy-soft fabric, usually of cotton or wool but sometimes of rayon or synthetics, with a brushed surface. The brushing process creates insulating air cells that provide more warmth than plain cotton. Thus, cotton flannel as well as wool flannel is considered a winter fabric. Three terms you'll see used with flannel:

Suede flannel is brushed on both sides, with fibers pressed into the fabric, almost like felt. It's the warmest flannel and is used for light outdoorsy jackets or heavy shirts.

"French" flannel is a fine twill-weave fabric, brushed on the outside only.

Viyella flannel means it's made from part wool and part cotton, and is guaranteed not to shrink.

Cotton flannel is one of the great American bargains. The Italians may print more beautiful cottons, and nobody can tan leather like the French, but if you're buying flannel, nobody makes a softer, more downy flannel than the Americans. With no import duties to drive prices up, there are real bargains in L. L. Bean's meltingly soft timberline flannel shirt ($17), or a Victorian wallpaper-print nightgown found in department store basements everywhere ($15). Brandywine's flannel nightie is particularly soft.

Care
Usually machine washable.

A flange shoulder manages to look both feminine and space-age at once, and is a good style for anyone with narrow shoulders. (Jacket by Mrs. H. Winter. Photo: John Peden)

Flannelette

A softer and lighter flannel, used a lot for children's clothes.

Flea Markets

probably have the best prices on clothes of any vendor, even better than thrift shops, which have a higher overhead and are sometimes run by eccentric women who charge more than department stores. At flea markets, the latest incarnation of those centuries-old open-air markets where shoppers crowd around, finger, and haggle heatedly over anything from black velvet capes to discount Adidas, dealers of-

ten have an overhead of no more than $5 for the day. Plus, once they've transported wares thirty miles in their vans, the vendors usually don't want to take the merchandise back home, so you can get bargains. According to a recent article in *The New York Times* (entitled "Flea Markets: New Retail Force"), five years ago there were only fifty large flea markets in the country. Today, 200 major ones and thousands of smaller ones are in operation in parking lots, pastures, drive-in theaters, and race tracks. A few are:

World Trade Center Flea Market, the largest in Manhattan, open Saturdays

Antique flea markets are terrific places to shop for vintage clothes; prices are lower because dealers don't have to pay rent. Pam Coghlan, a former associate fashion editor at **McCall's** magazine, sells at two of the biggest East Coast fairs: the Yankee Doodle Drummer show in Boston in October and the Meadowlands, N.J., racetrack show of 300 dealers in November, January, and March. (Photo: John A. Coghlan, Jr.)

through summer and fall on the 150,000-square-foot area a block north of the World Trade Center. Offers discount prices on everything from designer clothes and antique jewelry to jugs, kits and vegetables.

Roosevelt Raceway Flea Market, in Westbury, L.I., New York, where 600 sellers, many of whom are schoolteachers, hawk their wares every Sunday. You'll find lots of new clothing.

Rose Bowl Flea Market, Pasadena, California, open every second Sunday of each month, draws as many as 40,000 people a day.

Ventura Flea Market, Ventura, California, a bimonthly gathering which, in addition to the usual, has stalls featuring handicrafts of local artisans with items such as handwoven scarves and crocheted hats and bags. California has more flea markets than any other state.

A few tips on flea market bargain-hunting:

• *Learn how to find flea markets* Outdoor markets are the most ephemeral of activities—they're not listed in phone books or city guides because they're here for a day or month or season, vanished the next. Sometimes a flea market will appear in a parking lot in one place, and then you'll discover it months later moved en masse to a parking lot across town. Look in local newspapers under such headings as *Weekend Guide* or *Activities,* and when you see a tiny notice about a flea market, *clip the notice,* because while the flea market may go on all summer, the notice may not appear again. If you find a dealer whose wares you particularly like, and the flea market is only a one-shot affair, ask her to send you a

notice when she's going to be in your neighborhood—many dealers have postcards printed up for just this purpose.

• *Take a tape measure* You'll find no dressing rooms at flea markets, sometimes no mirrors, so what do you do when you see a mint-condition silk slip from the 1940s for $15? You either try it on over your jeans and bulky sweater with male customers trying not to notice, or you have a tape measure and a few notes about hip size and bust size all ready to go.

• *Take cash* For vague reasons having to do with IRS activities, most dealers detest checks and love cash. Cash will get you a lower price.

• *Go late* The ideal time to arrive is about an hour before wares start disappearing into clouds of newspapers for the trip home. It's also good to be the first customer, as the most beautiful items go quickly. At any rate, bargain, bargain, bargain—nobody will be offended, haggling is the name of the game.

• *Especially look for* antique jewelry, cashmere sweaters, interesting old handbags, mouton coats, hand-crocheted shawls and mantillas, the unexpected.

Fleece-Lined

Authentic fleece is real sheep's wool; "fleece-lined" today usually means the item is lined with a thick fleecy-*looking* acrylic. When the fleece is real, a hang tag will read, "authentic shearling lining." Synthetic fleece looks as cozy and cuddly as real fleece, but the real McCoy is much warmer. Especially beware "fleece-lined" rubber boots—rubber conducts cold, and acrylic fleece will be inadequate to keep your feet warm without heavy wool socks.

Flocking

A method of printing fabric. Glue is applied to fabric in patterns such as dots, stripes, or flowers, and then fibers of the same material are sprinkled over the glue and pressed on, giving printed designs a different texture from the background fabric. The dots in dotted swiss are often flocked on. Good-quality flocking is anchored on so securely you can wash and dry clean. To check, scrape with your fingernail—if fibers come off easily, forget it. Even with a good fabric of this type, however, normal wear will cause designs to fade in abrasion points such as the neckline, cuffs, and seat.

Folkwear Patterns

Tired of blazers and shirtwaist dresses? If you can sew, or pay somebody to sew, Folkway has easy-to-sew patterns for the antique and ethnic clothes you'll seldom find in department stores: a French cheesemaker's smock, a medieval dress with flaring sleeves, Navajo blouse, Missouri River boatman's shirt, even a pair of Turkish sarouelles, which are voluminous and comfortable drawstring pants. Patterns cost from $3.50 to $5. Write Folkwear, Box 98, Forestville, California 95436.

Fortrel

Polyester made by Celanese. (See POLYESTER.)

Foulard

A print. Small, all-over patterns of the sort used for men's neckties. First popularized by Oscar Wilde, today used mostly for scarves and shirtwaist dresses. Considered part of the preppy look.

French Cuffs

Cuffs that must be fastened with your own cuff links. Very elegant, though you may need a valet to fasten the links for you, as it can be frustrating to do with one hand.

French Cut

A term without much meaning today. At one time, American clothes were determinedly clunky, baggy, and sturdy. The French took American sportswear classics and working clothes, such as jeans and blazers, and cut them with narrower lines, higher armholes, and all-around better tailoring, transforming them into fashion items. Then they shipped our own national costumes back to us with a French designer label, advertising copy proclaiming "French cut," and a doubled price. American designers, beginning with Ralph Lauren, hastened to do their own refining of American sportswear, and now U.S.-made jeans, suits, and skirts fit well too. Sasson and Jordache are particularly known for cutting their jeans as tight and skinny as St. Laurent ever did.

French Sizes

If you're a hopeless clothes addict who is constantly looking through boutiques, resale and thrift shops, and department stores where salesclerks have vanished, tucking a little note with French sizes into your billfold can save a lot of frustration. Sizes run as follows:

For dresses, pants, skirts, French sizes 38-40-42-44 roughly equal our 6-8-10-12. For lingerie, 80-85-90-95 translates into 32-34-36-38; the American small-medium-large is scaled 1-2-3 in French, while French (and Italian shoes too) run 36-37-38-39-40 to our 5-6-7-8-9.

Frizon, Maud

(free-zon) French designer who makes sleek, futuristic shoes, definitely not the footwear you'll see at garden-party teas or prayer meetings. No discreet gray pumps here—Frizon pumps are pink and green, topped with angry jagged edges. Ballet slippers aren't pink satin but aqua snakeskin, while the ubiquitous slingback is a metallic bronze and pewter with a toe so pointed it could cut croissant dough. Cost: From $200 to $400 a pair, but Frizon often has half-price sales. Find in Bloomingdale's, Neiman-Marcus, Bergdorf Goodman, and other prestige department stores.

Frog Closing

A fastening for clothing in which material, usually matching the garment, is sewn into a cord. The cord can be sewn into a flowerlike pattern in the center, with two large loops on either side to loop over buttons, or it can be wound into a design with a looped cord which is joined to the opposite edge of a similar design with another loop of cord.

Fruit-of-the-Loom

is a 130-year-old American manufacturer best known for durable, inexpensive men's underwear. Lately, however, its T-shirts, in gorgeous deep blues, mauves, and blacks, and with those luscious clusters of fruit on the front, have been dominating everybody's T-shirt wardrobe. "The six dollar price is right, and besides, I knew if the T-shirt shrank, I'd get my money back," says one satisfied customer.

She's right: "For over a century of operation, if a customer has had a problem, we've refunded her money, no questions asked," says Peter Felberbaum, vice president of marketing.

The company was founded in Rhode Island in 1851 by the brothers Knight, one of whom had an artistic daughter who liked to draw fruit on the end of bolts of muslin. The bolts with fruit on them sold better than bare bolts, and in 1871 Fruit-of-the-Loom was registered as trademark #418. (A registration number today would be in the trillions.) Nobody thought of putting the trademark *outside* clothes, however, until four years ago, when the ever-fashion-conscious Italians recognized its possibilities.

Frye Boots

An American classic, Frye boots are to the East what Nocona and Tony Lama are to Texas. The present best-selling Frye boot to women is not a cowboy boot but a direct descendant of an 1863 boot made for Union Army soldiers during the Civil War. After the war, this plain, sturdy boot became workingmen's footwear, and was also worn by soldiers during World Wars I and II. The company is still housed in the same building in Marlborough, Massachusetts, where production began 117 years ago, and many of the procedures for making boots haven't changed, either. Much of the work is done by hand, as opposed to putting shoes through assembly-line machines, and Frye boots are recognizable by their "benchcrafted" look. Today, about 60 percent of the company's boots are still the classic boot; the other 40 percent has gone western. Boots for women are fitted *on*

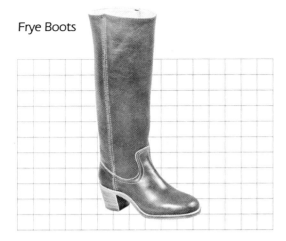

One hundred and eighteen years is a long time for a style to stick around, but everyone from Civil War soldiers to Wilhelmina models has enjoyed the rugged, handcrafted look of Frye® boots. This style is their biggest seller to women. (Courtesy of the John A. Frye Shoe Company, Inc.)

women—they don't just take a men's boot pattern and make it smaller. Average price is $110, but if you happen to be in Marlborough (between Worcester and Boston) you can get $40 off on seconds, which may have tiny scuffs, or colors that are a bit off.

Furs

Probably nothing makes us feel more pampered than a good fur coat. Fur plays so special a place in the wardrobe that men have judged their success as providers by whether or not their wives had a fur. Today, however, men buying status-symbol gifts for wives are no longer the biggest customers. The newest development in the fur business is that women are buying for themselves. "The women who come here to buy furs don't bring their husbands or boyfriends," David Stypmann, head of Henri Bendel's fur department, told *The New York Times*. "They're working women who find it perfectly normal to buy their own."

Should you buy a fur? The delights of owning a delicious fur coat are obvious. However, fur-owning has a negative side as well, and anyone about to spend thou-

sands on a coat should be well informed of all its aspects. The liabilities are:

- *Inconvenience* Most coat check rooms in restaurants and department stores won't take furs because they're afraid the coats will be stolen and they'll be held responsible. You have to either sit on your coat or carry it, getting hairs all over your wool suit. At parties, the best of which can turn into mob scenes seething with strangers, you may be afraid to leave your fur in the bedroom.

- *Fear* Presumably if you can afford a fur, you can afford taxis and automobiles, but sometimes taxis refuse to appear, and cars break down. A woman alone in a mink coat is more likely to attract muggers than someone in a cloth coat. There will be many places you won't feel safe in an expensive fur, such as the New York City subway, and there will be freezing weather when you'll be obliged to wear your last year's wool melton, leaving your $5,000 fox at home warming a coat hanger.

- *Hostility* Fur-wearers have to be prepared for verbal attacks from people who are opposed to animal cruelty. These people bitterly deplore the killing of animals for nothing but their pelts, and are especially incensed by wild-animal furs such as raccoon, lynx, fox, beaver, martin, and muskrat which are caught by use of a torturous device called the leghold trap. This trap, banned in twenty-one countries and a few states but still in use in much of North America, snaps shut on an animal's paws when it steps forward after bait, and the more it tries to escape, the tighter the jaws grip. "Behind every beautiful wild fur is a brutal, bloody story," remarked actress Mary Tyler Moore. Others resent animals raised on ranches, such as chinchilla, rabbit, nutria, lamb, mink (though not *all* mink—about 10 percent of mink pelts are still trapped). These people argue that at least wild animals had a good life, while ranched ones must spend all their days in tiny cages. "There's no doubt I get more respect from salesclerks and headwaiters," says one owner of a marten coat. "But there's also no doubt I get hostile glances as well. At any rate, here is an explanation of terms:

Dyeing	Changing natural color of a fur with chemical dyes. Dyed furs are thought not to hold up quite as well as natural fur. Persian lamb and Alaskan fur seal, however, do last longer dyed. You can tell if a fur is dyed by looking at the leather underneath: if dyed, fur and leather will be the same color; if natural, different colors.
Female skins	Usually lighter and silkier, but not quite so durable as male skins.
Guard hair	Longer outer hair that protects the downier underfur. Flat furs such as mink and mole don't have guard hair; on others it's coarse and is removed by plucking.
Leathering	(also called feathering). Sewing in strips of cloth or leather between fur strips, often done with long-haired furs to make them less heavy and bulky.
Letting-out	Cutting the pelt into diagonal strips and resewing into longer strips; eliminates bulkiness, enhances drape.
Piecing	Coats are sewn together from leftover fur such as paws and tails, also called sections; pieced furs tend to split at the seams and don't hold up as well as regular ones; on the other hand, they're one-quarter of the price.
Shearing	Cutting fur into a velvety, pilelike texture. Makes coats lighter in weight, but not quite as long-wearing.
Skin-on-skin	Skins are not cut into strips as in letting-out, but are simply cut to fit a pattern and sewn together.
Underfur	Shorter fur underneath guard hairs. The colder an animal's environment, the more dense and warm underfur will be.

The chart on the next page discusses the furs you're most likely to find in stores today. Inexpensive means you can get a midcalf-length new fur at height of the season for under $2,500; medium includes furs up to $9,000; expensive is over that price. Very expensive means $40,000 to $150,000.

Fur	What to Look For	Cost
BADGER	Heavy, sturdy, very warm; look for long silvery guard hair over thick, tan underfur.	Inexpensive to medium
BEAVER Sheared	Casual brown "knockabout" fur, very durable; look for rich dense plush; you shouldn't be able to see where skins are joined.	Medium to expensive
Natural	Look for long lustrous guard hairs over thick underfur. Very warm.	
CHINCHILLA	Has more hairs per square inch than any other animal; 200 skins of this squirrellike creature are needed for a coat. Look for short, dense, silky fur. White is most luxurious color, but pearl-gray and tan are also lovely. Very warm.	Expensive
COYOTE	Fur coarse but should be silky; long guard hair but thick soft underfur; shouldn't have a yellow cast.	
FISHER	Dark-brown weasellike creature, shading to blue-gray (most costly); look for thick underfur, rich color. Very warm.	Very expensive
FITCH	Also known as polecat, and a close relative of skunks and mink, found in Russia (most expensive), Poland, Germany. Very warm, silky.	Medium to expensive
FOX	Fluffiest, most longhaired fur, may be gray, white, blue, red, beige, brown, silver, or dyed. Look for long silky guard hairs, thick underfur. American wild gray fox is least costly.	Medium (gray) to expensive
LAMB American	See SHEARLING. Very warm, long-lasting.	Inexpensive
Russian Broadtail	Pelts from unborn lambs, beautiful, fragile, silky, may be brown or gray (most costly) or black.	Very expensive

Fur	What to Look For	Cost
LAMB Persian	Very warm, pliable, with silky, ripply curls, usually black, brown, or gray. Fur from southern Africa is called Swakara. All from newborn lambs, which infuriates anti-cruelty people.	Inexpensive
Mouton	See MOUTON. Very warm, heavy.	Inexpensive
LYNX	Called "bobcat" in the U.S., lynx elsewhere, the numbers of American lynx are so low that conservationists want the species declared endangered. Bobcat is spotted brown; Russian and Canadian lynx are white, creamy. All shed badly.	Expensive, often up to $150,000
MARTEN	A form of weasel, brown, with long guard hair and plush underfur; American is least costly. The best is "Stone" marten from Germany, Turkey.	Medium (American) and up
MINK	See MINK. Very warm, superbly long-lasting.	Medium and up
MOLE	A flat, dense fur, always dyed; make sure skins match in hair height.	Inexpensive
MUSKRAT	Aquatic animal indigenous to North America. Southern is flat and slightly less costly; northern has heavy underfur with long guard hair. Look for well-matched, dense fur. Very warm.	Inexpensive
NUTRIA	Aquatic South American rodent, akin to beaver, has coarse but silky fur. Wild nutria is less coarse. Very warm.	Medium
Sheared Unsheared	A flat, low-keyed fur, lighter than beaver. Look for long guard hairs, thick underfur. Very warm.	
OPOSSUM American	Gray to black marsupial, long guard hair, dense	Inexpensive

Fur	What to Look For	Cost
OPOSSUM	underfur. Very warm, often used for raincoat lining.	
Australian	Short plushy fur, gray most costly, brown most common. Very warm.	
RABBIT	See RABBIT.	Inexpensive
RACCOON	Very warm, striped, silvery, usually long hair but may be sheared.	Medium
SABLE	Lighter yet plusher than mink, very warm. A member of the weasel family, native to Canada and Russia; "Crown" Russian sable is considered the most desirable fur in the world.	Very expensive
SEAL Alaska or Fur Seal	Velvety, short brown fur, always plucked to remove coarse guard hairs; very warm and long-lasting. Alaskan is best seal fur.	Medium
Hair Seal	Short, shiny fur, coarser than Alaskan seal, with no underfur; very warm.	Inexpensive to medium
SQUIRREL	Lightweight, soft, fluffy, usually dyed; best country of origin is Russia, next best Poland, Canada, Finland.	Medium
ZORINA	South American skunk, black with white stripes, glossy flat fur.	Inexpensive

Tip: Best time to buy all furs: August and January.

Most long-lasting furs, lasting for fifteen to twenty years or more: mink and Alaskan fur seal; runners-up include unsheared beaver, badger, muskrat, unsheared nutria, raccoon.

Most fragile furs: rabbit, broadtail lamb, mole, squirrel. All other furs fall somewhere in between, with average life expectancy being around ten years for long-haired furs, somewhat longer for short-haired.

Under the Federal Fur Products Labeling Act of 1952 the consumer is entitled by law to certain information being provided on labels or hangtags. You should be clearly told the name of the fur and what country it comes from if imported. If a fur has been sheared or dyed, the label should so state; ditto if the coat is made in part or entirely of pieces. All this applies to second-hand as well as new furs.

Second-hand Furs

If the previously mentioned prices are out of your range, all is not lost. If you buy a used fur coat at the best store in town, you'll save half the price. If you buy a used fur privately or from a neighborhood store, off season and on sale, you can get prices down to an eighth or a tenth what they were originally. The New Yorker Fur Thrift Shop at Third and 50th in Manhattan had, in July, an Alaskan seal jacket with a mink trim for $75; a ranch mink, hip length, was $400; and a full-length mouton in perfect shape was $200. Some guidelines for buying used furs are:

- *Unless you're shopping at the best used-fur shops, such as New York's Ritz, which guarantees its furs, realize you're gambling.* You can buy still-lovely furs for $100 or so, but the pelt may be dried and brittle, which means it may have ten more good years or its demise could take place within a week. Never spend a lot of money on a used fur without guarantees. Says writer Elaine Louie, "trying to save an old fur is like trying to revive a dead pet."

- *Hints as to a fur's health are* furtively tug at the hair—if any comes out easily, don't buy. If possible, lift the lining and see if you can gently stretch the skin without it tearing. Of course, most proprietors of used furs are watching for just such maneuvers, so you may have to content yourself with feeling the skin all over—it should be soft and pliable, like chamois, with no hard or dry spots.

- *Mortally wounded coats can be saved (for awhile).* Just because a coat has a six-inch split doesn't mean it's hopeless. If you see a $35 fur with lustrous healthy hair but a torn pelt, and you're a gambler, buy and invest a few more dollars in furrier's tape. Any fur shop can tell you where to buy some. Open the lining and tape down the split. If the skin seems brittle in other spots, oil it lightly, from the back, with baby oil.

- *Don't overlook sling capes.* Hardest style to sell, and therefore low in price, are evening capes. You can get beautifully made hip-length furs, not heavily worn, for under $100. Wear over a regular cloth coat with an Inverness cape effect, when dressing up, or over suits.

Care

Avoid: Wearing shoulderbags, or other handbags over your arm, in the same place; sitting on the fur in a car for hours; sliding across car seats; spraying on perfume while wearing your fur; pinning on flowers or jewelry; exposing for long periods to direct sunlight; folding your coat inside out; wrapping in plastic; brushing or combing.

Do: Take the coat to a furrier if you spill something nasty on it, hang it somewhere dark and cool with space to breathe, wear a silk scarf to prevent matting of hairs on collar, have the fur cleaned and glazed by a furrier every year or so ($15–$30), and put in storage during summer ($15–$30). (Though don't clean more than once a year because the process does tend to dry out the pelt.)

If You Get Caught in the Rain

A little water won't hurt your fur—dashing from under an awning into a car, or even slogging a block or two is no big deal. However, should you be caught in a heavy downpour so long that the leather pelt gets soaked, that's more serious. "If water is beading on top of the coat, you're okay. If it looks like a drowned rat, you've got problems and should get professional advice," says Tim McCall, fur storage and repair manager at New York's Henri Bendel. *Never try to protect your coat from rain by turning it inside out*—linings aren't at all waterproof and may spot and pucker if they get wet. Gently shake the wet fur, and hang on a padded hanger away from heat, preferably near an open window where a little air is moving.

Your coat should be glazed every few years, which adds a measure of water-repellency in addition to giving the fur more sheen. Most furriers automatically glaze a fur when they clean it.

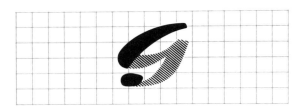

Gabardine

A light twill fabric, so finely woven it clings and swings like silk; it can be wool, cotton, rayon, or synthetic fiber. Even people who are allergic to wool can often wear wool gabardine. Everybody should have a pair of classic, straight-leg gabardine slacks, and not pay more than $60 for them.

Care

Gabardine develops a shine easily; never press while dry—use a steamer. Don't dry clean any more than absolutely necessary.

Galanos, James

(ga´-la-nos) Considered the most masterly American designer, Galanos lives in California, where his clothes are made by craftsmen often recruited from the defunct costume departments of film companies. His fabrics are beautiful and his workmanship comparable only with that of a few couture houses in Paris; prices for dresses run from $2,000 to $15,000. When Saks, Bergdorf-Goodman, and Neiman-Marcus advertise his clothes in the newspaper, they discreetly leave out any mention of price. He's best known for his billowing-sleeved evening clothes with a medieval air in chiffon, silk, and velvet. Galanos, one of the earliest members of the Coty Hall of Fame, designed Nancy Reagan's inaugural gown of white satin and bugle beads.

Gaucho Pants

Cowboys of the South American pampas wore midcalf-length divided skirts with a cotton shirt, silver belt, and poncho. St. Laurent copied the look in the 1960s and it's been around ever since. Gaucho pants are always midcalf; culottes can be shorter or longer.

Georgette

A sheer crêpe fabric, similar to chiffon, used for evening clothes. It can be made from silk, polyester, or many other fibers. See CRÊPE.

Gingham

A fabric woven into small checks or plaids. A printed fabric is not authentic gingham.

Cotton gingham was in its heyday on the American frontier.

Givenchy, Hubert de

(ghee-von-she) French couturier, to the manner born, known since the 1950s for clothes of classic, sober elegance. His $1,000 suits are worn by conservative women of international social prominence and his evening dresses are described by *The New York Times* as "important-looking and destined for grand balls and palaces." He designs everything from swimsuits to brassieres, and even his inexpensive garments tend to be quiet and demure.

Glacé

French for glazed, means a shiny, permanent finish has been applied to leather.

Gloves

Italian kidskin is softest and most luxurious. Warmest gloves are down-filled mittens. Also warm, and less bulky, are thermal skiing gloves, $20 up in ski shops. Lambskin shearlings are warm but costly. Mittens are always warmer than gloves, because fingers can heat each other; wool is always warmer than acrylic fleece. For moderate cold, cashmere-lined kid is warmer and longer-lasting than fur-lined.

Gold

is the one metal valued by every culture, including ours. Not only is gold jewelry a hedge against inflation, but it can be worn day and evening, swimming at the beach, or to dinner and dancing. Here are the terms to understand about gold jewelry:

Karat   A measure, from 1 to 24, used to indicate how much of the metal is gold and how much an alloy. Pure gold would be 24-karat, but this is too soft to use for jewelry. The most desirable jewelry is 18-karat, meaning that the metal contains 18 parts gold to 6 parts other metals. Fourteen-karat, also a good weight for jewelry, is less expensive and contains 14 parts of gold to 10 parts other metals. No jewelry less than 10-karat gold is sold in the U.S.

White gold is gold alloyed with nickel or palladium. Rose gold is gold with copper, pale gold has silver added. Cadmium and silver combined give gold a greenish hue, while iron makes it bluish.

Gold-filled   A layer of gold, at least 10-karat, has been bonded on top of another, less expensive metal. Gold-filled jewelry must have a layer of gold that weighs at least one-twentieth of total weight of the other metal used.

Gold-plated   Made by a process similar to gold-filled, but less gold is required.

Gold electroplate   means jewelry is coated with gold at least seven-millionths of an inch thick.

Gold-washed or *gold-flashed*   means that the gold finish is *less* than seven-millionths of an inch thick.

Vermeil.   Heavy gold electroplate over sterling silver.

Care

Wash occasionally with soap and water. To keep gold chains from tangling in your jewelry box, cut a drinking straw in half, slip chain through, and fasten the catch.

Gore-Tex

is the only fabric that's both entirely waterproof and somewhat ventilated. It has billions of tiny holes per inch that are *larger* than vaporized water molecules, the kind constantly evaporating from our bodies as water vapor, yet *smaller* than the liquified water molecules of rain. Though you may get the impression from Gore-Tex advertising that the fabric "breathes" nearly as much as cotton, it doesn't. It's usually laminated to nylon and is as ventilated as nylon (which "breathes" a lot more than other waterproof fibers that are chemically coated to close their pores entirely). So Gore-Tex is fabulous for rainwear, but it isn't really a new fabric for running suits on a sunny day.

Care
Gore-Tex is hand or machine washable but not dry-cleanable.

Greatcoat
Used to mean a man's army coat belted and reaching to midcalf; today it means any super-heavy warm coat.

Grès, Mme. Alix
(gree—rhymes with she) One of the classiest names in French couture, and the last to make ready-to-wear, which she considered a prostitution. A former sculptress, she's known for statuesque evening gowns cut out in ways that make bare skin part of the design. Socialites love to appear in ten- or twenty-year-old Grès dresses—the longer you've worn it, the more cachet it carries.

Grommet
A metal eyelet, used on belts, now being put on hems, cuffs, and all over the place for decoration.

Grosgrain
Ribbed ribbon fabric commonly used to reinforce the buttonholes on a cardigan sweater, now being used for evening pants and jackets, and for watchbands.

Gucci
One of the great status-symbol stores of the 1970s, this Italian-based, family-owned business has seventy-five shops around the world, sixteen of them in the U.S. Known for its dour clerks and absurdly priced luxury items, such as an $11,000 handbag with an 18-karat gold chain which can double as a necklace. Gucci does a nice classic walking shoe for under $200, and has lovely suede coats for under $2,000 and lots of its red-and-green-striped handbags with the double Gs for under $300.

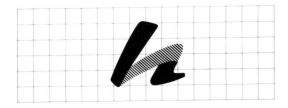

Hacking Jackets
are the tweedy riding jackets worn by horsewomen for over a century—one of the most enduring classics. These jackets, unlike blazers, always have slits at the sides so that when you sit on a horse, the back flap will fold out gracefully over the horse's back. They're very fitted from bust through waist, have higher-cut armholes than a blazer, and have only three buttons. People who never go near horses still buy hacking jackets for their beautiful tailoring, and wear them with slacks. Jacqueline Kennedy Onassis wears Pytchley of England. Miller's, special Coty Award winner and official saddlers to the U.S. Olympic Equestrian team, sells a similar English style jacket for $125; on sale jackets are reduced to $70, sometimes down to $50. For a catalogue of riding clothes from jodhpurs to hunt caps, write Miller's, 235 Murray Hill Parkway, East Rutherford, New Jersey 07073, or visit their New York store.

Nothing is more classic than a genuine riding-store hacking jacket. Wear with tweedy skirts, jeans, pants tucked into boots. (Jacket available at Approved Miller's Dealers)

Halston

"The Halston label on a dress or perfume tells a woman that what she's buying will be recognized as 'right,'" says *Vogue*, "that it's more than just stylish, it's in good taste." Corporate wives love Halstons, as do executive-level working women. And so do the world's most tasteful women, who made Halston the world's most tasteful designer in the first place: Jacqueline Kennedy Onassis, Lee Radziwill, Gloria Vanderbilt, Mrs. Vincent Astor, and Catherine Deneuve are clients.

Halston's philosophy about clothes is that they should be simple ("less is more"), and not draw attention away from the woman herself. He's a master of the figure-flattering bias cut, and made his reputation designing evening clothes that make even the more overweight look graceful—a silk tunic worn over a matching long gown, pyjamas, tiered chiffon dresses, caftans.

If you buy on sale, it's possible to afford a Halston. Halston boutiques in New York, Costa Mesa, and Detroit usually have a half-price sale after Christmas. Halston's lines run like this:

Halston Made-to-Order This is his couture line: clothes are fitted on you in the fabric of your choice. For someone who goes to a lot of posh parties, these clothes are a terrific investment: you can get a pair of the famed bias-cut evening pyjamas with a V-neck tunic top and a sash for around $700; a strapless floor-length evening dress in silk velvet is also $700, in silk chiffon, $900. Or you can spend more, much more, in which case you might even get to meet the master himself. Best to phone for an appointment (212 744-9033), but you *can* just drop into the Halston Boutique, 33 East 68th Street, New York, any day except Sunday. Clothes take three weeks to make up after they're ordered.

Halston Originals His largest-in-volume line, available in the designer dress section of department stores throughout the U.S. Here you'll find a selection of his silk evening dresses and pyjamas, for which you'll pay $500 to $1,000.

Halston Sportswear, found in the designer sportswear section of department stores such as Saks, are his separates—classic two-pleat slacks for $100, $200 blazers.

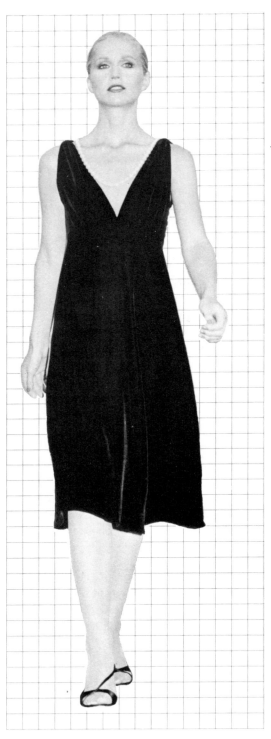

Halston believes clothes should be as simple as possible so as not to detract from the woman wearing them.

All other Halston labels are licensed, including his Halston IV line. Though Halston personally approves all designs licensed to use his name, devotees of his clothes say Halston IV "isn't the same feeling at all."

Halston has been in the Coty Fashion Hall of Fame since 1974.

Halter-Neck Dresses

have been around ever since Marilyn Monroe wore a white crêpe one in *The Seven Year Itch*. With its deep V-neck and vertical lines, it's a terrific look for women with broad shoulders or heavy bosom, not so flattering to thin women, unless you happen to have a very pretty back.

Handbags

are the only item of apparel carried day in and day out, so quality is of utmost importance. Here are a few facts about handbags.

- Best handbags, in the sense of finest leather and workmanship, are Italian imports of calfskin or reptile. Most durable—and not without a rugged charm of their own—are American cowhide bags (see COACH). Least well made, least durable, and almost aggressively unfashionable are synthetic bags.

- Highest-quality bags usually, but not always, are of the most fine, supple leather. They have sixteen stitches or more to the inch, and multiple compartments inside. They are usually *not* laden with a lot of superfluous brass, and often (but not always) have a highly polished finish rather than a dull matte one.

- Large women look best carrying large bags, small with small. (It's amazing

Marilyn Monroe launched halter tops in **The Seven Year Itch**. (Courtesy of The Museum of Modern Art/Film Stills Archive)

how many women choose to overlook this basic law of pleasing proportion.)

- Shoulderbags are unhealthy. Though these bags have been popular for years (originating during World War II as part of the WAC uniform), many orthopedists consider them an evil of the ilk of spike heels and girdles. Because one arm tends to rest against the bag instead of swinging naturally, and be-cause women usually carry the shoulder with the strap over it an inch higher than the other, gait is thrown off. This sort of cramped, asymmetrical posture won't cause trouble on short forays, but a three-mile hike with a heavy shoulderbag could give you a backache.

- *Most respected names in handbags:* Gucci, Hermés, Judith Leiber, Fendi,

Confused about styles of bags? Here are the six most common handbag shapes. (Courtesy of the National Handbag Association)

HOBO	<ul><li>Shoulder strap</li><li>Very soft</li><li>Top zipper</li></ul>	

SATCHEL	<ul><li>Wide, flat bottom</li><li>Top handles</li></ul>

ENVELOPE	<ul><li>Accordion or French (single) creased bottom</li><li>Flap opening</li></ul>

CLUTCH	<ul><li>Designed to be tucked under the arm, often features detachable strap or handle</li></ul>

CHANEL	<ul><li>Distinguished by chain handles and quilting</li></ul>

SWAGGER	<ul><li>Outside pockets surrounding center frame or zipper pocket</li><li>Double handles or shoulder straps</li></ul>

(Courtesy of the National Handbag Association)

Bottega Veneta, Madler, Prada, Morris Moskowitz, Coach, Meyer.

Care

Wipe dirt off bags with a clean, slightly moist cloth. Saddle soap is not recommended, according to the National Handbag Association, because it may remove natural oils. Rub matching Meltonian shoe polish into slight scuffs, and use Lexol (see LEXOL) frequently, especially after bouts with a rainstorm. Never overload bags, as this distorts shape and may break stitching. When storing out-of-season leather bags, they shouldn't come into contact with one another, as leather finishes have a tendency to stick together; best to wrap them in tissue paper, not plastic bags. For repairs, if you don't trust local shoe-repair shops, there's a New York store famous for repairing anything from linings to beads on evening bags, and accustomed to a large mail-in business with out-of-towners: Artbag Creations, 735 Madison Avenue (at 64th), New York, New York 212 744–2720. Prices are no bargain but neither are they unreasonable.

Handkerchief Linen

The finest, softest, most lightweight linen, which feels like baby clothes. Possibly the most delightful of all summery fabrics, and one of Ralph Lauren's big favorites.

Hardwick, Cathy

American designer; a beautiful Oriental, descended from Queen Min, last monarch of Korea. Her real name is Kashena Shura. She made her name making lovely silks we could all afford. Her clothes are low-priced, adventuresome, and her workmanship is as meticulous as that of many other designers selling for twice the money.

Harem Pants

Loose trousers, gathered into a band at the ankle. Buy only those made from soft, flowing materials, never corduroy or other stiff fabrics.

The most flowing, graceful harem pants come from countries where they were worn for real. These Adini label imports are Indian.

Harlequin Pattern

Brightly colored diamond checks, interspersed with white diamond checks, derived from the costume of the harlequin, a buffoonlike character from Italian comedy theater. The pattern is used occasionally for evening clothes.

Harp, Holly

A California designer known for her flowing bias-cut silk and matte jersey evening clothes with handpainted designs, in a $600 to $1,000 price range.

Harris Tweed

A soft, thick tweed woven on the Outer Hebrides Islands off Scotland, handloomed from yarns dyed with gentle vegetable dyes. The label will read: "Handwoven Harris tweed, spun, woven Outer Hebrides, Scot." Expensive but not out of sight, approximately $250 for a blazer.

Harvé Benard

An American sportswear manufacturing company noted for its beautifully cut blazers and wool flannel slacks.

Hats

Nothing confers a sense of presence and style quicker than a hat. Says designer Hubert Givenchy, "A hat changes a woman's behavior. A woman in a hat does not walk the same as one in jeans." The days when a stylish hat was *de rigueur* for every hour of the day are long past. The present sensible generation wears hats almost entirely to keep heads warm. However, a dashing Garbo slouch hat keeps a head just as warm as a dingy pullover. Here's what you should know about hats.

- *Heat*   Not wearing any sort of hat in winter is foolish indeed. Huge amounts of heat escape through the scalp, which in turn will cause hands and feet to freeze. Yes, hands and feet, because the body's first reaction to chill is to protect essential body organs, and that means cutting down on blood flow to arms and legs, sending it instead to liver and heart. The old adage, "If your feet are cold, put on a hat," is scientifically correct.

- *Buying a hat*   Most pliable, lustrous hats are felt velour made from rabbit's hair. They cost $20 to $40. Wool felt costs less, depending on quality: good felt hats are soft and touchable; cheap ones feel like cardboard. A cheap felt is a bad investment, because once it's dented, it stays dented; a good felt or velour can be restored to shape.

The horizontal line of a brimmed hat does wonders for a long narrow face. A short wide face looks better in a face-hugging cloche or knit hat. According to a spokesman for Betmar, America's biggest manufacturer of hats, the best-selling hat to women is the cowboy hat; after that, the fedora.

Care

The best way to store hats is on a styrofoam hat figure, obtainable from milliners. Should you live in an apartment with little closet space, store your hats stacked, one on top of the other, with a little tissue in between and lots of tissue in the bottom one. Make sure the bottom hat is stuffed enough to keep its shape and lift brim slightly off the flat surface below. If your hat has a ribbon around it, make sure the ribbon is lying flat in the direction it was meant to go. Otherwise, after three months of being folded in the wrong direction, it will stay that way. To fix a hat brim that's dented and funny-looking, moisten it slightly, cover with a cotton cloth, and iron gently with iron set on low heat.

Haute Couture

(oht koo-ture) The latest fashions put forth by the most expensive and celebrated designers.

Hawaiian Shirts

These brightly colored shirts, covered with patterns of orchids, banana plants, flamingos, and dancing girls with leis, and traditionally worn by American tourists in the 1950s, are back, and somehow they now look adorable. Imitations abound in department stores, but antique stores such as the Unique Clothing Warehouse in New York (718 Broadway) have the originals for $25 to $35. Most desirable are handscreened silks and rayons with labels such as Aloha and Made in Hawaii. Made in Korea or Japan doesn't have quite as much cachet, but if the shirt is bright enough, one accepts the trade-off. Buy them big and roomy, and wear belted over pants, tucked in, or with an A-line skirt patterned after the skirts worn at the same time as Hawaiian shirts.

Hems

Who knows where they'll be next? Only a few observations about hems escape the fickle whims of fashion. . . .

- *Width* Hems should not be too narrow, which can make a skirt look cheap and hang awkwardly, nor too wide, which makes skirts bulky. The more voluminous a skirt, the narrower its hem should be.

- *Stitching* The farther apart stitches are on a hem, the lower the quality of the dress. Look for small, neat stitches.

- *Permanent creases* Ever lowered a hem and not been able to get out the crease from the original hem? Permanent press clothes are processed in a way that makes them permanent *as is*. Most permanent press garments are of synthetic fibers or natural fabrics blended with synthetics. Hems on 100-percent wools, cottons, and linens can be successfully lowered.

- *Pant hems* On classic, tailored trousers, hems should touch top of shoe in front without wrinkling and come to top of heel in back. A small feminist battle was won at Macy's last year when a woman sued because she had to pay for hemming slacks, while men got free alterations. "Since women sew, they like to do their own alterations," a Macy's manager told the irate customer, making her irate enough to sue. Now Macy's will hem any slacks priced over $30 free for both sexes.

Type of Skirt or Dress	Width of Hem
Straight, narrow (except sheer fabrics)	2 to 3 inches
A-line, flared, dirndl or pleated (except sheers)	1 to 2 inches
Voluminous, circle	$\frac{1}{8}$ to 1 inch

Hermès

(ur-mez) The French house of Hermès, established in 1837 as a royal saddle and harness maker, is known for its luxurious, status-symbol handbags and luggage, and its silk scarves with horses on them, printed in as many as twenty-two different colors—more colors than are in most paintings. These scarves ($90 apiece) have been framed as wall hangings by connoisseurs such as Jacqueline Kennedy Onassis.

Herringbone

A twill weave with a tiny "V" pattern, found on wool suits. Gives a conservative, classic look.

Herringbone weave (Photo: Herb Dorfman)
Houndstooth weave (Photo: Herb Dorfman)

High-Tech Clothes

Not everybody likes sweet, soft, natural fibers. A thriving segment of the clothing industry thinks the future lies in more and better synthetics. "We've had years of silks and tweeds," says Patricia Field, owner of a Greenwich Village boutique bearing her name. "People want clothes that are easy to care for, affordable, and modern." High-tech stores are not for the middle-aged. The music is rock, the furniture of inflated rubber. Clothes run toward sweaters with industrial zippers down the side; silvery, shimmery windbreakers made of polyester coated with crushed mirror dots; shiny, aggressive polyurethane leather, which can be washed; stretchy bodywear; water-repellent Scotchlite, which reflects light. You might wear any of these with a see-through vinyl handbag, and dark sunglasses, very narrow and menacing, like the ones worn to watch 3-D movies in the 1950s. Some high-tech stores are:

Patricia Field, New York
Up Against the Wall, Washington, D.C.
Urban Camouflage, Houston
Rain, Atlanta

Hook, J. G.

See J. G. HOOK. There is no person named J. G. Hook—it's a company name.

Horn, Carol

American designer. Her label is Carol Horn's Habitat. If Greenwich Village had to vote on a favorite designer, it might well be Carol Horn. Her clothes have an ethnic look about them without *being* ethnic. One year she went to Guatemala and traveled from village to village buying up blankets to make into skirts. One of her latest best-sellers is a black cotton fiesta skirt ($120) with lines of brightly colored appliqués

No, it's not the photograph—the dress glows. Some people are weary of silks and tweeds and prefer "high technology" synthetic fabrics. Scotchlite®, the material used here, is a polyester/cotton blend coated with microspheres of the same substance used to make mirrors. (Courtesy of Patricia Field Boutique, New York. Photo: Maria Robledo © 1980)

running round and round. A pair of long pleated Carol Horn culottes costs around $100, a linen blouse $80. In 1975 she won the Coty Award.

Hosiery

See PANTYHOSE.

Houndstooth

A pattern of broken checks, woven into the fabric.

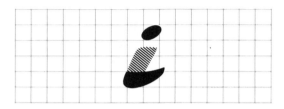

I.L.G.W.U. Label

This label means the item was made by members of the International Ladies Garment Workers Union, those who sing "Look for the Union Label" on TV. In 1900, when the ILGWU was organized, garment workers labored seventy hours a week in stifling, poorly lit sweatshops. The first big strike came in 1909, with members—most of them women and young girls—getting beat up by police and going hungry on picket lines all through the freezing winter. In the end, they won a 15-percent wage increase and a fifty-two-hour week, considered a great victory. Ever since, the union has battled determinedly for its members, winning a thirty-five-hour week but being unable to get wages even half as generous as those of steel or construction workers. Has 350,000 members in thirty-nine states, Puerto Rico, and Canada, 80 percent of whom are women.

Indian Clothes

cross all boundaries. Hippies wear them on communes, socialites grab them for their beach houses, older women who don't want to be condemned to sedate navys but aren't ready for Jordache find they bridge the gap. Everyone who's poor but has some taste should have a few. You can wear a $6 wraparound Indian skirt bought from a street peddler and look chic, while a $6 polyester knit from a shopping mall sale would look cheap and detract from your image. Here's what's going on in clothes from the other side of the world:

- *Fabric* What's desirable about Indian fabric is not perfect smooth silkiness but its very defects—tiny slubs and nubbinesses spun into the cloth. Indian cotton is still woven, embroidered, dyed, and printed by hand in village homes. No chemicals are added, no synthetics blended in; the fabric is pure, porous, and incredibly cool. Cotton voile is currently much in demand, and so are crinkly cotton and madras. Genuine Indian madras, unfortunately, has no label distinguishing it from imitations.

- *Design* After much disastrous misunderstanding, a compromise on design has been reached between East and West. At first, Americans tried to get Indians to make the sort of tailored clothes in demand in the West—blazers, skirts with pockets, zippers. Indians, who wear unconstructed clothing such as saris for women and tunics for men, could never grasp the concept of tailoring. "We told them we wanted a pocket on a shirt, and they put it in the middle of the back," says one importer. Today all Indian-made clothes are designed in America, but in styles consis-

- *Printing* In some sections of India, such as Jaipur, you can drive through the desert and see mile after mile of block-printed yardgoods laid out in the baking sun to dry. When buying Indian prints, look for clarity in printed patterns—colors should never be smeared and run together.

In the stores, look for caftans, tiered skirts, harem pants, soft peasant blouses. Adini is a good label. Much of the best cotton is found under designer names, but with a "Made in India" label also. Willi Smith of Williwear and Dominick Avellino of dddominick both spend about five months a year in India, and their products are superb. Carol Horn works well in Indian cottons, and so do two French firms, St. Michel and Panache. The Panache people have learned to take full advantage of Indian craftsmanship, and turn out beautiful scalloped trims, tucks, embroideries, and lace trims.

Care

You can wash or dry clean, though the beautiful colors on some of those $6 skirts may be from dyes that didn't set properly and will run when washed, especially the reds and blacks. Wash alone until you see whether they'll run or not. "A lot of people set colors first in vinegar," says Linda Anderson of Adini. "Pour vinegar into cool water until it smells dreadful, then soak clothes ten or twenty minutes before you wash." Indian cottons dry speedily and need only touch-up ironing. Crinkly cottons need no ironing.

tent with Indian concepts of dress. To get the best-made Indian clothes, buy *without* zippers, pockets, tight straight lines; *with* ties, gathers, unpressed pleats, shirring. Be prepared to be good-natured about little eccentricities, such as one side of a collar standing up sprightly while the other hangs limply, or a pucker between the second and third blouse button that no amount of ironing can flatten.

Intarsia sweater. (Sweater by dddominick.® Courtesy of Ann Taylor. Photo: Deborah Turbeville)

Intarsia Sweater

A design has been knitted only into certain parts of the sweater, such as neckline or cuffs. Fair Isles are one type of intarsia sweater. If the design were an all-over one, it would be called a jacquard knit.

Inverness Cape

A cape with a shorter cape on top, usually very tweedy. The design originated in Inverness, Scotland, and spread to England in the nineteenth century, where Sherlock Holmes became its most famous devotee. They are warmer and more convenient than regular capes because your arms are covered, and you can keep your handbag outside the cape. Holmes, James special-izes in designing inexpensive capes. For a brochure, write: Postique, 216 West 89th Street, Studio 5A, New York, N.Y. 10024.

Inverness cape

Ivory

The mellow white jewelry called ivory comes from the incisor tooth, or tusk, of elephants from Africa or Asia. Though ivory is also obtained from other sources, such as walrus and whales, when it's called simply "ivory," that means it's from elephants. Otherwise, it would be labeled "walrus ivory," "celluloid" (plastic), or "vegetable ivory." Vegetable ivory is made of nuts from a South American palm tree, and can so resemble authentic ivory that you need a microscope to tell the difference. Elephant ivory is most valuable, vegetable ivory relatively inexpensive. Ivory from Africa is sometimes called green ivory even though it's a pale white, and is more common than Asian ivory. Asian ivory is even whiter and finer but more likely to yellow with age.

Conservationists have been trying to get international trade in elephant products banned until African and Asian countries learn better management of their starving elephant populations. At the moment, the very African officials who are supposed to be protecting elephants are accused of being the biggest poachers. It is not ecologically responsible to buy ivory.

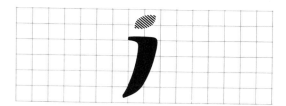

Jabot

(zhah-bo´) Ruffles which fill in the V-neck of a dress or blouse; can be either detachable or sewed on.

Jacquard

(jah-card) Designs of flowers, geometrics, etc., have been woven into the fabric. Michael Milea and Fenn, Wright, and Manson both make beautiful wool jacquard sweaters for under $50.

Jade

An exceptionally hard mineral, commonly green or white but can be red, yellow, gray, mauve, or blue. The Chinese valued "imperial jade," pure green and translucent, above all other jewels; ancient Central American civilizations considered jade vastly more desirable than gold and gave it to their Spanish conquerors as tribute; Eskimos carried the mineral for luck when hunting. Yet, dealers such as New York's Astro Minerals Gallery of Gems sell an 18-inch green jade necklace for only $18, matching earrings for $7. Along with China, sources of jade now include such diverse locales as California, Wyoming, Alaska, Guatemala, and Japan.

Jabot

Jaeger

(yea-ger) A 150-year-old British haberdashery of impeccable reputation, celebrated for its fabrics. Trendy dressers consider Jaeger somewhat dowdy, "leftover Peck and Peck," but they miss the point: though Jaeger isn't the place to shop for vinyl jumpsuits or décolletage evening clothes, it's superb for cashmere sweaters, camel-hair coats, gabardine slacks, Harris tweeds. A blanket-check flared skirt is $185, a double-breasted velvet blazer $300, but Jaeger has good end-of-season sales at its thirty American stores.

Jag

originated in Australia in the late 1960s, moved to New York after the huge success of its soft, loosely made denim separates with the glittery silver-and-black label outside. The great loose cut makes Jag clothes flattering to heavier women. Price is steep, around $60 for a pair of jeans. Find Jag clothes in good department stores, and at their breezy 21 East 57th Street flagship store in New York.

Jeans

Last year, $4 billion was spent on jeans in the United States, and another $2 billion spent on American jeans shipped abroad. Levi Strauss & Co. alone sold close to a billion dollars' worth, with Blue Bell, Inc., makers of Wranglers, not far behind. Gloria Vanderbilt sold 150 million dollars' worth, Calvin Klein $75 million, and Jordache grossed $40 million. It's been announced over and over that jeans are "out," but apparently the dedicated jeans consumer isn't found among those privileged ultrafashionables who change their wardrobes every few months at the whim of *Women's Wear Daily.* No matter what skirt lengths and pant shapes are doing, jeans seem to be as constant as the Cape Hatteras lighthouse among the shifting dunes.

As nearly everyone interested in history knows by now, the planet was without jeans until 1850, when a Bavarian immigrant named Levi Strauss arrived in San Francisco planning to panhandle for gold. Instead he ended up making pants for other prospectors, first from canvas and then from a sturdy cotton fabric woven like the French *serge de Nîmes* (pronounced, of course, denim). Western horsemen also quickly adopted the new pants, making them form-fitting (wrinkles cause saddle sores) by sitting in a horse trough and then wearing them while they dried to the same pelvis-hugging fit we adore today.

Jeans have gone on to become, ironically, the uniform of technological man, mass-produced by the billions, yet so form-fitting that each pair is as individual as each human form. Most people think jeans are a good thing, the most comfortable outfit in the world. You don't have to worry about dirt, abrasion, wrinkles. They breathe. And after you've laundered them a few times, they get soft and bend easily where you do. A few people *don't* think jeans are a good thing. "Jeans have taken on the characteristics of torture chamber instruments," say Maggie and Rollo Nussdorf in *Dress for Health.* "They're constructed to hug the body in the culturally desirable right places and, like tightly laced boots, leave the tattoo marks of seams and thread embedded in the thighs. They also provide a breeding ground for bacterial growth in the crotch and have a tourniquet effect on the abdomen."

Buying Your Jeans

A little controversy stops nobody in pursuit of the sexy jean look, so here's how to

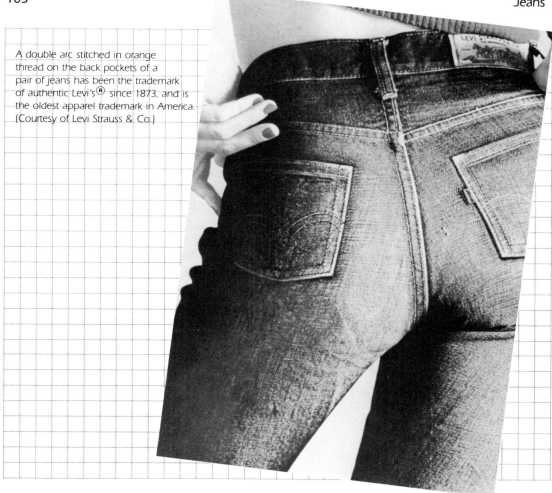

A double arc stitched in orange thread on the back pockets of a pair of jeans has been the trademark of authentic Levi's ® since 1873, and is the oldest apparel trademark in America. (Courtesy of Levi Strauss & Co.)

be as comfortable or uncomfortable—however you choose to look at the matter—as you wish.

- *Fit* Most important, and hardest for curvy women to find, are jeans that don't gap at the waist. For this reason, forget about trying on men's jeans unless you're as straight up and down as a telephone pole. Men's jeans also have extra fabric at the front of the crotch, superfluous, obviously, on a female. Jeans should be tight but not straining over the pelvis, with no fabric bagging under the buttocks and no hiked-up wrinkles at the knee. Advises Jerry Hart of New York's French Jean Store,

"Lie down to pull jeans on, pull in your stomach, and have someone standing by to zip you up."

Possibly the easiest way to get a proper fit is to shop in a Wrangler store, brimming with charts showing hip and waist measurements of each size. Jean connoisseurs claim that Wranglers are the better jean for ladies with large behinds, while thinner-cut Levis look best on slim figures. Stretch jeans are still *declassé*.

- *Labels* Designer jeans cost from $35 to $60 and up; Levi's cost $21. Is the designer label worth the extra money? Practically everybody who knows clothes thinks buying labels in jeans is foolish. In *Money* magazine's special-report-on-quality issue, designer jeans were knocked by designers themselves. Said menswear designer John Weitz, "Anyone who buys a pair of blue jeans for sixty-five dollars in order to wear a designer label deserves to lose her money. If she'd bought Levi Strauss, she could get the same thing for twenty dollars from people who've been around for a hundred and thirty years and know how to make blue jeans!" Levi Strauss, incidentally, is the only jeans manufacturer to receive a Coty Special Award for its product. Still, for those who do adore those expensive designer labels, *New York* magazine recently took a perfect size 8 model and went around town trying on designer jeans to see which fit best. Gloria Vanderbilt's jeans won raves, number two was Adolfo, with his tight European fit, number three was Ralph Lauren ("his leg has just the right degree of skinniness"), number four was Calvin Klein, and fifth was Liz Claiborne. If you buy designer jeans, be on the alert for counterfeits—at least 10 percent of name-label jeans are produced illegally. The imitations, sold mostly in "factory outlet" stores, are characterized by shoddy workmanship. Another giveaway: plain fly buttons and metal fasteners; on authentic designer jeans, they're embossed with the designer's name or logo.

Care

Buy a teeny bit too big, because no matter how you proceed, they'll shrink 2 to 3 percent in the first washing. This means one inch for every thirty inches in the length or waist. Jeans take about five washings to fade to a weathered look (never wash new jeans in the same wash with lighter clothes), and adding plenty of fabric softener helps. After the first three or four washings, which gets rid of the worst stiffness, put them on while they're still a little damp so they can be molded to your body. *Warning:* a teen-ager wearing damp jeans was crippled recently when the jeans shrank while he took a nap, cutting off blood flow to the legs.

To bleach jeans: fill a tub with enough lukewarm water to cover jeans, stir in half a quart of Clorox, and add jeans. Should take about half an hour for mild bleaching, more time for really light jeans. Keep them soaking until they look right, but don't forget that a wet fabric looks darker. You can also hasten a soft, worn look by rubbing jeans with fine sandpaper.

Jerkin

A sleeveless, close-fitting jacket; most jerkins have no buttons and slip over the head. It looks good on overweight women because it's a long, vertical type of garment; also makes short women look taller. Designer Bonnie Cashin is celebrated for her sleeveless leather jerkin.

Jersey

A plain-knitted elastic fabric of cotton, wool, rayon, or synthetic fibers, first knitted on the Jersey and Guernsey Islands in the English Channel. One of the great summer fabrics in cotton; what could be fresher than a Popsicle-colored jersey dress? For winter, a heavier, pure wool jersey makes the perfect "little black dress."

Care

The National Cleaners Association says jerseys tend to shrink and those Popsicle-colored dyes are poor, so wash tenderly in cold water.

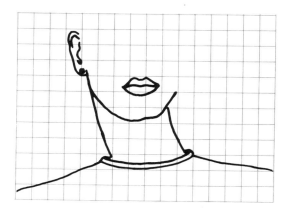

Jewel Neck

A plain round neckline at the base of the throat, used on sweaters, blouses, dresses. Since this simple, uncluttered line acts as a frame for the neck, it's flattering only if you have a lovely neck. Otherwise, add a scarf or plenty of jewelry.

J. G. Hook

A five-year-old American company which has won much praise for its tailored women's classics made in menswear factories. Fabrics are natural fibers, buttons are brass. Biggest sellers are blazers ($165) and pima cotton shirts ($44). The anchor logo conveys an outdoorsy, "yachting" feeling.

Jodhpurs

Riding pants cut full over the hips, tight from knees to ankles. Named after a former state in India. For the real thing with knee patches, visit a store selling riding equipment; otherwise, department stores sell them in tan or olive cotton twill for about $40.

Johnson, Betsey

One of the groundbreaking and internationally influential American designers, Betsey Johnson makes clothes that are young, space-age, and inexpensive. She was married for a time to a member of the Velvet Underground rock group, and got a lot of publicity in the 1960s for such styles as her clear vinyl slipdress, which came with a kit of paste-on stars and numbers, and her "noise" dress with loose grommets on the hem. For the last few years, she's been making "body wear." "I like clothes that are stretchy, second-skin, soft, pajamalike," she told *Ms.* magazine. "Nonconstricting, seasonless, packable, washable and affordable.

"I think bodywear will be the eighties' statement—modern, pure and clean . . . an architectural, futuristic look. Women have finally been accepted as healthy, moving, active people, and I want to celebrate that." She has said that she's a "mass market designer." She doesn't do a high-priced couture line but sells her inexpensive clothes directly to department stores and boutiques.

Jones New York

Founded in 1970, one of the first American sportswear manufacturers to bring a sleek European cut to moderately priced American sportswear. Also among the first with the concept that a woman who's a size 8 on top might be a size 12 on bottom, and want to buy "related separates" rather than a suit. Jones makes classic, conservative pants, sweaters, blazers in handsome fibers that last forever.

Jumper

A one-piece, sleeveless dress with a low scoop neck or square-cut neck, which can be worn with a blouse or without. Because of their long, unbroken lines, jumpers are terrific for short people, and for overweight and big-busted women.

Regina Kravitz's $125 tissue faille jumpsuit has sold over a million dollars' worth and is still going strong. Copies abound, but this is the original.

Jumpsuits

are jumping off the racks these days. Like jeans, they originated not with the haute couture but from the workingman, in this case grease-splattered mechanics. Amelia Earhart was the first woman to wear a jumpsuit, her costume on all her flights including the last. The jumpsuit business got its biggest boost from the movie *A Clockwork Orange*, which established them as proper attire for a futuristic look. Since pants and tops are combined into one piece, the unbroken vertical lines are flattering to almost everyone except possibly someone tall and too thin. Another plus is that jumpsuits are convenient—you don't have to worry about coordinating bits and pieces of an outfit.

Big names in jumpsuits: Regina Kravitz, with her best-selling rayon faille eve-

ning jumpsuit for $130; Stewart Richer's Reminiscence line, which won a special Coty Award citation for its parachutist-type cottons and corduroys.

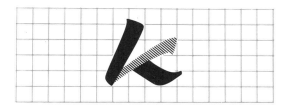

Kamali, Norma

American, and one of the world's most innovative designers. She likes to make flamboyant clothes out of unusual fabrics, such as jumpsuits from used silk parachutes or evening dresses from gold lamé curtain fabric, and most of her clothes are designed, cut, and sewn under one roof. Her

Norma Kamali's daringly cut swimsuits are the sexiest in the business. (Fashion by OMO Norma Kamali Swimwear Collection. Photo: Robert Michael Lambert)

best-selling ready-to-wear items are her wild, sexy swimsuit designs, though her puffy red sleeping-bag coat helped launch down coats. Swimsuits range in price from $35 to $100 and are sold in department stores; regular clothes are expensive and sold only in her three boutiques—one in New York at 6 West 56th Street, one in Beverly Hills in Neiman-Marcus, and one in Brown's of London. However, she always has a few playsuits or dresses in her boutiques that working girls can afford. This year you could have owned an original Norma Kamali flannel wrapdress—dubbed the "Ethel Mertz dress" (for Lucy's friend Ethel, in the television show "I Love Lucy") with broad shoulders and a high collar—for $145.

Kasper, Herbert

An American designer with superb credentials, including a Coty Award. Kasper doesn't go after publicity as do Calvin Klein and Ralph Lauren, but he's aiming at the same customer and his style and workmanship are equal to theirs, while his prices are lower. He designs a sportswear line, J. L. Sport, quiet and nontrendy, but best Kasper buys are his Kasper for Joan Leslie evening separates—a jumpsuit or long dress and jacket for under $200, even less on sale. Definitely a designer to look at if you need an evening outfit in impeccable taste but don't have hundreds of dollars to spend.

Kente Cloth

A famous African fabric, handwoven by Ashanti tribeswomen in four-inch strips that are then sewn together.

Kenzo, Takada

A Japanese designer who lives in Paris. Though not one of the big-volume design-ers, he's super-influential, and his new shapes are much copied. Look for his famous jacquard knits. "Kenzo's mingling of patterns can be as complicated and effective as the mixtures in an old kimono," says Bernadine Morris of *The New York Times*. Many of his knits have a cabbage-flower motif, and he's also fond of reindeer and snowflakes. Find his clothes in good department stores for $200–$400 for an outfit, or in his "Jap" boutiques in Paris, London, Munich, and Rome.

Keyhole Sweater

has a neck fastening with one button and a small, keyhole-shaped cut-out below. Sexy, in a demure, discreet way.

Keyhole sweater

Khaki

is an ancient Hindu word meaning dusty, which came to be applied to the light brown cotton used for Indian army uniforms. British troops stationed in India in the 1850s found that their white uniforms would be dusty within hours, and began soaking them in mud to turn them the same practical "khaki" color as the Indians'. More streamlined dyeing methods were soon developed, and khaki has been used for tropical military uniforms ever since.

The best label in khaki these days is British Khaki. Thirty-year-old Robert Lighton, an American whose family owns the Woolf Brothers department store in Kansas City, fell in love with the fabric on a trip to India. He commandeered an old British khaki mill in operation more than 100 years, a mill still using authentic nineteenth-century dyeing processes, and designed a snappy line of bush jackets, shirts, and pants to be made up *with* this khaki. (The khaki is woven in India, the clothes are sewn in America.) "True Indian-made brown khaki is a fantastic fabric," says Lighton. "It's colorfast, sturdy, and the more you wash it, the softer it gets." British Khaki clothes are sold at Saks, Woolf Brothers, Ann Taylor, and many other department stores and boutiques. Pants cost $40, jackets from $70 to $150.

Khanh, Emmanuelle

French ready-to-wear designer who made a huge splash in the 1960s, as Mary Quant did in London, with "New Wave" dresses that had a 1930s feel. She's married to a Vietnamese interior designer, Quasar Khanh. Especially look for: featherweight scallop-edged cotton and crêpe ensembles hand-embroidered in Rumania. Moderately expensive.

Kidskin

The tanned leather of goats about two and a half years old, used for gloves and the softest of shoes. With meticulous care, kidskin is just as durable as a stiffer, less comfortable leather. If you love soft kidskin shoes and ever shop in New York, go look at the handmade shoes at Eddris Shoes, 314 East 78th Street. They're seldom more than $40–$60 and have developed a local cult following.

Kilt Skirt

Kilts, the regimental skirts of male Scottish Highlanders, take up to nine yards of wool and weigh five pounds; kilt skirts are scaled-down versions. Though American designer Ralph Lauren makes them for $270, the world's most pedigreed kilt skirt is easily obtainable and sells for much less. Kinloch Anderson Ltd. of Edinburgh, founded 113 years ago and still operated by the same family, holds the Royal Warrant as kiltmakers for Queen Elizabeth and the Duke of Edinburgh. Their kilt skirts, complete with label reading "by appointment to the Queen," cost only $150 and are found in department stores around the world. In January, prices are cut in half. (To find the store nearest you, write Kinloch Anderson, c/o Frank L. Savage, Inc., 17 East 37th Street, New York, New York 10016.) You can also buy authentic imported Scottish kilt skirts in registered tartans at Scottish import stores, such as New York's Scottish Products or San Francisco's Scottish Tartan Shop, for under $100. A true kilt skirt such as Kinloch Anderson's is hand-pleated so that plaids match up all the way around, and the waistband is sewn so that plaid matches apron, the front section of the skirt. Each skirt is supplied with a kilt pin, which does *not* function as some sort of safety pin holding edges together, but acts as a weight to maintain proper drape of the apron. Ask to see a skirt in "muted blue Dress Stewart," a beautiful mixture of browns and blues.

Care

Good Scottish kilt skirts last for generations, and are passed down from mother to daughter. Wash them in Woolite, and press in the pleats (takes about fifteen minutes) by covering with a damp cotton or linen napkin and ironing.

Klein, Anne

American designer, who died in 1974. Anne Klein & Company, established in 1968, is now headed by designers Donna Karan and Louis Dell'Olio. Donna Karan, picked by Anne Klein as her successor, took over at age twenty-five and soon ended up on the best-dressed list herself. She got her clothes savvy from her father, she likes to say, who made custom-tailored suits for theater people and gangsters. She likes the 1940s style herself, and was married in a long knit dress, ten yards of pearls, and a fedora.

From Anne Klein & Company, look for clean-cut, beautifully tailored sportswear in indestructible fabrics, classic style, often double-breasted. Her wools don't get shiny, her silks behave perfectly when you handwash them against "dry clean only" directions. The line is interrelated from year to year: if you buy a pair of pants one year, usually you can still buy a sweater to match the next. Find Anne Klein in the designer section of all good department stores. Her winter ivory colors are much admired, and so are her evening silk separates. A pair of lambswool trousers go for $220, a silk charmeuse blouse for $220. Hint: Anne Klein gabardine pleated trousers can be found in the jeans department for only $50, and look exactly like the trousers in her more expensive line.

Anne Klein & Company is known for spare, beautifully tailored separates.

Klein, Calvin

American designer. Now thirty-eight, Calvin Klein is the youngest designer to be elected to the Coty Hall of Fame. His clothes are admired for being chic but without clutter. Instead of ruffles being used to get a soft, feminine effect on an evening tunic, say, you'll find the tunic cut simply but made in an exquisite silk with delicate checks or hair-thin stripes. An avowed health nut (his office complex includes a gymnasium), he likes to say that fashion today is not as much a matter of buying the right clothes as it is keeping your body in shape to wear them. His clothes are made to "feel good against the skin," and he takes pride in the softness of his fabrics—silk charmeuse, cashmere, handkerchief linen.

Calvin Kleins are found in 300 American stores, usually at prices below those of his two major competitors, Anne Klein and Ralph Lauren. His separates are coveted by upwardly mobile career women, both for day and evening. A wool twill jacket might be $300, his silk charmeuse evening separates $200–$500. You might resist paying $140 for his plain, beige, simply cut silk blouse, so simply cut that decent knock-offs may often be found on another floor for $60. However, he's mostly good value. If he were French, we'd be paying twice the price.

This tweed suit is a perfect example of the uncluttered, businesslike tailoring for which Calvin Klein is known. His suits are particularly longed for by upwardly mobile career women.

John Kloss revolutionized the industry by designing a bra that looked as if you weren't wearing a bra. The style is now called the "Lily of France Glossie"® and is still a best-seller.

Kloss, John

Winner of two special Coty Awards for lingerie, Kloss designs nightgowns that are shimmery and made for romance, and his name is legendary in bra history. In the early 1970s, the "ban the bra" movement badly hurt the bra industry. Not until 1974, when John Kloss took on an assignment from Lily of France to design a bra that looked as though you weren't wearing a bra, did women start buying again. Lily of France style #1803 was the biggest blockbuster bra of all time, and has sold over eight million in colors such as amethyst, mocha, ruby, and indigo. The bra has an underwire, and is sheer, unconstructed, stretchable, and seamless. Today called the Lily of France "Glossie," it can be bought inexpensively at any department store.

Knickers

Pants gathered just below the knee. Italian designers are making them in flowering silk prints and plaids and charging a fortune; one alternative in the knickers market is a gorgeously rugged L. L. Bean model in taupe corduroy for $32, superb with boots.

Krizia

(kreet-zia) Most adventurous of Italian ready-to-wear houses, founded in Milan in 1954 by a schoolteacher named Mariuccia Mandelli, who had $200, a flair for fashion, and a clever name from Plato's unfinished dialogues. "Crizia was a rich man who ruined himself by spending too much on women," she says. "Everyone in the dress business hoped for customers like him."

Mandelli has always had a penchant for improbable contrasts: corduroy with satin, wool lace over accordion pleats. Krizia clothes sport a different animal motif every year—last season's $1,200 sweater-dress with a large leopard knitted in front became a status item. Find Krizia at Saks and other prestigious department stores, where one of her "little nothing" silk camisole dresses with a leopard print costs $700, a 1940s-looking rayon blazer with large shoulder pads runs $500. If you find yourself in Milan, visit the Krizia boutique on the Via della Spiga and save all that added-on import duty.

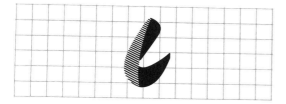

Lace

Because so much tacky polyester lace adorns so many clothes of questionable charm, lace has fallen into a state of mild disrepute. Yet, many beautiful cotton laces are still being made, and the delicacy of good lace has a way of making any woman look soft and nice.

Lace has been treasured for so long that archeologists have found fragments over 4,500 years old. The most famous names in lace—Alençon, Valenciennes, Chantilly—date from the seventh century A.D., a time when nuns made lace-making the great convent industry, and these cities were leading centers.

Early lace was entirely handmade with a special needle, often from linen thread so fine it couldn't be felt between finger and thumb. So heavy was the demand for lace, and so high its price, that for centuries vi-sionaries tried to invent machines to make lace. Finally, in 1830, an Englishman named John Leavers did indeed invent such a machine, an event that quickly became so important to the English economy that for a time exportation of a lace machine was punishable by death. His extraordinary machine comes close to being one of the wonders of the world. It has 40,000 parts, all in motion at once; it takes two weeks to thread and, when the machine is started, contains enough thread to stretch halfway around the planet. Even more extraordinary, the machine is in use today much as he originally designed it. "Today's Leavers makes exactly the same product that it made during the nineteenth century," says Mitchell Ostrover of American Fabrics, the largest manufacturer of lace in the world. To become a Leavers operator, you have to apprentice nearly as long as it takes to get through dental school. Though the twentieth century has produced machines that knit synthetics such as polyester or nylon into "Rochelle lace" cheaply, cotton Leavers lace is by far the loveliest of new laces.

Buying Lace

Avoid buying stiff, plastic-looking nylon lace. If you like a dress or blouse except for the lace, do as French women do—take off the lace and substitute a cotton Leavers lace collar, found in any good department store. When buying lace from antique dealers, don't believe them when they assert their lace to be handmade. Except for a small amount of absurdly expensive imported French lace, along with pre-1830 lace and the output of 1,500 people who are members of a worldwide group called the International Old Lacers (most of whom consider lacemaking a hobby and don't sell their work), from 1830 on virtually all good lace has been Leavers. Even when the lace is "handmade," it's not been made with a needle since the fifteenth century. It's made with tiny bobbins which are manipulated by hand, a vanishing art except for the Old Lacers' work. To make an inch of lace with bobbins takes fifteen minutes and, when you're finished, only an expert can tell it from good Leavers lace. The more intricate and delicate the pattern, the better both are considered.

Care

Old lace acquires a patina with age, turning a lovely ecru color. Since this patina is what makes vintage lace more desirable than new, you don't want to bleach it out. However, much old lace is stained and would have to be thrown away without aggressive laundering. In this case, proceed as follows: soak the lace in cold water for about an hour, and then transfer to a pan filled with a sudsy mixture of water and Ivory Snow. Bring slowly to a boil, simmering for five to fifteen minutes, or until the stains disappear. If the stains *don't* disappear, try dabbing at the still-damp spots with a Q-Tip soaked in a solution of water and chlorine bleach, and then wash and rinse again. For black or green mould stains, dab with hydrogen peroxide. If all this leaves the lace too bleached-out, you can restore much of its antique ecru color by soaking it for a few minutes in weak tea. (Also works for too-white new lace.) If you want to stiffen your lace, add a little sugar to the final rinse water.

If your piece of lace is black, try dabbing at discolorations with distilled white vinegar, then washing in Ivory Snow.

Lacoste

(la-kahst´) Anytime you see a little alligator with its tail curving forward used as an emblem on clothes, the trademark name Lacoste has to accompany it. An American classic, the original Lacoste tennis shirt was proposed to the David Crystal Company in 1956 by Rene Lacoste, a French tennis champion, and David Crystal has been manufacturing the style ever since. When the shirt is for men, it's called Izod for Men; for women, it's called Haymaker for Women or Izod for Her. The Lacoste shirt is part of the "preppy" look, and though not expensive, is a bit of a status symbol. Writer Peter Benchley described it, some years ago, as "a five-dollar shirt with an eight-dollar alligator." Probably the most classic way for women to wear a Lacoste shirt is in red or pink, with a white cotton or denim skirt.

The Lacoste® polo shirt (here a shirtdress) with its sewn-on alligator is a preppy classic. Imitators have spawned foxes, horses, and cute dogs, but none have succeeded like the Lacoste alligator. (Courtesy of David Crystal®)

Lagerfeld, Karl

Karl Lagerfeld for Chloé is considered one of the most important pace-setters in French design. If skirts are short, he makes his long; if everyone is wearing pants, his collection may well be all skirts. When lesser designers, like Lagerfeld, try to break new ground, they run a great risk of people snickering and not buying their out-of-the-mainstream fashions. However, Lagerfeld manages to make his new silhouettes refreshing rather than weirdly extreme. For instance, he recently took ugly old bermuda shorts and split them at the sides so that they now look graceful.

Though Chloé is a ready-to-wear house, prices are extremely high. Visit the Chloé boutique in a Saks Fifth Avenue store, and you'll find that a raincoat is $1,500, a silk blouse $580, a wool bias-cut skirt $550.

Laine

French for wool.

Lamaine

The softest wool, from a special breed of Australian pedigreed merino sheep. Only 1.5 percent of the total Australian wool industry is Lamaine, making it one of the most luxurious natural fibers, selling for only slightly less money than cashmere.

Lambswool

The first shearing from lambs seven to nine months old; it's baby soft and much finer than regular wool, yet because it's from homegrown lambs, lambswool is an inexpensive luxury. You'll find it mostly in sweaters mixed with angora and nylon, a truly luxurious and comfortable natural-fiber sweater for as little as $20.

Care

Lambswool isn't as durable as sturdier wools such as Shetland, and isn't meant for heavy-duty wear day in and day out. Dry clean or handwash and lay it flat. If you get a few fuzzballs at points of wear, pluck them off with your fingers or rub with a dry sponge.

Lamé

(lah-may´) A fabric either entirely or partly woven or knitted with metallic yarns. Beautiful, but not too practical: according to the Neighborhood Cleaners Association, metallic yarn is fragile and snaps easily, perspiration causes it to tarnish, and some yarns dissolve in dry-cleaning chemicals. Buy lamé dresses only from a reputable store and keep the sales slip.

Latex

The rubbery, clammy stuff in old girdles and the elastic panty bands that would snap on you used to be made from latex. This horror has now been almost entirely replaced by the lighter synthetic spandex.

Lauren, Ralph

"You don't have to live in Connecticut to wear classic clothes," says Ralph Lauren, who grew up in the Bronx as Ralph Lipshitz but made his fortune by taking such drab old country-club items as blazers and button-down shirts and giving them a sleek, French cut. His customer's image is that of a refined, well-bred woman who does *not* wear a lot of makeup or elaborate coifs.

Lauren began his career working as a necktie salesman, and got the idea that a wide, expensive, handmade tie might sell better than the skinny, stingy ones then in vogue. His tie was a runaway success, giv-

Ralph Lauren's Romantic
look (he also has an Ivy
League look, an Old West
look, and an Outdoor look)
is accomplished here with
an imaginative combination
of such classics as hacking
jackets, shawl-collared vests
with crocheted buttons, his
famous linen blouses, and
dirndl skirts.

ing him the means to start a menswear company. In 1972, he showed his first collection of women's sportswear, and his natural fibers, impeccable craftsmanship, and Ivy League look was "in" overnight. His 1978 westernwear collection—fringed buckskin jackets, flounced prairie skirts—coincided with the country's frontier fever, his 1980 romantic collection of hooded capes, ruffled cream linen blouses, and bias-cut silk and cashmere skirts was a big hit, and his new Sante Fé look, with its earthy Navajo colors and blanket skirts ($650) is a trend-setter. He's the only designer to have been elected to the Coty Hall of Fame for both his menswear and women's clothes.

Lawn

A fine, sheer cotton fabric first woven in Laon, France. Slightly stiffer than batiste, and wrinkles easily.

Leather

is the hide of an animal that's been chemically treated to make it soft and supple and to prevent it from rotting. Since most leather is a by-product of the food industry, it can be worn in good conscience. A leather coat improves with wear, molds itself to your body, and is a superb windbreaker. Before discussing leather coats, here's a list to help you know what the labels on *all* leather products mean.

Alligator	Has lovely markings and a longer-lasting hide than lizard or snakeskin. "Crocodile" skins are nearly always alligator. Though the American alligator is out of danger and being commercially trapped again, alligators from Africa, South America, and Indo-Pacific are endangered, yet countries such as Italy and France allow trade in them. Check the label of alligator or crocodile goods for country-of-origin of the leather, and don't buy if the leather originates anywhere but the United States. Old alligator handbags from the 1940s are adorable and can be found in antique and thrift shops for $20–$40; not bad when you consider that new ones cost up to $3,000!
Buckskin	From deer and elk. See BUCKSKIN.
Cabretta	Sheepskin from Brazil, very long-wearing and inexpensive; used in a good percentage of American-made coats.
Calfskin	Soft, supple, and takes a high polish; used for the best shoes; best patent leather is calfskin.
Chamois	Yellow, pliable, and washable; originally from goats but now from sheep and deer also. See CHAMOIS.
Chrome	An inexpensive leather tanned by chromium salts and used for shoes.

Cordovan	Soft, heavy, costly. Made from horsehide, used mostly for expensive boots.
Cowhide	Coarse, heavy leather, the strongest. Because cowhide is so thick, the skin is "split"—peeled, like layers of salami, into a more usable thickness. The top layer becomes "top-grain leather"; underlayers become suede.
Doeskin	A luxury leather, the soft skin of white lambs and sheep. Used for gloves, some coats.
Glacé leather	Glazed, finished to a high gloss.
Kidskin	Goatskin, when used for gloves from young goats; shoe kidskin is from older animals. See KIDSKIN.
Lizard	A beautiful, unpliable leather used mostly for handbags and belts, but an ecological disaster. See LIZARD.
Mocha	Fine, soft sheepskin from Arabia and other parts of Africa.
Nappa	A tanning process making leather extremely soft and pliable, first used in Napa, California. Tanning is done with soap and oil, on skins from sheep or goats; used mostly for gloves.
Patent	Leather is coated with varnish for a hard, glossy finish. Make doubly sure "patent" isn't synthetic.
Peccary	Fine, lightweight, washable pigskin, a glove leather, but from a wild pig in Central America. Since killing wildlife for leather upsets the ecological balance, it's better to buy domestic pigskin.
Pigskin	Durable, sporty leather, pockmarked where bristles are removed.
Seal	From the hair seal. The leather is soft and durable, used for coats.
Shearling	Sheepskin tanned with the wool left on. See SHEARLING.
Snakeskin	From the world's largest and most needed wild snakes. An ecological misfortune. See SNAKESKIN.
Suede	The flesh side of calfskin, buffed by machine to a velvety napped surface. Suede (the word is French for Sweden, which first produced suede) outsells smooth leather by about 50 percent.

A few considerations:

- What kind of leather—lamb, split cowhide, pig, sheep—doesn't matter so much as how it's been finished. The softer, richer-looking, and more supple, the more high-priced. European coats tend to be of more exotic skins (ostrich, seal) and to be more finely crafted, glossily finished, less durable, and certainly more expensive than American ones.

- Be wary of exceptionally low prices from sell-and-run stores—animal skins are weaker toward the belly, a part discarded by makers of quality coats and scooped up by makers of cheapies.

- One test of a poor product: rub a Kleenex up and down a coat to see how much color rubs off. Some rub-off, called "crocking," is natural, and stops after a few weeks of ownership, but if your Kleenex changes color, don't buy.

- Be sure to buy only coats with linings, as a lining helps prevent skins from stretching out of shape. Don't buy a suede coat if the lining and hem are sewn together, because it will eventually curl under.

Care of a Leather Coat

Spot clean with a damp cloth and mild soap, such as Woolite, in lukewarm water, and rinse. Never use saddle soap or cleaning fluid. Don't store in a plastic bag, since lack of air may cause discoloration.

Care of a Suede Coat

To deal with minor crocking on a new suede, rub it briskly with a clean, dry towel, which should get rid of excess particles. For spots, rub lightly with a fine sandpaper. (Don't be afraid—though sandpaper sounds like the tool of some rough fellow in carpenter's overalls, it *works*.) For water spots, brush with a good suede brush.

Legwarmers

are heavy, warm, footless stockings ending at the ankle on bottom and at mid-thigh on top. You can wear them over pants, over or inside boots, under skirts. For a more outré look, you can wear them with shorts over tights. Their engineering works—they never slip or fall down around your ankles when you wear them over pants or tights (some people report they slip an inch or two when worn next to the bare leg); they're comfortable because they don't tug anywhere, and they're more healthful to wear than warm synthetic pantyhose, which can prevent air from circulating around the crotch, causing vaginal infections. Danskin's $9 wool legwarmers sold out last winter. Since best styles vanish by January's first cold spell, buy well before Christmas.

Leotard

Only a few years ago, leotards were something you had to make a boring trip into a hosiery shop to buy for your exercise class. They were regulation black and looked like tank-top swimming suits from the 1930s; if your figure wasn't perfect, you'd suffer in embarrassment. Today, imaginative designers are doing styles that are both chic and flattering. They have a high, cut-out leg that makes your legs and thighs look longer and slimmer and your waist tinier, and engineered stripes to direct the eye where it should and shouldn't go. You can choose among styles that are halter-topped, scoopbacked, see-through, sprinkled with glitter, strapless, wrap-waisted, spaghetti-strapped, lace-edged, or iridescent, and wear as a swimsuit, or with a matching skirt for streetwear, or as thermal underwear in winter. All last summer the favorite uniform of the collegiate female was a Danskin top, short shorts, and impenetrable sunglasses. Among the disco crowd, the look was a one-shouldered leotard, preferably leopard, worn with a clingy, bias-cut matte jersey skirt. Jules Leotard, a nineteenth-century trapeze artist who designed the outfit for circus wear, would probably have been astonished.

Here's a glossary of leotard terms:

Leotard A skin-tight, second-skin sort of garment which reaches from neck to crotch; can be sleeved or sleeveless.

Tights Opaque pantyhose worn by dancers underneath their leotards.

Unitard (also called a solotard). A one-piece head-to-ankles leotard, with a stirrup strap fitting under the instep of the foot.

Danskin Largest manufacturer of leotards in the U.S. They make dozens of different styles with matching pants, skirts, and shorts in forty different colors from shocking pink to plain black.

Capezio Oldest manufacturer of leotards and dancewear in the country.

Rudi Gernreich, designer of the topless swimsuit, designs Capezio dancewear.

Milliskin Du Pont's blend of Lycra spandex and Antron nylon used for leotards that double as swimming suits or disco tops. Basic dancewear leotards are usually made of 100 percent nylon.

Big names in designer leotards Norma Kamali, Betsey Johnson, Maya, Sant'-Angelo. Most leotards cost from $10 to $20; a designer label can add $20 or more to the price, but some of the styles are stunning.

Care

Wash and wear. Hanging the leotard to dry rather than putting it in the dryer extends the garment's life.

What's Bad about Leotards

Wearing one for an hour's exercise class in a gym is one thing, but adding a skirt or pants and going discoing is another. The disadvantage never mentioned in the Danskin catalogue is that in order to go to the W.C., you have to take off virtually everything. Standing in a drafty, semi-public ladies room stall almost completely naked is an experience most of us can do without.

Both Danskin and Capezio have catalogues of their wares. Send $1 to:

Danskin
Dept. C-1
P.O. Box 822
Times Square Station
New York, NY 10036

Capezio Ballet Makers
1860 Broadway
New York, NY 10023

Lexol

Leather can last for hundreds of years if properly cared for, but if it's neglected, environmental pollution causes it to become acidic in a year or so; its oils break down chemically and it becomes dry and discolored. If you rub leather with oils alone, such as neat's foot, they oversaturate the leather, staying messily on top and rubbing off on fabrics that brush against the surface. Lexol, developed as a tack and saddlery conditioner, "feeds" leather and prevents acidification while *not* remaining greasily on the surface. It also acts as a mild cleaner and provides a low-gloss luster for shoes, boots, handbags, attaché cases. Shoes treated regularly with Lexol, along with Meltonian shoe polish for scuffs and discolorations, become softer and more lustrous with time, like old wood.

Liberty of London

is a fabric-printing operation, famous for its complicated, finely etched designs, largely in tiny flowers or paisleys. "We're a very old-fashioned printer," says Jeffrey Phillips of Liberty's New York office. "We use the same methods and machinery we've used since the business started a hundred years ago." Which means Liberty prints its fabrics with copper rollers as opposed to the wood or rubber method used by mass-market fabric printers. Wood or rubber produces a thick, splotchy design; with copper you can print exquisitely fine lines. "We work almost entirely in natural fibers, because colors print better on cottons and silks," says Phillips. "You simply can't do the same work on nylon or polyester." Liberty fabrics are printed almost entirely in England. Price depends on the designer or manufacturer who makes the fabrics into clothes, or you can buy Liberty in yardgoods stores at moderately expensive prices.

Linen

is as much a luxury now as it was in biblical times, as was mentioned so often in both the Old and New Testaments. In America, for much of our own century the only real linen around has been on the dinner table. Only lately has this beautiful fabric crept out from under the Sunday roast and reclaimed its rightful place on the racks of our best clothing stores. You can now buy snowy pure handkerchief-linen blouses, handwoven blazers, shirtwaist dresses with exquisite tucks and lace. Linen is being knitted, used for shirts, woven into tweeds. "Americans had a polyester mentality for years," says Pauline Delli-Carpini of the Belgian Linen Association. "Nobody wanted to wear linen because it wrinkled and they felt badly groomed. Now, it's hard to import enough to fill the demand."

Linen has practicality as well as good looks, or it probably wouldn't have been so treasured for ten thousand years. Here are some characteristics:

- *Strength* A product of the flax plant, linen is the strongest naturally occurring cellulose fiber—stronger than wool, three times as strong as cotton. This means linen holds up. Egyptian mummy wrappings, in pristine condition after thousands of years, are made of linen. The Shroud of Turin is made of linen. Fragments of the fabric were found by archeologists in the Swiss lake dwellings of Stone Age man, making linen the oldest known textile fiber.

- *Comfort* Linen absorbs moisture and dries faster than any other fabric, which is why it's been used for table napkins and handkerchiefs for hundreds of years. Put a drop of water on linen and it will be blotted up and evaporated before your eyes. This makes linen extremely cool and comfortable for summer wear.

- *Cleanliness* Linen fiber has no fuzz, which means it doesn't trap dust and soil and is terrific for the allergy-prone. The more you wash linen, the more vitality and luster the fabric will have.

Here are the terms most used with linen in clothes:

Irish linen The finest of soft, white linens.

Moygashel (moy-ga´[as in gag] shell) Trade name for highest quality Irish linens used for clothes. Moygashel is the name of an Irish company that weaves fabrics, linen among them.

Oatmeal linen An unbleached, home-spun-type fabric, used for blazers. It's a brownish cream color like oatmeal. Most oatmeal linen is imported from Poland and is a little less expensive than handkerchief linen. The term "butcher's linen" usually means imitation oatmeal linen.

Oyster linen An unbleached, homespun-type linen in an off-white color.

Handkerchief linen The softest, creamiest linen, the best of which is from Ireland, where they spin finer cloth than anywhere in the world.

Why Linen Costs So Much

Obviously, most of us would like to cherish a linen blouse of our very own, but then we're confronted with cost: $80 and up for a blouse. (Fortunately, there are sales.) Linen is expensive because the process of obtaining it has stubbornly resisted modern technology. Egyptian tomb paintings from around 3000 B.C. show flax plants being converted to linen, and the hand operation used then is still the basic *modus operandi* today. In Ireland, the business of turning flax to linen has been passed from father to son for hundreds of years—the people who made the linen for your blouse are probably direct descendants of the craftsmen who wove linen sails for ships of the sixteenth century.

Producing cotton is child's play compared to linen. Cotton is simply picked, seeds are ginned out, and it's ready for spinning into fabric. Flax plants disgorge their fibers from the woody stalks only after seven days of soaking in water, which dissolves the gum so fibers can be pulled away. The water used for soaking can't be any old water— it must be totally free from minerals and other impurities, which harm the flax. Few countries have such water, which is why the best linen has always come from Ireland and Belgium, both abounding in pure ponds, lakes, and rivers. The fiber must then be broken up, cleaned, straightened, combed, beaten, bleached, and doubled into fibers strong enough for yarn. Because so much labor is involved, and since much linen comes from Ireland, Belgium, France, and Italy where the dollar doesn't go far these days, linen is a costly fabric.

Cambric Another name for handkerchief linen.

Care

Do try to wash white linens yourself instead of dry cleaning; a good cleaners will return a sparkling white garment, but, according to the American Apparel Manufacturers Association Consumer Affairs Committee, some cleaners don't use fluid pristine enough for white natural fibers, and they turn yellow or gray (a condition that can easily be laundered out). "It's so silly, really, to put a 'dry clean only' label on linen, but it's a way of protecting oneself against people who abuse things," says Harry Banks of Hamilton Adams, the leading import firm of Irish linens.

Wash your linens in Woolite or Ivory Snow and lukewarm water. Never add a vinegar rinse—it burns linen. You have to iron linen wet, on both sides for luster. Damp linen is a delight to iron—as fast as wrinkles get into linen, they come out just as effortlessly when your iron glides over the fabric. Don't succumb and buy wrinkle-free linen. It doesn't breathe as well as the pure variety, scorches easily, and isn't as strong. Should you run across a marked-down linen blouse with lipstick or some other such stain, buy it. Should all routine methods of removing stains fail (see STAINS), you can boil linen, like cotton, with a little Ivory.

Hint: Best imitation linen is made from rayon. Anne Klein and Ralph Lauren adore the real thing, but Halston unapologetically fakes it. "Rayon linens are terrific," he says. "I think they take color better than real linens and customers love them because they don't wrinkle so much."

Linings

are a sign of good tailoring. The lining helps preserve shape and reduces wrinkling, covers rough inner construction work, and makes things easier to slip on and off, reducing wear and tear. This is why linings are always made of slippery fabrics such as acetate, nylon, or Cupro. The color of a lining should match the color of the exterior fabric.

Linsey-Woolsey

A fabric heavily used in Colonial America, mentioned often in books by such writers as Nathaniel Hawthorne and Herman Melville. It was a coarse fabric woven with varying proportions of linen and wool. Similar fabrics are still made, but they're called linen-wool blends.

Lizard

Probably the most exquisite handbags, belts, and watchstraps made today are lizard, which has exceptionally delicate markings. However, lizards can't be farmed because they won't lay eggs in captivity, so all this gorgeous leather (six to twelve lizards required to make a bag) is coming from wild creatures that are an important part of the natural food balance. Argentina, Colombia, Peru, and Paraguay are the biggest exporters, according to the International Institute for Environment and Development, with the monitor lizard, tegu, iguana, and false monitor the most important skins. These lizards are on no "endangered" lists, but many wildlife experts think they soon will be. "We don't have reptile scientists out in the field counting lizards, but we know certain species are getting very hard to catch," says David Mack, of Traffic U.S.A., a group that monitors trade in international wildlife.

Nobody with an ecological conscience should buy lizard, especially when so much beautiful leather is available as a by-product of the food industry. Also consider that lizard is an expensive and non-sturdy leather that often starts to peel quickly.

Llama

A large, South American mountain camel, close relative to the alpaca, used both as beast of burden and producer of fleece. Llama herds are owned and tended by South American Indians, who shear the animals in early December, and either weave the wool themselves or sell it to textile manufacturers. It's used mostly for blending with wools and other hair fibers, and, like cashmere, provides much warmth in proportion to its light weight. Llama coats are wrinkle-resistant, lustrous, light, and warm, and cost $200 or $300 on up, depending on design.

L. L. Bean

Want the softest cotton flannel shirt in the world, the same worn by woodsmen and lumberjacks for a century? The same Mackinaw cruiser jacket worn by prospectors during the 1897 Alaskan Klondike Gold Rush? Or how about a buffaloplaid woodchopper's vest, or a coat made from the same blanket wool used to make the famous Hudson Bay blankets? How about some moosehide slippers, buckskin gloves, snow boots with real sheepskin lining? A name synonymous with cold-weather gear, with rugged outdoorsmen—and outdoorswomen—with clear-eyed, rosy-cheeked campers, hunters, fishermen, cross-country skiers, hikers, backpackers, mountain climbers, is the name L. L. Bean.

You'll find this original, cozy, folksy New England establishment in Freeport, Maine, a town eighteen miles north of Portland. Should you be in the vicinity, you can go shopping in the plain three-story building on Main Street at any hour of the day or night. The store has been closed only three times—when L. L. Bean died in

1967, for President Kennedy's funeral, and once when a snowstorm was so heavy everyone thought the roof was going to cave in. For the rest of the time, nobody even bothered to get a lock for the door, though along about 1940 someone did attach some sleigh bells.

Though the store is always open, its parking lot crammed with every sort of vehicle from jeeps to Mercedes 320s, and though inside you can wander down the aisles between the snowshoes and Labrador parkas and hear Norwegian, French, and Irish accents mixed right in with the plain speech of locals, most Bean business is transacted by mail order. The L. L. Bean catalogue goes out to eight million customers around the world every season, and Bean's new IBM computers handle some 2.2 million mail orders and 500,000 telephone orders yearly. Within forty-eight

L.L. Bean's Scotch plaid lumberjack shirt.

L.L. Bean's Chouinard Double Seated Trail Shorts

hours after an order comes in, the merchandise is packed and on its way down a conveyor belt into U.S. Mail or United Parcel Service trucks waiting at loading docks. Customers pay no shipping costs, and if they don't like the goods for any reason, they get a refund, without protests or questions. Along with the merchandise, customers get service as personalized as they'd get in any small-town general store. If you need a button for your northwoods shirt, Bean's will mail it. If you want reassurance that you really can wash your sheepskin coat, someone will tell you exactly what to do.

The L. L. Bean catalogue business was begun in 1912 by Leon Leonwood Bean, a man who ran a small clothing store with his brother but spent most of his time out hunting. Tired of always coming home with wet feet, he designed a rubber and leather hunting shoe, had it stitched up by the local cobbler, and sent out a description of the boot to holders of Maine hunting licenses. The catalogue grew from one page to a dozen pages by 1920, and to 128 pages by 1980. Today the company is run by L. L.'s grandson, who has continued its stated policy of "sell merchandise at a reasonable profit and treat the customer like a human being," and the company expects sales of $120 million this year.

Bean's catalogue contains plenty of gear for women. Indeed, *Newsweek* called L. L. Bean's "one of the most sought-after fashion labels," which caused a certain amount of astonishment at company headquarters. "Lots of our products haven't been changed in more than fifty years," said assistant advertising manager Lee Bois. Best sellers to women are:

Oxford cloth shirts ($13.50) in pink, blue, white, and maize. Of great simplicity, these shirts are usually worn under crewneck sweaters.

Handloomed Shetland sweaters ($30), both plain and Fair Isle pullovers.

Tartan wrap skirts ($60) from Scotland in authentic Scottish plaids.

Chamois cloth shirts ($15.50). The same as Mr. Bean used on his own hunting trips, these solid-color red, blue, and green shirts have been in the line since the 1920s and are probably Bean's most famous item. Made of fine cotton flannel thickly napped on both sides, the shirt is as soft as velvet and is not only machine washable, but the longer you wear it, the more it looks and feels like chamois leather.

Items not yet big sellers but which Bean feels have special merit are their canvas sailcloth pants and their pima cotton shirts.

To get a catalogue
Write L. L. Bean, Inc., Freeport, Maine 04033, or phone (207) 865-3111, any time day or night (not a toll-free call, though). You can use Master Charge, VISA, or American Express credit cards to order. The catalogue explains how you can be assured the right fit when ordering by mail.

Loden Cloth

A thick, napped wool fabric, heathery green in color, used for coats and jackets. Originated in Germany, where it's still worn everywhere.

Long Johns

See UNION SUIT.

Loré

(lore-ray´) American lingerie designer. The first collection of sensuous, bias-cut, pure silk lingerie since World War II was designed five years ago by Loré Caulfield, a former Los Angeles film producer. She'd finished an NBC documentary on the American housewife and decided to reward herself with the most delicate, lacy silk underwear she could find, never mind the price. What she found was that silk, that delicious lingerie fabric, had vanished from the marketplace. Hunting down a bolt of the stuff and a seamstress, she designed an ivory bikini panty with an appliquéd lace flower. That was the first item in what turned into a million-dollar business and today, all the best department stores have Loré boutiques. Her swirly gowns with French lace and hand embroidery cost $230, camisoles $90, and slips $135. Though Loré designs are expensive, she believes that just as we now buy silk lingerie from the 1920s in antique stores, in sixty years *her* things will still be as usable and as highly prized.

The original bias-cut Harlow gown (worn here by none other than Jean Harlow), probably the most clingy dress in American fashion history.

Loré's celebrated silk satin Harlow gown is a copy of the notorious 1930s version. Now, as then, the daring wore it both as party dress and nightgown. (Copyright © 1980 by **Playboy**. Photo: Mario Casilli)

Lucite

Du Pont trade name for a hard, transparent acrylic used occasionally for handbags and shoe heels.

Lumberjack Shirt

A rugged shirt not without romance, worn by Paul Bunyon *et al* when felling the giant spruce and pine of Canada and the great Northwest. It was always plaid, always a thick cotton or wool flannel. Outdoorwear and army-navy stores sell them for both men and women for $10 to $20. Good brand names are: Klondike, Woolrich, Boston Traders, L. L. Bean. Some of the plaids are beautiful, and look terrific over turtleneck sweaters or tucked into tight jeans.

Lurex

Trade name of the Dow Badische Company for metallic yarn, called lamé. See LAMÉ.

Lycra

Du Pont's trademark for spandex fiber. See SPANDEX.

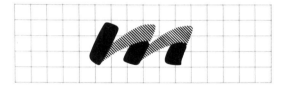

McFadden, Mary

Everything about Mary McFadden is exquisite, from her shiny little Dutch-girl bob to her enormous brown eyes to her showroom, with its white ceramic sculptures, straw baskets full of brass Easter lilies, and mat rugs from Africa. At forty-one, she's a member of the Coty Fashion Hall of Fame and has been ranked by *Women's Wear Daily* as one of the top twelve designers in the world.

The famous pleats and braided ropes any real partygoer would kill for are modeled here by Mary McFadden herself.

She's best known for her eveningwear: skirts and dresses with hundreds of tiny pleats and lots of twisting, braided belts; floaty silk tunics over pants; hand painted quilted jackets. Though fashion writers are continually talking about her pleated silks, she doesn't do pleated *silks*. Pleats don't stay *in* natural fibers, and to get her sculptural, Grecian-column effect, she uses a polyester satinback fabric developed for her in Australia; once it's pleated, you can handwash it forever and the pleats will stay put. A McFadden dress costs anywhere from $1,000 to $2,500. Her clothes are in department stores, but you have to phone the couture department and make an appointment, or ask especially to see them. Don't be timid—often, the more expensive the merchandise, the more gracious are salesclerks.

Mackinaw

An American Indian word for a heavy wool plaid jacket. Indians made the plaid blankets they got at a Mackinac, Michigan, trading post into jackets, an idea soon copied by trappers and hunters.

Mackintosh

In the early 1830s, a Scottish chemist named Charles Macintosh invented a heavy rubber-coated fabric used for raincoats. Since rubber is seldom used to make rainwear anymore, "macks" are obsolete, but the name remains in popular usage for raincoats.

Madras

is a handloomed Indian cotton with plaids, checks, and stripes all colorfully intermingled. Because the yarn is dyed with natural vegetable dyes, colors run together (called "bleeding"), producing a lovely muted effect. The fabric often has an odd swampy smell from being washed many times in India to promote bleeding, and the weave itself has many slubs and imperfections. Genuine madras is woven in village cottages, with spools and spindles kept wet so that bleeding begins even as the fabric is woven. Imported madras costs somewhat more than the imitation polyester and cotton blend "madras type" fabrics manufactured here. You can tell the real thing by its bumpiness.

Brooks Brothers sells genuine madras shirts.

What's bad about madras: it sometimes fades a little *too* easily. If you're wearing a madras jacket and perspire under the arms, you may find your blouse has changed color.

Care

Naturally, you wouldn't throw it in with a full machine load because it would fade all over everything else. But handwash as often as possible—the more washing, the more bleeding. *It will shrink the first time it's washed.* You can also dry clean madras.

Maillot

(my-oh) A one-piece swimsuit. See SWIMSUITS.

Mainbocher

(main-bo-shay) A name to know if you're trying to be knowledgeable about fashion, even though he's long since retired. Mainbocher, the most prominent American designer during the 1940s and 1950s, dressed the Duchess of Windsor and other *crème de la crème*. Unsurprisingly, he was known for his quiet good taste and prices only the wealthy could afford.

Mandarin Collar

Chinese in origin, a narrow collar that stands up instead of lying flat, and has square corners which don't quite meet in front. A mandarin jacket is usually in rich, embroidered fabric; when the fabric is plain, it's called a coolie jacket. Collarless, front-button bodices help reduce a top-heavy look.

Mantilla

A lacy Spanish shawl, nice to wear with formal or party dress in spring and on cool summer nights. Crocheted cotton is much nicer than polyester. Get them at South American import shops.

Maribou Feathers

Jean Harlow made maribou-trimmed negligées and feather-bedecked mules the most glamorous of boudoir wear. Though a maribou is a beautiful wild African stork, happily "maribou feathers," as we're concerned with them, are the breast feathers from our Thanksgiving turkeys, shipped overseas to be skillfully dyed and made floaty. Oomphie's classic Harlow satin mules are a great bargain at $21.

You certainly can't wear sneakers with a filmy nightgown. Oomphies® "maribou" slippers are perfect.

Mark Cross

offers the ultimate in status leather for business—the $650 mocha calfskin attaché case for women announces clearly but with the best possible taste that you enjoy worldly success. The store's envelope briefcases, only $190, deliver the same message for less money. Mark Cross is an old and elegant American firm, founded in 1845; however, the leather it sells is crafted in Italy, France, Switzerland, and Germany.

Marquisette

A light, loosely woven fabric formerly used for mosquito netting and curtains, now used for vests and T-shirts to be worn on top of other clothes.

Mary Jane Shoes

A pump with a strap across the top of the instep. It's what Alice wore in Wonderland, and what little girls' dolls often wear. In cotton, the national shoe of China for women.

Masandrea, Frank

(mah-sahn-dray-ah)An American designer who's been getting a lot of praise for his slinky eveningwear with a 1930s look. He made his name designing bridal gowns, now takes pride in keeping costs of his natural-fabric clothes between $180 and $330. A good designer for women who don't like ruffles and frills and who do appreciate designer clothes but usually can't afford them.

Matte Jersey

Matte means a lusterless, dull surface. Matte jersey is a particularly swingy, clingy fabric, usually bias-cut. If you're svelte enough to wear matte jersey, few fabrics move more gracefully with the body, which is why the material is a big favorite with designers such as Halston, Stephen Burrows, Scott Barrie, and Clovis Ruffin.

Care

Bias-cut jersey dresses stretch out of shape rather easily, so better to treat yours as a sweater and fold loosely in a drawer than to put on a hanger, and certainly *never* put one on a wire hanger.

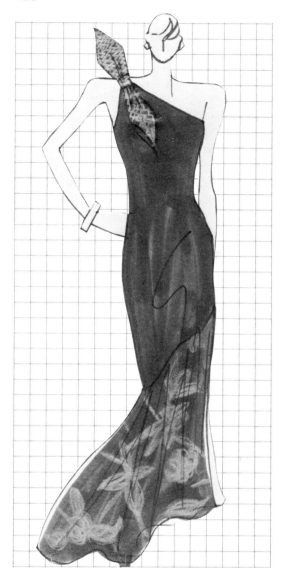

Frank Masandrea is a young designer known for his evening clothes with a 1930s look. (Drawing: Frank Masandrea)

Melton Cloth

is what most coats are made from when they're not tweeds. Wool melton is a closely woven fabric with a slight nap. Better meltons feel almost velvety to touch; others, such as the recycled wool used for pea jacket meltons, feel rough.

Même Soie

means "same as silk" in French and is a polyester crêpe de Chine. This imposter is almost impossible to tell from silk by the naked eye, is washable, and is relatively inexpensive.

Minaudière

(min-au-dee-air) A metal handbag for evening—some are so beautiful they could be sculptures. Macy's sells minaudières from India, made of bronze and shaped like envelopes with chain handles, for $38. Most minaudières, found in the handbag section of department stores, cost around $150. Art Deco motifs with inlaid copper, brass, and German silver are lovely; others have gold-plated designs such as butterflies, and are carried by woven gold chains. Best minaudières are Judith Lieber's (Nancy Reagan carried one to the Inaugural Ball), who became famous making them and has won a Coty Award for her handbags. Her

For anyone who goes to a lot of black-tie parties, a gold-plated minaudière by Judith Lieber would be a good investment; this style has sold steadily for seventeen years.

minaudières have a soft cuddly look but are made of Florentine hand finished gold plate, and cost from $300. Garnet, lapis, cornelian, jade, onyx, rose quartz, and rhinestones are all used lavishly, and should a stone be lost, you send the bag back to Leiber headquarters (14 East 32nd Street in New York) and it will be replaced.

Mink

Over 55 percent of all furs sold in the U.S. are mink, possibly because mink is one of the great status symbols of all time. Also, mink happens to be warm, long-lasting, and ranchbred rather than cruelly trapped. (Only 10 percent of mink are still trapped; since they don't have the advantage of controlled diet, their pelts are not considered as good as ranchbred mink.) The mink industry likes to point out that while fake fur is made from petroleum, a nonrenewable resource, ranched mink is a renewable resource that has no bearing on the balance of nature. Mink is also soft, lustrous, and irresistibly beautiful. "Looking at a great mink coat is like looking into a deep, clear lake where you can't see the bottom," says mink rancher Ronal Gengel. Of course, nothing is *all* good. The average price of a mink coat is about $5,000 (though you can cut that during sales in August, January, and pre-Christmas). After the initial outlay, you still have to insure and store the fur during summer. Plus, not everybody feels comfortable in a mink. "I felt like a Rich Bitch," says one mink owner who sold hers and got a nutria, which doesn't even look like fur. "I seemed to be saying, 'I have money and you don't.' " Undoubtedly this conspicuous consumption element is why Jacqueline Kennedy Onassis and other First Ladies have been careful never to be photographed in mink.

These considerations aside, never have mink pelts been lovelier, or manufacturers more skillful in putting coats together. Minks are native only to America, and American mink is considered the world's best. In 1980, 80 percent of the more than six million pelts grown in the U.S. were exported; however, that still leaves enough mink for you to buy the sort of coat that would cost French or Japanese women twice as much. Indeed, a thriving part of the U.S. mink business consists of women from abroad making shopping for a mink part of their visit to America, just as we'd make looking for cashmere part of a trip to Scotland. Always look for country-of-origin on the label. American mink costs a little more, but knowledgeable shoppers pay it.

Anyone shopping for a mink should be familiar with the following terms:

Blackglama The label of the Great Lakes Mink Association (GLMA), formed in the early 1940s to perfect the lustrous black pelts of ranch mink. (Minks are naturally a medium brown, not nearly so rich-looking.) The animals were first ranched in the 1920s, but the pelts weren't big sellers because women staggered under their weight. Through selective breeding and diet, milk pelts became lighter in weight and darker in color, and today the best of these rich, dark furs are sold under the Blackglama label. With luck, you can find one on sale for $3,000; a designer name adds another $3,000.

Natural ranch mink Mink sold by the Great Lakes Mink Association that doesn't rate the Blackglama label is sold as natural ranch mink. "Natural" means the fur was handsome enough not to need dyeing. A coat costs around $2,600 at a good sale.

EMBA Call letters for the association of American mink breeders who raise mink with pale or colored fur, as opposed to black fur. When mink was first ranched, off-color minks were greeted with dismay; soon breeders realized that if they could raise these animals in any numbers, there might be money there too. The Mutation Mink Breeders Association was formed in 1942, but the word mutation was dropped because people were confusing it with "imitation." Now, the association is simply called EMBA, and genetic research has resulted in eleven different registered colors, from brown to platinum to the latest triumph, a natural pale rose called Rovalia.

Top-of-the-line EMBA furs are stamped "Rare Quality" and sold by their registered color names. Thus, you'll see "Natural Lutetia Mink" advertised, which means the coat is a gunmetal gray and the best of its kind. EMBA mink that doesn't rate the Rare Quality label is stamped "Royal Quality" and sold simply as "EMBA gray natural mink." Two other EMBA colors you'll see frequently advertised are Lunaraine, which is a dark brown, and Tourmaline, a pale beige. Lesser qualities of these two colors would be advertised as "EMBA dark brown natural mink" and "EMBA pale beige natural mink." Cost depends on the rarity of the color. Tourmaline and Lunaraine are around $3,000 on sale, Lutetia more like $6,000.

SAGA Trade name of Scandinavian minkgrowers for their finest pelts. They raise more mink than the United States, but Scandinavian mink, while good quality, isn't admired quite so much as American.

NORKA Russian mink.

MAJESTIC Superior mink from Canada.

Oxidation

After about twenty years and/or much exposure to light, some mink dulls and turns an unattractive reddish shade, much like hennaed hair. "While an animal is living, there's a continuous renewal of the nutri-

ents its fur needs to be lustrous and maintain its color," says Carol Speed of the American Fur Association. "All animal furs will oxidize gradually over the years." If a coat is natural to begin with, it can be dyed to recapture its lost color. When a mink has been bought dyed, *re*dyeing it properly is much harder, which is why a natural coat is a better investment than the coats dyed green, red, or even black. Dyeing mink costs about $200 and, with a little remodeling, can make a twenty-year-old coat look stunning. A good furrier should open up the lining and check to make sure the leather hasn't dried out and redyeing is worth the trouble.

For care of mink see FUR, Care.

Missoni

Tai and Rosita Missoni of Milan, Italy, are the world's most applauded knitters. At Bloomingdale's in New York, Missonis are the only clothes chained to racks—the ultimate compliment to their work.

The complex Missoni knitting machinery turns out fabrics that are a haze of beautiful, intricate colors, in varied textures, richly nubbly and feathery and clingy. They do sweaterdresses, knitted coats, and glittery evening clothes, and knit equally well in wool, cotton, linen, mohair, angora, or metallic yarn, or with combinations of these. You pay substantial import duty for a Missoni. After Christmas, however, Bloomingdale's usually has a Missoni dress marked down from $445 to $110, others from $300 to $150. Find them in chic department stores across the country.

Moccasin

In a recent *Time* magazine article, a Bloomingdale's buyer said, "We all want to be cowboys and Indians. We were all cowboys and Indians as kids. It's one of the last great fantasies left." Whatever the reason, the Urban Pocahontas look abounds these days, complete with fringed buckskin jackets, squash-blossom necklaces, and, naturally, Indian moccasins. Biggest seller is the beaded white Minnetonka moccasin, "Indian-type" footwear manufactured for over thirty years in Minneapolis, Minnesota. The Minnetonka sells for $18 in American stores, $60 in Paris. Most *authentic* moccasin, however, is real Indian stuff made by Cherokees, in the traditional tribal manner, on North Carolina's Qualla Reservation. These deliciously soft moccasins and squaw boots are made of American deerskin, sell for under $18, and are found in small stores throughout the country. To find the store nearest you, or order directly, write: The Cherokees, Qualla Reservation, Cherokee, North Carolina 28719 (704 497-4051).

Modacrylic

The warm, furry synthetic used mostly for fake fur coats and very fleecy fabrics. It's made from natural gas, coal, air, salt, and water, is flame retardant and mothproof, resists stains and mildew, dries quickly when caught in rainstorms. The thicker the fabric, the warmer the coat. On the minus side, modacrylic doesn't breathe as wool does.

Trade names: Union Carbide's "Dynel," Monsanto Textiles Company's "Elura," and Eastman Kodak's "Verel."

Care

Coats should be dry cleaned or fur-cleaned, according to label instructions. Washable items can be machine washed in warm water. Add a fabric softener during the final rinse cycle. If you are drying by machine, use a low setting and remove clothes as soon as tumbling has stopped; otherwise

wrinkles may set in permanently. Never use a hot iron on modacrylic, or leave a fake fur near a hot radiator—heat distorts the fibers.

Mohair

With its long curved horns, silly-looking face, and thick ringlets of fleece, the angora goat looks like something from a children's fairy tale. Fleece from the angora goat is what provides us with mohair, and at present the largest concentration of these animals is not some exotic Oriental mountain peak but the limestone hills of Texas, north of San Antonio. For thousands of years, these goats were bred in Angora, Turkey, and exporting a goat was a serious crime. But in 1849, two bucks and seven does were given by the sultan to a Columbia, South Carolina, man in gratitude for his work on improving Turkish cotton, and today the United States, not Turkey, is the largest producer of mohair fleece. The goat liked the Lone Star state best, and Texas is now home to over four million of the animals, which are shorn twice a year.

Mohair is a light, airy fiber, providing warmth way out of proportion to its weight. You can dye it more vivid colors than the other animal fibers, and it has a lovely luster. Though you can buy pure mohair sweaters, most often mohair is blended with wool to add sheen and fluffiness. Mohair is so soft because in its final stages of production, mohair fabric is always brushed with a French thistle, called a teasel, cultivated especially for the purpose. No mechanical device has ever been invented to take the place of a natural teasel.

Because of their fluffiness, mohair sweaters look best on tall, thin women, add too much bulk for the short, plump figure.

Care

Mohair is wrinkleproof, doesn't shrink, and, according to the Mohair Council of America, can be handwashed. Turn inside out, wash in Woolite in lukewarm water, and blot out excess moisture in a Turkish towel. Lay it flat and pat into shape—no blocking is necessary. When completely dry, turn to right side and shake to fluff up the fiber.

Moiré

(mah-ray) A rippling pattern, similar to a wood grain, mechanically produced on the surface of fabrics, most commonly taffeta, but also on rayon, silk, acetate, and synthetics. Moiré patterns are permanent on synthetic fibers, but natural fibers must be resin-finished to make the pattern permanent, a process which interferes with the fabric's breathing ability. Without the finish, perspiration or a spilled drink will dissolve the pattern. Moiré is most often used for evening clothes and lingerie.

Monk's Cloth

A coarse, loosely woven cotton fabric, usually used for slipcovers but, in the continuing search for exotic but inexpensive fabrics, sometimes used for clothes.

Montana, Claude

A young French designer celebrated at thirty for his *Star Wars*-style jackets with shoulders extending six inches on either side and worn atop the skinniest of leather pants. His futuristic but beautifully made clothes lean toward $1,000 leather jumpsuits, coats with football shoulders, and dramatic flying-saucer hats, all unapologetically masculine in style. Look for his leathers.

Mori, Hanae

A Japanese designer, living in Paris, who does spectacular silk and chiffon creations printed in flower patterns suggesting Japanese paintings. Her designs are western and sedate, and cost up to $5,000; butterflies are a signature motif.

Mother-of-Pearl

The iridescent lining of certain sea shells used for buttons. Most "mother-of-pearl" buttons are plastic; if they're the real thing, usually somebody will tell you so.

Mousseline

French muslin, a plainly woven cotton cloth a little finer and softer than the usual run of muslin.

Mouton

The sheared pelt of a lamb, with hairs straightened and dyed. Water-repellent, durable, ecologically correct, inexpensive, and no fur is warmer. The drawback: mouton weighs a ton. You don't just lightly fling a mouton coat over your arm; you usually stagger a bit. Mouton enjoyed great popularity in the 1950s, gradually disappeared in the 1960s. You can buy mouton new for $600 or $700, used for $100 or $200.

Mucker

A short, ankle-high boot, rubber on the bottom half, leather on top, with a tread design on the shoe's bottom for a firm grip. L. L. Bean himself first designed the style, and still sells it as the "Maine Hunting Shoe." Most outdoorwear stores have them under one brand or another, usually for around $35.

Not only does a muffler keep your neck warm, it can also make a terrific vest. This one is hand-loomed in Brooklyn by Black Sheep.

Muffler

A long knitted wool scarf, usually fringed at the ends. An indispensable cold-weather accessory, as heat always escapes in large doses through the neck. If you're warm everywhere else and your neck is bare, you'll be cold.

Mugler, Thierry

(tee-erry moog-ler) French designer, avant-garde, who made a big splash a couple of years ago with his plastic breastplate molded with nipples and navel. He's been compared to the artist who does things nobody likes but whom everybody is in awe of. Mugler is written about a lot, but found in only a few American department stores,

selling $300 silk blouses and $500 dresses with a space-age look. His seams make angular, angry zig-zags at the cuffs and shoulders, and feminine frills are definitely not present.

Muir, Jean

England's best-known designer, admired for her soft, feminine leather clothes and, lately, for her loose, calf-length dresses with puffed Victorian sleeves. She's found at a few of the best U.S. department stores, such as Henri Bendel's in New York.

Mules

High-heeled slippers with no ankle straps, also called slides. In the spring, F.W. Woolworth always gets in a great collection of canvas and wood mules for under $10.

Mulqueen, Jack

Volume manufacturer of silk shirtwaist dresses in the middle price range. Most Mulqueen silks aren't as fine as Italian and French silks, though some are, and his dresses tend to be made with labor-saving cuts in dressmaker detail, such as having an elasticized waist instead of a waistband. His designs, though simple, are flattering to everyone, and in only four years he's made breathing, sensuous silk, long considered a luxury fabric, available at polyester prices. His operation is unique in a business in which most designers buy their fabrics in one place and hire contractors to make them up in another. Mulqueen does everything himself: fabric patterns and dress designs come from his workshop; his Korean operation does all else, from growing silkworms and spinning the silk fiber to printing, dyeing, and sewing the dresses. His operation is so efficient that two of the world's most respected designers, Mary

McFadden and Zandra Rhodes, have designed collections for him (which cost a
fraction of their own expensive lines), and
Rome's leading designer, Valentino, is said
to be on the verge of signing up.

Mulqueen himself, a former president of
Jaeger, has yet to get a Coty Award, but
he's made millions while still under forty
and is considered the wonder boy of Seventh Avenue.

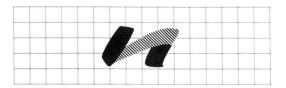

Necklaces

While many of those old rules about how to
camouflage faulty face shapes are silly
("rouge the end of a long nose," etc.), camouflage with necklace shapes is quite sensible. A few basics:

Round face or short neck   Wear beads in
a long oval to the bust, or a long silver or
gold chain with a pendant hanging below
the bust. The vertical lines have a definite
elongating effect.

Long face, long neck   Wear choker necklaces, keep beads at your throat. Large,
wide chunky beads, worn right at the
collarbone, make a nice contrast against a
long, thin bone structure.

Thick   neck   Avoid   delicate,   fragile
chains—the contrast emphasizes the bulk
of a bull-like neck. Wear long, medium-size
jewelry.

Football shoulders   Never wear necklaces right at the neck—they add to horizontal line. Wear wide necklaces hanging
in a diagonal "V" line, to break up broad
expanse.

Nipon, Albert

The Philadelphia-based designer of the
fabulously successful Albert Nipon line is
neither Japanese nor male. Pearl Nipon,
wife of Albert, chooses fabrics and designs
the dresses; Albert runs the factory and
sets prices. The Nipon name comes from
Albert's father, a Russian immigrant, who
changed his name from Niepomaczyczk.

Albert Nipon dresses are most admired
for their lovely detail: the "Nipon tuck,"
delicate pleats, shirring, ruffles. They're
soft, feminine, perfect for dinner dressing
and for non-black tie occasions when you
just want to dress up a *bit*. Nancy Reagan
appeared at the Republican convention in a
Nipon. Nipon Boutique dresses start at
$150, and have the same styling as, but less
expensive fabrics than, regular Nipon
dresses, which start at around $275. The
couple has never won a Coty Award, and
doesn't move in the chic circles of Halston

Single-strand necklace
lengths are:

Dresses are the forte of Albert Nipon®, as are artful pleats and tucks.

and Oscar de la Renta. However, in the nine years since they formed their partnership, they've quietly made retailing history. The company grew from a small maker of maternity-wear into the largest designer-dress manufacturer in America—a $30-million-a-year business—practically overnight.

Nipon is a master of cotton-polyester blends for fresh, crisp summer dresses that can be wadded up in a suitcase and then miraculously unfolded in nearly perfect condition. You'll find little snobbism over synthetics vs. natural fibers here—many styles are in practical synthetics such as polyester or acetate.

Nomelle

An acrylic that looks like cashmere.

Norell, Norman

The late Norell, who died in 1972, was considered the dean of the American fashion industry. He was the first designer elected to the Coty Hall of Fame in 1958, and was best known for the conservative elegance of his slinky sequined sheaths and double-breasted coats, and for the introduction of pant suits for women.

Notch-Collared Blouse

A tailored blouse, which provides instant conservative good taste. The perfect blouse to wear on job interviews.

Nylon

was the first totally man-made fiber, spun from petroleum, natural gas, air, and water by Du Pont in 1938 and used to make hosiery. Elastic, wrinkleproof, and mildew-resistant, nylon caught on immediately. The fabric doesn't breathe well or absorb perspiration, and in 90-degree weather a dainty nylon blouse or slip will start to feel like a plastic tablecloth. However, nylon has wonderful "slippage" characteristics, meaning the abrasion it causes against your skin is minimal. A nylon T-shirt would be too clammy for running, but nothing is less likely to rub your skin raw than jogging shorts of nylon. Its smoothness also makes it superb for slips, nightgowns, and other lingerie. You wouldn't want to wear nonabsorbent nylon underpants while exercising, but for sensuous everyday comfort, nylon panties are fine as long as they have a cotton crotch. Synthetics have been accused by doctors of causing bacteria and germs to form in the vaginal area, promoting infections.

Trade names: Monsanto's Actionwear, Du Pont's Antron and Antron III (see pp. 9–10); American Enka's Enka, Du Pont's Qiana (see p. 159).

Care

Usually can be machine washed, and tumble dried at low temperatures. Nylon easily

picks up colors from other fabrics, so you may want to wash separately. Use warm, not hot, water, and you can add fabric softener to the final rinse cycle to reduce electricity. Because it's so low in moisture absorbency, nylon dries almost before you can get it hung up, and is certainly a good lingerie choice for vacations. Don't hang nylon in the bright sunlight for long periods of time, as it tends to discolor.

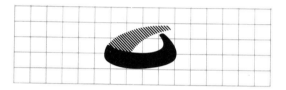

Oatmeal Linen
See LINEN.

Obi
(oh´-be) A broad, stiff sash, fastening in back, worn by generations of Japanese women with their kimonos. Designers often borrow the style for evening clothes.

Oilcloth
is a fabric with a synthetic coating making it waterproof; at one time, oil was used as the waterproofer.

Ombré
(ahm´-bray) An ombré design has graduations in color, like a rainbow; it can be shades of one color, or can change colors, such as from red to green.

Organdy
is a light, transparent cotton or silk. Stiffening is added to give it that crisp finish, which means that it may waterspot easily. A professional cleaner can remove water

Notch-collared blouse

rings. Don't handwash unless the label says you can.

Organza

is the same stiff, sheer fabric as organdy, but is made of silk or a synthetic silk look-alike. Bill Blass does ruffly blouses in pale pink silk organza for around $100, a terrific buy. Again, follow label instructions for cleaning.

Orlon

The acrylic and modacrylic fibers made by Du Pont.

Outdoorwear

Time magazine called the boom in rugged outdoor clothes the "urban mountaineer look"; Seventh Avenue calls it "chilly chic"; city officeworkers think longingly of "camping and backpacking" clothes, while designer Ralph Lauren has taken many of the staples of the determinedly nonfashionable look, made them look fashionably nonfashionable, and called his new line "Roughwear." Ragg wool crew-neck sweaters, Klondike lumberjack shirts, Sierra Designs goosedown vests and parkas, Hudson Bay blanket jackets, chino pants with flannel linings, Duofold's itch-free cotton/wool thermal underwear, Lee Riders, L. L. Bean's chamois cloth shirts, Herman-Survivor boots—the clothes alone seem to give fresh-air-starved cityfolk a heady glimpse of wide open spaces. The granddaddy of clothes purveyors for the outdoors is, of course, L. L. Bean, yet some purists—those who really *do* go backpacking through the Canadian wilderness and mountain-climbing in Alaska in winter—say snobbishly that Bean clothes are wonderful for suburbanites out for a four-mile hike through the fall leaves, but aren't nearly hardy enough for really serious outdoor stuff—you'd freeze to death.

Everyone has her own favorite among the hundreds of new outdoorwear stores that have opened all over the country, particularly around college campuses. Most "army-navy" stores are really outdoorwear stores. A lot of them operate thriving mail-order-catalogue businesses, among them:

L. L. Bean, Inc.
Freeport, Me. 04033
(207) 865-3111

Kreeger & Sons
387 Main Street
Armonk, N.Y. 10504
(914) 273-8520

Sierra Designs
247 Fourth Street
Oakland, Cal. 94607
Toll free: (800) 227-1097

Columbia Sportswear Co.
6600 North Baltimore
Portland, Ore. 97203
(503) 286-3676

Eastern Mountain Sports, Inc.
Vose Farm Road
Peterborough, N.H. 03458
(603) 924-9212

The North Face
1234 Fifth Street
Berkeley, Cal. 94710
(415) 548-1371

Wilderness Experience
20120 Plummer Street
Chatsworth, Cal. 91311
(213) 998-3000

Eddie Bauer
Department AW2
Fifth & Union
Seattle, Wash. 98124
(206) 622-2766

Early Winters, Ltd.
110 Prefontaine Place South
Seattle, Wash. 98104
(206) 622-5203

Outlander Sweaters

are found in practically everybody's sweater drawer. "Sweaters are our business, not fashion," says Philip Shapiro, executive vice president of the eleven-year-old company. Outlander started making affordable natural-fiber sweaters in a decade when most people wanted the machine-washability of acrylic, yet sold enough to become one of the biggest sweater manufacturers in the country.

Though most Outlander care labels say Dry Clean Only, they don't really mean that. "Our wool and fur blend sweaters can be handwashed in Woolite," says Shapiro. "You wouldn't want to wash them in a detergent, because it would take the oil out of the fibers. Oil is what gives a wool sweater its resiliency. Also, hot water will ruin wool."

Outré

(oo-tray´) Exaggerated, eccentric; slightly beyond the limits of convention. A light-reflective Scotchlite dress worn with a see-through vinyl handbag would be outré.

Overalls

are made by attaching a bib and suspenders or a pinafore top to pants. They originated in the late nineteenth century among workmen such as farmers and painters, who liked them for their comfort: they're held up by shoulder fastenings, making them less constricting and looser-fitting than clothes held up with belts. Overalls are actually a rather flattering garment for the overweight because the line is a

long one, and because they're usually made of dull-textured materials, such as khaki, that make you look slimmer.

Overblouse

A blouse that's worn outside, rather than inside, a skirt. A good style for the sway-backed.

Oxford Shirts

are made from oxford cloth, a cotton fabric woven with tiny, delicately colored stripes and first worn in England at Oxford University. Button-down oxford shirts sell for under $20 in boys' departments of department stores, and are usually a cotton polyester blend, but all-cotton ones can be found at Brooks Brothers. The more polyester, the less oxford cloth breathes—but also the less it wrinkles.

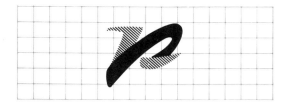

Paillette

A large sequin, which is a round, glittery metal disc pierced in the center for thread. See BEADED CLOTHES.

Paisley

A woolen fabric patterned with colorful, curvy shapes that gets its name from Paisley, Scotland, where wool paisley shawls were first woven in imitation of Indian cashmere shawls. Weaving the patterns proved too costly, and most paisleys are now printed. Some paisley fabric is still woven, and is more expensive than printed paisley.

Panne Velvet

(pan-a´) A particularly clingy, shimmery velvet with the pile pressed flat in one direction. Most expensive panne velvets are made of silk; most commonly, you'll find it made of a blend of triacetate and nylon. A beautiful fabric for thin, willowy figures, especially in evening pyjamas. Dry clean only.

Pants

are possibly the oldest fashion classic, having been worn by anybody who wanted to ride horses ever since it occurred to someone that horses could be ridden. Modern straight-leg, floor-length trousers are an American innovation, first worn during the War of 1812 as a symbol of disassociation from the British, who wore knee breeches. Other styles abound: you can wear soft, drapey evening pants, harem pants gathered into a cuff at the ankle, loose midcalf-length pants called culottes, pants with tapered legs, bellbottoms. A few guidelines for buying pants are:

For large hips, thighs, or waist Buy regular-length straight-leg pants without pleats, gathers, slit side pockets, or pocket detailing. Wear your pants with a sweater, blouse, or jacket of a matching color, so that you don't have a horizontal line in the middle. (Avoid polyester pant suits, possibly the country's most declassé outfit.) Stick to the long vertical lines of full-length trousers. Never wear Bermuda-length short pants, though the looser, more flowing cuts of midcalf culottes worn with boots may be flattering. When pants bunch around the crotch, that means you need a cut that's longer between the waist and crotch, particularly important if you're a tiny bit outsized there. Avoid wearing underpants with elastic at legs and waist—

they cause tiny bulges you don't need. Buy stretch panties designed for wearing under pants.

For short legs Avoid wide pants, and try for a close-fitting straight-leg cut. You, too, should wear a matching blouse or sweater, avoiding a horizontal line at waist that chops you in two and makes legs look even shorter. A wide belt the same color as pants has an elongating effect.

For a pot belly Avoid velour or clingy knits in favor of a more tailored cut giving a little support. Never wear pants with a short sweater or blouse tucked in—wear a tunic, overblouse, or long, loose sweater. If you're thin and pot-bellied, drawstring pants slightly gathered at the waist should provide some soft camouflage.

For a swayback and protruding buttocks- Wear pants cut smooth in front, gathered in back. Wear with a tunic, an overblouse, a long, belted, or loose sweater, or a blazer.

Hem length Classic floor-length trousers should cover the instep of foot in front, come to midheel in back, never drag the ground.

Care

Hang wet pants upside down from a pants hanger, then clamp another pants hanger at bottom. The added weight pulls out wrinkles and ensures that the legs hang straight.

Pantyhose

Sheer nylon pantyhose are probably one of the most foolish fashions in all history. They're cold in winter, hot in summer, and when you pay $3 for a nonexchangeable new brand, it will invariably hang two inches too short at the crotch or bag at the ankles. Many gynecologists believe that the lack of ventilation in the tight-fitting crotch of pantyhose causes vaginal bacteria to flourish, contributing to infections and possibly even cervical cancer; as a result, most—but not all—pantyhose now come with cotton crotches. In addition to these liabilities, few last more than a few weeks before running. Since nylons are made from petroleum, a nonrenewable resource, they're ecologically irresponsible. A far more sensible alternative is, whenever possible, bare legs and sandals in summer, midcalf skirts with knee-highs or boots, and wool/cotton thermal knee-length underwear in winter. (You can remove these in an overheated office.) Or wear wool or cotton pantyhose—you can try on "thermal tights" in department stores, but no stores let you try on wares from the stocking department. Textured or opaque pantyhose look better with low-heeled shoes than sheer stockings anyway.

For those hooked on the sexiness provided by a lustrous, sheer stocking, however, here are a few guidelines:

Buying the right shades Always try to match up stockings with shoes rather than skirt—if you blend stockings and shoes you get a slimmer, leggier look. A light stocking with a dark skirt and dark shoe creates a choppy look. You won't want to wear dark, dark stockings, especially in daytime or summer, but a *tint*-of-black stocking, such as Dior's Black Orchid, will keep the line going. If you're wearing white or bone shoes in summer, a lighter, more nude stocking would be appropriate. Brightly colored nylon stockings are nearly always *too* bright; better to keep exciting colors for blouses or sweaters around your face, and buy stockings in more subdued colors. "If a bright color is selling particularly well in ready-to-wear clothing, we'll always do a matching stocking, but in a gray, *muted* tone," says Brenda Tellman, product manager of Burlington. "The more muted and grayer a tone in an Ultra Sheer, the prettier on the leg." More advice: if you're trying to match up a shoe with a stocking, bring the shoe along with you. Pull sample stockings not just on your hand but over your arm, and hold them against the shoe, buying the most toned-in shade. Of course, if you're wearing a brightly colored metallic evening shoe,

---

For the Most Beautiful, Aristocratic Stockings

Look for the packages that say Ultra Sheer, as this is the key word used by most manufacturers to indicate their luxury hosiery. Ultra Sheers sell for around $4 as opposed to $1 or $2 for everyday pantyhose. Since the yarn used is more delicate and lighter in weight, Ultra Sheers aren't as sturdy as everyday mesh pantyhose. Also, since the yarn isn't crimped as is yarn used in heavier mesh stockings, Ultra Sheers don't stretch as much, making them harder to fit. If you have slender ankles, they may bag slightly, especially if you buy drugstore Ultra Sheers. Better to go to a department store or hosiery shop (the nice ladies who operate hosiery shops will sometimes even let you exchange ill-fitting pantyhose) and buy one of the top brands—Burlington, Dior, Hanes, Round-The-Clock. These masters take more care in knitting stockings proportionally, graduating the fit so they're narrower at the ankles.

then you wouldn't tone but would wear a neutral, nude shade.

A few more stocking terms to know:

Demi-Sheer Not as beautifully sheer and lustrous as Ultra Sheer, but sturdier and not as expensive. The terms Sheer and Demi-Sheer are used interchangeably by different manufacturers.

Mesh The most coarse stockings; also the sturdiest and least expensive.

Opaque Means you can't see through the stockings. Opaque and textured stockings are generally worn with low-heeled, sportier shoes, delicate Ultra Sheers with light, dressy footwear.

Sandalfoot Stockings without a reinforced toe, to be worn with bare sandals. Don't buy sandalfoot unless you need it, because they don't last as long as reinforced toes.

Control top Means the top, but not legs, has extra spandex to help hold your stomach in. A control top isn't as firm in its support as a girdle, but does help a bit to smooth things out. Control top pantyhose should be worn without panties, and provide the smoothest possible line for wearing under knits and other clingy fabrics.

Support hose Spandex is in top *and* legs, the idea being that extra support will hold your veins in firmly, helping circulation and preventing varicose veins if you're on your feet all day. Though support hose sell well, and some women report less fatigue in their legs and feet when wearing them, not everyone in the medical profession approves of them. "Support hose are a commercial gimmick," says one Manhattan internist specializing in Sports Medicine. "There's no medical documentation whatever showing that these hose support the

---

Alternative to Pantyhose

Some women have never accepted pantyhose or synthetic stockings. One company whose natural-fiber stockings have been selling steadily by mail order since 1920 is the English Funn company, which has a distributor in California (Funn Stockings, P.O. Box 239, Menlo Park, California 94025). In silk ($18), the stockings are sheer and lustrous and, though they will snag, they won't ever ladder or run; they breathe and feel good next to your skin. Bamboo is the best-selling color, but you can get them in black, navy, cocoa, and lots of other colors. Cotton ($9) and wool ($15) stockings are opaque, lightweight, and colorfast; if you wash them in cool water, they won't shrink.

Another alternative to synthetics is Danskin's new line of 80 percent cotton, 20 percent nylon pantyhose. Ribbed, they cost $8.50. Plain tights, 95 percent cotton, 5 percent lycra, are $9.50. Danskin stockings can also be ordered from the Funn distributor, or they can be bought in department stores.

Since most hosiery can't be returned after you've opened the package, buying by mail may actually be more efficient than buying in a crowded hosiery department. When you order by mail, you provide all relevant measurements, and from long experience they pick the most likely size. In stores, the responsibility is often yours to guess your size from charts. In hosiery shops, you'll find more pains taken for a good fit than in understaffed department stores.

muscles or veins. We prescribe strong supportive surgical stockings for people with varicose veins, but even then they don't always help.''

Full fashion knitting   This means stockings aren't just shaped like tubes but have been designed to be larger on top, and taper down at the ankles, as real legs do.

Parachute Weave

A weave so tight air can't get through, usually in nylon, but also in cotton or silk. Used mostly for weightless tote bags, but also as the outer layer on down-filled vests and jackets.

Parka

A jacket with a hood that keeps out icy air more efficiently than any other wrap, as even the warmest coat, muffler, and hat leave slivers of neck and ears exposed. Parkas are the best cold-weather outdoor gear because they don't flap around your legs when you're out walking, and don't tug at your neck and arms when driving. Here are some of the different kinds of parkas.

Down   The warmest, most ventilated, and lightest, though bulky, parka. See DOWN.

Thinsulate has been winning raves as the most efficient new synthetic insulating material, an alternative to down. Thinsulate parkas have two qualities lacking in down: they don't lose their warmth when they get wet, and they are thin, not bulky. While down keeps you warm by expanding to keep body heat in, thinsulate compresses millions of microfibers, each 3 percent of the size of the human hair, into a thin layer of insulation. Though down is still warmest, thinsulate is warmer than any other synthetic fiber and sometimes is preferred to down because a thin jacket is eas-

ier to move in. Thinsulate is both washable and dry-cleanable.

Gore-Tex (See GORE-TEX). The most fabulous new rainwear-type parka around, which breathes more than any other 100-percent waterproof material. Early Winters has the biggest selection of Gore-Tex parkas of any of the mail-order catalogues, and much other wet-wear gear as well. Write Early Winters, Ltd., 110 Prefontaine Place South, Seattle, Washington 98104.

60/40 Not a waterproof fabric (though reasonably water-repellent), 60/40 cloth is lightweight, wonderfully wind-resistant, and reasonably ventilated. The cloth is a weave of 60 percent cotton, 40 percent nylon, with cotton yarn as the fill and nylon yarn as the warp. It was developed in 1967

Parkas can be so warm you just want to crawl into them. When worn in Arctic weather, a fur trim means frost will collect on the fur rather than on your face. (Parka by Woolrich.® Courtesy of Paragon Sporting Goods Co., New York)

by California's Sierra Designs, the founders of which yearned for a wind-resistant motorcycle jacket. Parkas of 60/40 work both as lightweight jackets for spring and fall, and over warm sweaters in winter. 60/40 is also used in down parkas. Though the cloth is now widely imitated, Sierra Designs still makes the original for their trim Mountain Parkas ($105). Find them in over 500 stores in the U.S. or write: Sierra Designs, 247 Fourth Street, Oakland, California 94607. (Toll-free 800 227-1097).

America's best parkas sell for from $100 to $200, half that during January/February sales. (One advantage of buying in a store rather than ordering is the sales.) Of the mail-order catalogues, Columbia Sportswear Company of Portland, Oregon (see OUTDOORWEAR), has the best all-around selection of parkas—everything from superwarm down with attached wool-lined visored face masks to knee-length parkas to anaraks (lightweight pullovers, wind resistant and good for biking and skiing).

Parnis, Mollie

(par´-nis) An American designer who specializes in clothes for "women over thirty." Customers include Lady Bird Johnson, Nancy Kissinger, and Barbara Walters. Her evening clothes are considered her best work.

Passementerie

(pas-ment´-e-ray)An ornate trimming, usually some sort of mixture of beads, braid, tassels, fringe, lace, or embroidery.

Patch Pocket

Any pocket stitched on top of a garment.

Patent Leather

See LEATHER.

Pea Jacket

A short, warm, double-breasted naval jacket of dark blue wool, also called a reefer jacket. Buttons are a matching navy blue, with an anchor design imprinted on them. This classic has been made exactly the same way for a hundred years, though only in the last twenty has it been worn by women. You can pay $380 for Calvin Klein's wool-and-cashmere designer version, but authentic pea jackets are sold in

A genuine Navy pea jacket is as well-tailored as (and somehow more fun than) designer versions selling for three times the price. (Photo: John Fleming)

army-navy stores for $40–$60. Good labels are Woolrich (first company to make them in America, starting in 1880), Schott, Lee, Levi, Fox Knapp. Many will say "Made for U.S. Navy," which means the manufacturer got an order from the Navy, and made some extra for commercial sale. Most are made from warm, sturdy, reprocessed wool. Reprocessed wool is made from ends of yardgoods, or from garments that couldn't be sold; buttons are taken off and the wool is shredded and made into yarn again.

In addition to being worn over pants, pea jackets are perfect over midcalf skirts that are an inch too long for your regular coat. On anyone five feet five and over, they look tailored and feminine in that trim, neat way military uniforms achieve.

Pearls

The most serene and sensuous of jewels, long cherished by seductive women for the way they emphasize the softness of bare shoulders and throat. Ancient astrologers thought pearls were under the influence of the moon and had an aphrodisiac effect upon the wearer, while publishers of such men's magazines as *Playboy* and *Penthouse* obviously believe them to be erotically stimulating to viewers, as their centerfold ladies often wear nothing *but* pearls!

We're *all* wearing pearls these days—the tiny pearl choker made famous by Jacqueline Kennedy Onassis, long strands cascading suggestively down the cleavage, pearls with jeans, *faux* pearls sewn on collars. Elizabeth Taylor owns and wears the world's biggest pearl, La Peregrina, formerly owned by Mary, Queen of Scots, and France's Louis Napoleon. It was given to Liz by Richard Burton, at a cost of $150,000. What's really wonderful about pearls, however, is that of all the world's

beautiful gems, pearls are the only ones we can all afford. Because a Japanese oyster farmer learned how to "culture" pearls back in the early 1900s, the price of a choker dropped from thousands of dollars to under two hundred. Even at Tiffany's, which sells the best pearls in the country, you can get a sixteen-inch choker for around $425, $375 on special sales, such as they often have before Christmas.

All pearls are made by an oyster building layers of nacre (pronounced nay´-ker) over an irritant. With wild pearls, the irritant is usually a grain of sand; in cultured pearls, the farmer implants the irritant—a tiny shell bead—himself. In either case, the oyster takes three or four years to build a pearl, and should the water be too hot or too cold, or polluted by some passing oil tanker, the farmer will find chalk instead of pearls. Here are the terms you should know to understand pearls:

Oriental pearls Natural, noncultured pearls, still considered the most beautiful and desirable, and therefore the most expensive. They come from parts of the world's oceans where oysters breed naturally: the Caribbean, off Venezuela and Panama, the Pacific Islands, Australia, Japan.

Cultured pearls Pearls formed over an irritant, as described above; they can be told apart from natural ones only by experts.

Simulated pearls (also called *faux* pearls). Glass beads coated in ground-up iridescent nacre from fish scales. The more times a bead is dipped into this "pearl essence," the more iridescent and expensive. *Faux* pearls don't have the subtle luster of real pearls, though the difference can be so slight that sometimes you can only distinguish imposters by the *feel*—fakes are completely smooth; real pearls have a slightly gritty feeling, and tiny irregularities.

Baroque pearls are the ones with irregular shapes. Less expensive than round pearls, they may be cultured, natural, or fake.

Freshwater pearls Pearls made by mussels instead of oysters, which come from lakes and rivers. They're not as lustrous as saltwater pearls, are usually baroque, and are generally less expensive; perfectly formed teardrop shapes are the most coveted.

Biwa pearls Small, particularly lovely baroque pearls from freshwater lakes in Biwa, Japan.

Seed pearls Tiny cultured or simulated pearls used mostly as embroidery pearls.

Mobi pearl Half of a round pearl.

Shopping
To get the loveliest pearls for your money, go to a high-quality jeweler in your city and look at strands that cost twice as much as you can afford. Study their luster—good pearls seem to glow from within, shining so much that you can see a reflection on the surface, as well as rainbow colors shimmering softly. Then, try to get pearls in your price range that look as much as possible like the good ones. You'll pay more for perfectly round, smooth ones than for freshwater baroques. Size makes a difference in price, also—the bigger a pearl, and the more perfectly matched a strand, the more costly; tiny-to-large graduated pearls will cost more than a string of mediums. As for color, black and green pearls are rarest and most expensive. Biggest-selling shades are "champagne," a deep cream shade, and "rose-white," which is stunning on blondes. Some of the pearls

sold in America today are dyed; though it's against the law to sell a pearl dyed *black* without informing the buyer, buyers of white pearls usually never know whether their pearls are as the oyster made them or not, simply because they don't bother to check. *Ask,* because natural-colored ones have a more lustrous sheen and are not necessarily more expensive. The most reputable stores, such as Tiffany's, never dye their white pearls. All pearls should be strung with silk thread with knots in between to prevent scratching. One way to save money: buy a simple clasp and spend your cash on the pearls themselves.

Care
In spite of the myth that pearls lose their luster when their owner dies because they need body contact to glow most beautifully, wearing pearls is more likely to cause them to *lose* luster. Body oils, perspiration, perfume, hair spray—all erode nacre. Wearing pearls against the skin often may indeed give them a lovely subtle shine, but these body oils should be wiped off with a soft cloth. Don't wash pearls in soap and water, or forgetfully wear your pearls in the shower, as getting the string wet will rot it. If your pearls are good ones and you wear them often, have them professionally washed and restrung every now and then. Handle pearls gently—nacre is a form of calcium, which is a soft mineral, so don't drop or accidently whack them against hard surfaces; keep them wrapped in soft cloth or tissue so they won't get scratched in your jewelry box.

Peasant Skirt
A tiered skirt, or a cotton skirt with a large ruffle around the bottom, and a classic that's been around for hundreds of years in one culture or another. Many a clotheshorse has been chagrined to find herself

unnoticed in her designer skirts and blouses with gold chains, and then sets a man aglow with enthusiasm over a $20 ruffled skirt. The fact is, no skirt has more life than a peasant skirt: it swirls gracefully and rhythmically with every step. A woman who walks into a roomful of men in such a skirt is going to be noticed more than one wearing straight, simple lines. With a sexy, off-the-shoulder blouse, one makes a particularly nice hostess outfit. Crêpe evening pyjamas may be perfect if you're greeting your guests while the maid prepares dinner, but if your dinner is being served on a coffee table by you, a casual yet feminine tiered skirt, over which you can tie an apron without looking silly, is perfect.

To Buy
Well-cut peasant skirts get voluminous only toward the *bottom*. If they're too gathered at the top, they're bulky even on a thin person. Indian import shops are brimming with tiered cotton skirts. Buy in a darker color and you can also wear it with a sweater and boots in winter, or sandals and knee-highs in fall. Never wear with loafers or pumps.

Peau de Soie
A heavy, satinlike fabric with a dull sheen. The black bowed peau de soie pump is a classic, and most black evening bags are made of peau de soie. Soie means silk in French, but the fabric is usually made from either polyester or rayon.

Peignoir
(pen-war-as in *are*) The shapeless, tired old robes worn by the stereotypical housewife with her hair in curlers are called housecoats. Filmy, lacy robes with matching gowns are called peignoirs.

Pencil Skirt
A skirt as straight as a pencil from hips to hem. It can look particularly bad on a woman with wide shoulders, as she needs a graceful flare at bottom for balance.

Pendleton Woolens
Coveted classics of the 1950s and still going strong, Pendleton woolens are spun, woven, and designed under one roof. The entire operation is engineered so that there are no polluting waste products. Pendleton Woolen Mills was established in Portland, Oregon, in 1909 and was a big success with its bold, bright Indian blankets. It started making women's separates in the 1940s, and is known now, as then, for its pleated plaid skirts and classic hacking jackets at affordable prices.

One **must** have a peignoir for all those before-and-after-the-occasion moments.

A peplum is great to hide swaybacks or pot tummies.

Peplum

A short flounce attached to the snugly fitting waistband of a jacket or blouse. A feminine, nineteenth-century look, terrific on slender women, too bulky for anyone who's hippy.

Peretti, Elsa

American jewelry designer, born in Italy. Her organic, freeform designs are to jewelry what Henry Moore and Barbara Hepworth sculptures are to art. Halston showed the first pieces of sterling silver jewelry she designed—the famous flask and a horseshoe belt buckle—with his 1969 collection, and both became instant classics. You can buy Peretti at Tiffany's, where her sterling silver pieces were the first silver jewelry Tiffany's had carried in twenty-five years and are still among the great bargains of the store. Prices vary according to the silver market, but right now

you'll find a plentiful selection of Peretti bean necklaces, hearts, flasks, and belt buckles in sterling at prices from $22 for a tiny heart to the flask for $160. Wrapped in their Tiffany's boxes, they make the most impeccable graduation presents. Peretti won a Coty Award for her jewelry designs in 1971.

Perfume

is as important an accessory as any you can see. Most women don't feel fully dressed without their favorite perfume, and certainly most men connect fragrance with femininity and romance. Obviously, any female desiring to please the opposite sex should have a small collection of perfumes, light and subtle for day, heavier for evening. Though the world's top-selling perfume is Revlon's Charlie, connoisseurs

Two silver classics by Elsa Peretti. You can put a tiny flower in the urn or wear the well-known organic bean inside a V-necked blouse. (Courtesy of Tiffany & Co.)

usually buy French perfumes. Here's how to apply:

- Always spray, never dab. When you dab, perfume is wasted on your finger; if you use a dipper stick, oils from your body can subtly alter the perfume when the stick goes back into the bottle. When you spray, you use less perfume and it counts more.

- Spray parts of the body where blood vessels are closest to the skin—wrists, back of the knees, between breasts, inside elbows—*warm* places. Warmth somehow brings out the best in a perfume, and your pulsebeat wafts it into the air in the most delicate of invitations. Perfume lasts about four hours.

- *Use* your perfume once opened. Perfume is a live, unstabilized liquid altered by heat, light, and air; after three or four months an opened bottle will start to oxidize and won't smell as good. After a year, forget it. If you can resist keeping lovely little perfume bottles on top of your dresser for decoration and keep them instead in a cool dark drawer, or even the refrigerator, they'll last longer.

- Spray tissue paper with perfume and spread around your lingerie drawers. For some reason, tissue paper absorbs perfume beautifully and retains the fragrance for months.

Permanent Press

Synthetic or partly synthetic clothes can be chemically treated and baked for about fifteen minutes in a 300-degree oven, which will set them permanently in the shape they're in at that moment; pleats will stay pleated forever, and no wrinkles will appear after washing. Such "permanent press" clothes are nearly always of synthetic fibers, mostly polyester and cotton-polyester blends. One disadvantage is that you can never let down a skirt hem without a permanent crease being left behind. On natural wools or cottons, you can lower hems after years of wear without a line (unless there has been wear at the site of the former crease).

Peter Pan Collar

A small round collar. Not a good look for women with round, moon-shaped faces, but on most of us it looks softer and more feminine than pointed collars—men have never worn Peter Pans. Peeping over a crew-neck sweater, these collars are part of the preppy look. J.G. Hook specializes in $40 blouses in tiny plaids with Peter Pan collars.

Petites

are women under five feet four inches tall, who usually have narrower shoulders, smaller busts, shorter arms, and shorter waists than taller women. According to the

U.S. Department of Health and Human Services, there are fourteen million women in the U.S. between four feet ten and five feet four—nearly 25 percent of all adult women. Just in the past year, small has become beautiful in the apparel business, which has discovered that a lot of shoppers aren't built like the tall, willowy sixteen-year-olds who model their clothes. One of the first companies to design for petites has been Evan Picone, which shipped a collection of blazers and skirts to the stores last summer and was astonished to find that every last item had sold out in three weeks. Other good labels making petites: L. F. Petites, a division of Leslie Fay; Ciao; Princess Sumi; Abe Schrader. One resale shop has even begun specializing in used petite clothing: Julie's Resale Shop, 6920 Northeast Sandy Boulevard, Portland, Oregon 97213 (503) 284-1336.

Picot

(pee´-koh) An ornamental edging formed of tiny loops of twisted thread.

Pierrot Collar

(pea-ehr-row) A narrow, stand-up collar with ruffles around the top, much favored by Princess Diana.

Pima Cotton

See COTTON.

Piping

A strip of material, usually contrasting, used to finish an edge such as a neckline or armhole, or to trim collars or pockets. It shouldn't be too bulky.

Piqué

(pee-kay´) Raised patterns, such as wales or small puckers similar to those of seer-sucker, are woven into cotton fabric. Used frequently for white collars and cuffs on dresses, and for tennis dresses.

Plaid

A pattern of stripes that cross each other, forming squares or rectangles. Manufacturers don't much like plaids, because if plaids don't match up at the seams, their product is inescapably exposed as poor quality. So far, matching plaids has totally defied machinery, and has to be expensively done by hand. Plaids have made a comeback in, of all things, silk taffetas for evening. They're the kiss of disaster on anybody more than five pounds overweight, as are large plaids on petites.

Pleats

Long folds of fabric that give life to skirts, as ruffles do. Pleats are permanent only on synthetic fabrics. On a natural-fiber skirt, including rayon and wool, pleats have to be pressed after each cleaning; they also tend to disappear in the rain. Pleats in a bias-cut skirt are even more ephemeral. Unless you want to pay a dry cleaner a fortune, or spend an hour at your ironing board every time you wash it, don't buy a skirt with intricate accordion or knife pleats unless the fabric is at least 55 percent polyester, nylon, or acetate. A few simple pleats, such as box or kick, are no problem and dry cleaners will press them back in free of charge. Neither are pleated blouses a problem, as they're invariably unpressed pleats and nothing is more flattering to a small-bosomed woman.

Plissé

(plee-say´) A puckered fabric similar to seersucker; the fabric is saturated at patterned intervals with a chemical that causes shrinkage and, since the unprinted fabric doesn't shrink, a permanent pucker is formed. Plissé is usually made of cotton, is washable, and doesn't need ironing.

Pockets

are a tell-tale sign of Mr. Good Work or Mr. Poor Work. They should be well hidden in the side seams—when they gap or bulge, they're badly made and add inches to your hips. Ninety percent of all skirts found on sale have gaping pockets, and many of them are by top male designers, who don't seem to understand that the Rubenesque look went out centuries ago.

Polo Coat

A straight, double-breasted coat with a half belt in back; a favorite tailored, upper-middle-class style introduced to America in 1910 by Brooks Brothers. Polo is a game played on horseback with long-handled mallets and a wooden ball, and the polo coat was thrown over the athlete's shoulders between periods of play. Small women look particularly good in this straight up-and-down style. Not for older, heavier women.

Polo Sweater

A finely knitted, short-sleeve pullover sweater, which has a collar and opens about three inches down the front, usually with three buttons.

Polyester

If silk is the queen of fabrics, polyester is the sturdy workhorse. It's the prevalent fabric in America—close to 50 percent of all fibers used for clothes and other products are polyester. Industry estimates make a good case for its being a practical fabric as well: "It would be impossible for cotton or wool to meet America's fiber

Brooks Brothers® introduced the first polo coat to America in 1910 and is still selling almost exactly the same style.

needs," says a spokesman for the Man-Made Fiber Products Association. "Twenty million additional acres of cotton land would be required, much of it at the cost of food or grain crops, while to replace man-mades with wool would require grazing on all the agricultural land in the country." A single polyester plant located on 300 acres of land in Alabama produces as much fiber as all the cotton grown on 600,000 acres in Alabama in a year. As to the argument that polyester is not ecologically sound because it's made from coal, petroleum, air, and water—coal and petroleum are nonrenewable resources—the answering argument is that cotton is nearly as bad because petroleum-based fertilizers are needed to grow it. (Statistics show that while every one-dollar price rise for oil increases the cost of polyester production by one cent per pound, it increases the cost of growing cotton by nearly seven-tenths of a cent per pound.) Furthermore, cotton clothes usually have to be ironed, which takes energy, while polyester is drip-dry. Polyester can be made to look so much like silk that the naked eye can't tell which is the imposter; it's strong (blends of cotton and polyester outlast pure cotton); it's wrinkle resistant, will retain pleats, doesn't fade or discolor in sunlight, and doesn't wilt or droop as do cottons and linens. Says one television personality, "Nothing is better than polyester for traveling. I spilled a whole Coke on a white linen-look polyester suit and was able to completely eradicate the mess with water and paper towels. Then I slept on the suit for three hours in a plane seat and it still looked good."

The most common criticism of polyester is that it isn't comfortable in hot weather. Though recent improvements make it breathe more than acrylic or nylon, it still doesn't have much "wickability." Lacking the spongelike structure of natural fibers, which absorb body moisture and allow it to evaporate, polyester simply traps moisture, making you feel clammy. On cool days when you're not perspiring heavily, this quality is less noticeable than on 90-degree days. And though you don't have to iron polyester as you do cotton or linen, polyester needs washing more often; it ab-

Providing you're tall and willowy, nothing looks better with tight pants and good leather boots than a hand-woven, earth-toned poncho such as this one in Icelandic wool. (Courtesy of L.L. Bean)

sorbs body oils and odors more than do natural fabrics, meaning cuffs and collars get dingy faster, and odors develop faster, tending to cling under the arms.

Trade names: Du Pont's Dacron (the first polyester, marketed commercially by 1953); American Enka's Encron, Celanese's Fortrel, Eastman Kodak's Kodel, Hoechst Fibers' Trevira.

Care
Machine wash in warm water, tumble dry in low heat, but remove from dryer immediately, so wrinkles don't heat-set. Use a fabric softener every few times you wash.

To remove underarm odors, rub with deodorant soap before washing. A presoak in cool salted water also helps remove odors.

Poncho

Probably the oldest American classic, the poncho has been worn by South American Indians for thousands of years. A square of handwoven wool with a hole in the middle, usually patterned in Aztec geometrics, it doubles as a blanket. Ponchos hang below the waist and are the most nonconstricting of wraps. On really Arctic-type days, you can wear one over your regular full-length coat and be as warm as in the warmest fur, as layers trap air.

Look for them in the import shops sprouting near college campuses. The best ones—of thick, handknit wool or alpaca—are imported from Ecuador or Colombia. Ponchos look wonderful on tall women with long legs; a brown-and-white-patterned alpaca poncho worn with tan chinos or cords tucked into brown boots looks spectacular. Resist the look if you're short and plump—ponchos are too shapeless for you.

Poorboy Sweater

A ribbed, slightly boat-necked sweater with elbow-length sleeves, the rage around 1965. The style is so classic that a lot of women have kept theirs all this time, wearing them alone in summer, over blouses in winter.

Poplin

A finely ribbed, medium-heavy silk, cotton, or wool fabric, used since medieval times (it was used for church vestments and known as papalino; around 1800 the English began weaving it and called it poplin). You'll see it a lot in trenchcoats and raincoats. Rubberized poplin—cotton poplin with a thin sheet of rubber sprayed on—makes the lightest of raincoats, and the Neighborhood Cleaners Association is rapturous over the fabric. Poplin also makes nice durable pants—Liz Claiborne has a pair of pleated silk poplin trousers in her present line for only $45.

Portfolio Case

Also known as a briefcase, a portfolio has soft construction rather than hard sides, and is lighter in weight than an attaché case. Portfolios usually come with handles that retract into the sides, so you can carry one as a briefcase or tuck it under your arm as a clutch. A good portfolio should have at least one zippered inner pocket for change and keys, so that you needn't carry a handbag, and an outside pocket or two is even more convenient. It should also have a detachable shoulder strap with a shoulder pad, in case you want to carry it with luggage.

Care

See ATTACHÉ CASE. Unlike the hardsided attaché, portfolios get easily bent out of shape, so if you don't use it for weeks at a time, make sure it's lying flat, or it may emerge curved like a discus. Storing it stuffed with paper helps keep the shape.

Prairie Dress

A high-necked, long-sleeved calico or gingham dress with a large ruffle around the bottom. From 1850 to 1910, Sears & Roebuck and Montgomery Ward sold them by the thousands to homesteading women of the Great Plains states. Vintage-clothes dealers get the original dresses in stock more often than you might think, though not in perfect condition, since pioneer women had only two dresses—one for work and one for church. Antique Ward and Sears dresses aren't considered as interesting as dresses handmade at home from yard-goods; they go for around $60, handmade ones for $80 up. All the old buttons are made of such natural materials as lava stone, bone, or horn.

The style looks charming on almost anyone. If you have a taste for the old-fashioned, it makes a great informal hostess dress—you're romantic and definitely non-office, yet if guests come in jeans, nobody feels inappropriately dressed. And if you have a fireplace to sit around, it's even more perfect. Folkwear sells an authentic prairie dress pattern, their biggest seller (Folkwear, Box 3798, San Rafael, California 94902). Neiman-Marcus stores sell prairie skirts with matching blouses under their own label—Red River Westernwear.

Preppy Look

According to one wit, what the fashion-un-conscious woman has been wearing for years. WASP and upper-middle class, it's called the County look in England, the Brooks Brothers or Ivy League style in the American East. Clothes are neat, under-stated, and classic. Many preppy items were worn as far back as the Eisenhower years: Shetland crew-neck sweaters, Fair Isle sweaters, madras jackets, seersucker suits, houndstooth jackets. The idea is that you make a substantial initial investment, and then wear the clothes for years. To keep up with what's selling in preppy clothes, peruse the clothing ads every week in *The New Yorker* magazine, or get on the mailing list for Brooks Brothers (see p. 30) or for Talbot's catalogue, 164 North Street, Hingham, Massachusetts 02043 (toll-free [800] 225-8200). Talbot's is a refreshing catalogue, if only because the models look nice instead of lascivious, as in so many fashion magazines, and some are even over thirty.

Prêt à Porter

(pret-ah-por-tay´) French for ready-to-wear. The English say "off the rack." Americans have never developed a similar phrase, as 99 percent of the population have always considered couture (expensive made-to-order clothes) complete foolishness; what would be "ready-to-wear" to the French are simply "clothes" to Americans.

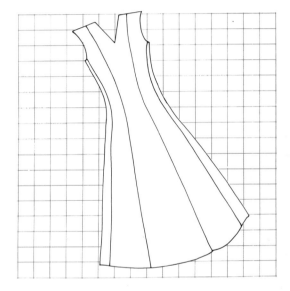

Princess Line

A flared dress style, with bodice and skirt cut out of the same piece with no waistband or belt. The nicest ones loosely follow curves of the body, flaring into a gentle A-line skirt. Probably the most flattering cut ever devised for women who need to lose twenty pounds. The style doesn't look good on thin women, who need the horizontal line of a belt or waistband. Designer Pauline Trigère is the designer most famous for princess-line dresses.

Princess Sumair

A designer headquartered in New York, though not exactly as American as apple pie. Princess Sumair was the daughter of an Indian maharaja, was brought up in a quarter-mile-long palace with 400 rooms, 3,500 downstairs servants, and fountains that flowed with gallons of French perfume. Her dresses are the most expensive in the world: an evening dress costs from $1,200 to $12,000. However, she's designed a collection of petite dresses (Princess Sumi label) for Don Sophisticates which will cost as little as $120 apiece, and can be found at stores such as Saks, Neiman-Marcus, and I. Magnin.

Pringle of Scotland

Absolutely the prestige label in cashmere sweaters. Founded in 1815, Pringle is the world's largest manufacturer of cashmere and holds the royal warrant for making Queen Elizabeth's sweaters. Of the 400,000 sweaters they turn out a year—on machinery unchanged since the dawn of the Industrial Revolution—50,000 are shipped to department stores in the U.S., where they sell for around $175 apiece. Since the sweaters last up to twenty years, and can be sent back to the factory to be reshaped after that, most people regard their Pringles as heirlooms. Pullovers and cardigan styles are untrendy to the point of boredom, so as not to detract from the thick, soft beauty of the cashmere itself. See CASHMERE.

Pucci, Emilio

(Poo´-chee) Italian designer from Florence. His silk jersey dresses printed with bright, geometric patterns were big status symbols during the 1960s. Find his little $600 silks in the designer section of department stores, where they are bought devotedly by wealthy older women. He has a boutique in New York at 24 East 65th Street.

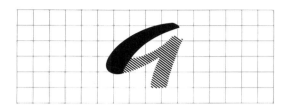

Qiana Nylon

(kee-ah´-na) is made by Du Pont, using a more complex method than for regular nylons. Though made from petroleum, gas, air, and water, it looks and feels like a high-quality silk, and doesn't wrinkle, shrink, or stretch. Top designers such as Christian Dior use it for their most luxurious $100 nightgowns. It isn't as absorbent as real silk or cotton, meaning it won't breathe as well and gets clammy on hot days, but it can be so beautiful that nobody cares. Like all nylon, it has wonderful "slippage," meaning it's among the least abrasive of fabrics against your skin.

Care

You never have to worry about Qiana water-spotting or mildewing, and, when washed, it dries in an instant. It's usually machine washable in warm, but not hot, water. However, like all nylons it easily picks up colors from other fabrics, so you may want to wash separately. Also, like all nylons, it may discolor if hung in bright sunlight.

Quilting

sandwiches materials such as down or polyester fiberfill between layers of another material, most commonly cotton poplin or a cotton and nylon blend, then stitches through all these layers to form diamond or geometric patterns. Quilting can be done very cheaply by machine, and makes the warmest possible coats, jackets, and bathrobes. As with down, the fatter a coat the warmer, and don't buy if you see a fuzzy film anywhere—stitching is loose and stuffing is escaping, which will cause lumps. Some people like their quilted fiberfill coats better than down because they're more resistant to rain and snow, and because they're not as warm as down, which sometimes provides more warmth than anyone needs or wants. Fiberfill coats are flatter and less bulky, so that you look more like a human being and less like a large puff.

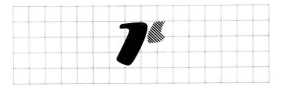

Rabbit

is the most inexpensive of all furs—you can buy a good quality full-length coat for from $300 to $600, jackets for under $200. Should you bother? Yes, says a spokesman for one of New York's busiest furriers, who does a lot of business in rabbit. "Rabbit is one of the best values in fur. Sure, it sheds some, but so does any long-haired fur such as lynx, fox, and coyote, which cost a lot more than rabbit. It's not as long-lasting as mink, but neither are the other long-haired furs. You can pay fifteen thousand dollars for a lynx coat, and if you wear it every day with a shoulder bag, it will only last a year. A mink lasts fifteen years and a rabbit five, but then a mink will cost five thousand dollars and a rabbit five hundred." Here's what you should know when shopping for rabbit:

- Don't buy the pieced skins that shopping mall stores sell for $75—their lifespans are depressingly short. The pieces not used to make a good coat are

the weakest parts, and a pieced coat is riddled with seams. Better to buy a "full skin" coat on sale.

- Look for coats that say France on the country-of-origin tag. French rabbits have been ranch-bred for fur longer than any other rabbits, and have developed a coat that is silkier and doesn't shed as much as that of rabbits of other nationalities. Also look for French rabbit that is manufactured in the U.S. Though coats made up in the Orient cost less, the skins shipped directly to America are better. Next best is Spanish, then American, which will shed quite a bit at first, but then slow way down. Chinese rabbit is most likely to keep *on* shedding.

- The more plush the fur feels, the higher its quality. Rabbit fur comes in three grades, depending on size of the rabbit when it's killed. As rabbits get bigger, the fur gets heavier, but the meat isn't as tasty, so money is lost there, making fur prices higher. No hang tags tell you what grade you're buying, but price should: the plusher coats will cost more.

Ragg Wool

A rugged, heavily textured yarn woven with two strands of colored wool and one strand of raw, undyed wool with all its natural oils and lanolin intact and in the same color as it grew on the sheep. Ragg-wool sweaters have a hearty outdoor flavor and a high-quality expensive look, but cost only $20 in camping stores. A lot of runners wear them over their running suits in midwinter 20-degree weather, find them to be windproof yet able to breathe; others wear them over cotton blouses in drafty houses and stay toasty. There's something addictive about them. Ragg-wool socks, mittens, hats are also inexpensive and warm. Boston Traders is a good label in Ragg wool, and so is Cambridge Supply.

Care

Dry clean or handwash in Woolite. Ragg wool has a wonderful earthy smell when it's wet, and emerges from its wash soft and fluffy. Be sure to dry flat—*heavy wool will stretch* if laid over the side of the bathtub.

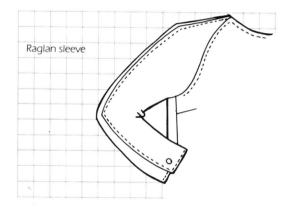

Raglan sleeve

Raglan Sleeve

A sleeve seamed diagonally from neckline to underarm, a good look for top-heavy women because it breaks the broad expanse of the chest and shoulders. Definitely a no-no for sloping or narrow shoulders, or on very thin women. Used a lot for coats because it's a comfortable and unrestricting cut. Raglan sleeves are named after Lord Raglan, the British general who led the charge of the Light Brigade in the Crimean War.

Rainwear

We need no longer splash along perspiring under rubber weighing several pounds. Water-repellent coats are now bantamweight, with fleece linings for winter,

vents and slits for ventilation in summer. Here's what's what in rainwear:

Raincoats

*   The big sensation in raincoats is Gore-Tex, the only completely waterproof fabric that breathes somewhat. (See GORE-TEX.) Other raincoats are handsome and wonderfully lightweight, but if they're truly waterproof, the vinyl or plastic waterproof finish has closed the fabric's pores, making it warm and extremely clammy to wear. So don't buy a raincoat hoping it will double as a lightweight coat for spring and fall.

*   Don't think that just because you're wearing a waterproof coat, you can go without an umbrella. With long exposure to a heavy rain, every fabric except rubber and Gore-Tex will finally get damp.

*   Know that if you buy a water-repellent coat, such as a chemically treated cotton twill trenchcoat, it won't stay water-repellent forever. Water repellency lasts through only two or three cleanings; after that it has to be reprocessed with each cleaning at a cost of $4 or $5 extra. Gore-Tex and rubberized fabrics are true raincoats, and *will* stay waterproof indefinitely.

*   That deliciously rubbery canary-yellow rainwear you sometimes see *is* rubber and is a fashion classic made by the Swedish Helly-Hansen company. The $50 full-length coat has a hood, industrial snaps, and deep pockets, and glistens in the rain. (The cast of *Jaws* wore Helly Hansens when they were fighting the shark.) Find Helly Hansen in stores that specialize in outdoorwear for the ocean, such as New York's eighty-year-old Fulton Supply Company, 23 Fulton Street.

Raincoats cited by Consumer Research as superior: Misty Harbor, London Fog.

Regular Clothes

Avoid wearing jeans outside on a wet, cold day. Because cotton absorbs water so efficiently (which is what makes it comfortable on a 90-degree summer day), it has no insulating power when wet and will rob you of body heat. *Wool* thrives on dampness, which is why it's been the national fabric of cold, rainy Britain for so many centuries. Because of the oils in lanolin, wool is mildly water repellent. When it does get wet, it doesn't feel as uncomfortable as other fabrics. "Wool is the only fiber that absorbs up to thirty percent of its weight in moisture without feeling wet," says The Wool Bureau. Peter Storm's oiled wool sweaters, found in outdoorwear stores, are super-water-resistant in foul weather, as are Icelandic wool and Ragg wool.

Footwear

Everyone should have a pair of "rubber" boots. Slush, water, and salt ruin leather, and a $20-to-$60 investment quickly pays off by saving your good footgear. Besides, it's such fun to go striding through puddles of melting slush, while others cautiously pick their way from one dry spot to another.

Except for fisherman's boots, which are made from real rubber, all rainboots are made from rubber-looking vinyl. The formula is much the same no matter who the manufacturer is, and there are no poorly sewed seams to come apart, so as far as water-repellency goes, you're just as well off buying in the cheapest shopping mall. All everyday-wear rainboots are only reasonably waterproof—if you stand a long time in water, wetness will seep through. Vinyl boots, even those lined with acrylic

fleece, don't keep out really serious cold, so buy boots roomy enough for you to wear heavy wool socks inside. They should also have a side zipper, or you'll have to have them pulled on and off as did the military men of yore (only they had valets). Most fashionable label in rainboots is Andrew Geller's. One low-cost rainboot that breathes is the New Market boot, rubber on bottom and cotton canvas on top, which sells in riding stores for $22.

For summer, buy a pair of waterproof Gore-Tex sneakers, wear high wooden clogs to lift feet out of puddles, or wear an old beat-up pair of shoes. Nobody has yet come up with the ideal summer rain shoe.

Rainhats

Probably the country's best-selling rainhat for women is the Totes hat in cotton duck, modeled after Irish walking hats. You can buy them in shopping malls and department stores for $13.

Umbrellas

(See pp. 214–215.)

Rawsilque

Trade name of Collins & Aikman for an easy-care synthetic fabric that feels and looks like raw silk.

Rayon

is a fabric not without poetry. It is not, as commonly thought, a synthetic fiber, but is made of cellulose from pine, hemlock, and spruce trees and is biodegradable. By far the oldest of "man-made" fibers, it was called artificial silk and worn at Queen Victoria's funeral in 1901. The designer who introduced its charms to the wider world and who made the fabric a big success in 1915 was the beautiful Coco Chanel. However, this aristocratic but definitely non-wash-and-wear fabric went into a nearly terminal eclipse after World War II, when people wanted the polyesters and nylons that didn't wrinkle or need ironing, and not until just recently has it made such a comeback in a new form that nobody can praise it enough. "Rayon has a warmth and lushness," says a designer at Auburn Fabrics. "I love its antique-like quality." "Rayon has a lovely fluid quality and a muted shine," says designer Evelyn De Jonge, who puts it in her knits. Ralph Lauren uses rayon to make his $460 black velvet Victorian dresses, and says Halston, "Rayon takes color so well. I like clean, clear colors and many of the Oriental dyes I use simply wouldn't work on any other fabric."

Before World War II, rayon was made by a process in which cellulose was dissolved in copper and ammonia, and spun into a lustrous thread. This relatively expensive "filament rayon," from which beautiful old rayon lingerie is made, has disappeared from the market and can only be found in antique shops. Today's more versatile and easily washable variety is made by treating wood pulp with alkali and carbon disulfide, controlling luster by introduction of pigments into the spinning. It can be made to look much like a soft cotton (cellular structure of cotton and rayon are virtually the same), can be crimped for crêpe or woollike styles, can be iridescent, may be made into velvet or velour, can even be made to look like broadtail lamb.

Trade names: Avril, Avron, Lirelle, and Zantrel are the new, higher-strength rayons that behave like cotton and may be washed and ironed without special care. Avron, Bemberg, Cupioni, Skyloft must be dry cleaned. Coloray, Cupracolor, Jetspun, Kolorbron are rayons dyed when coloring is added to the actual spinning solution, giving them exceptionally lovely colorfast colors. Viscose rayon is simply another name for rayon.

Care

Most of the newer rayons can be handwashed and ironed with a warm iron. Rayons more than three years old should be dealt with cautiously, as older rayon shrinks easily and loses shape. In other words, if you buy a rayon skirt in a resale shop, and it says Dry Clean Only, or has no cleaning directions label at all, you'd better

---

What's Good and Bad About Rayon

In addition to its versatility, the fabric is ecologically responsible. "Unlike synthetics, rayon is made from a renewable resource," says Dr. Thomas E. Muller of ITT Rayonier, Inc. "We get our cellulose from trees which grow on marginal land not suited to the production of food." Rayon absorbs moisture and breathes nearly as well as cotton, yet is a more flowing, more sensuously clingy material.

Rayon isn't nearly as strong as cotton, linen, silk, or wool, and probably shouldn't be bought for anything from which sturdy wear is desired, such as knockabout pants. It is nearly as cool as cotton, linen, or silk but not as warm as wool or acrylic. It mildews easily and, like cotton, burns easily. According to Dr. Muller, chemical flame retardants, considered carcinogenic by environmentalists who want them withdrawn from all clothes, are seldom added to rayon.

dry clean. Antique rayon, the sort from which those lovely bias-cut gowns and slips were made, can be washed in lukewarm water with Woolite or Ivory Snow; you'll have to iron before drying sets in or you'll never get all the wrinkles out. *Never iron rayon, especially antique rayon, with a hot iron*—you'll burn it irrevocably.

Redingote

A long, full princess-line coat, with no fastenings below the waist in order to show the dress beneath. The word is shortened from riding coat.

Reefer Coat

A descendant of a semifitted, double-breasted Navy jacket, today's reefer is a regular-length, double-breasted, semi-straight style (it flares slightly toward the bottom), with a half belt in back. Usually made of wool melton, sometimes with a velvet collar. A coat in impeccable, if conservative, taste for around $140.

Resale Shops

sell pristine-condition, still-in-fashion used clothes on consignment. Clothes usually go for a third their original cost, with the donor getting half of the selling price. (At thrift shops, all merchandise is *donated*, and will be accepted torn, stained, or forty years out of style.) The best resale shops make a big point of letting you know in their ads or telephone-book listings that they specialize in designer-label clothes; this means they have *some* designer labels, but *all* their clothes are high quality. Used-clothing stores without these standards sell second-hand shopping-mall or J.C. Penney-type clothes and are generally not as good as good thrift shops.

If you ask shopowners where they get the clothes they sell, they'll tell you that all their customers are wealthy, compulsive shoppers who sell their Halstons and Kleins without ever having worn them. If you sell clothes of your own, and watch other women bringing in clothes and haggling, you get the impression that most sellers are probably extremely *careful* shoppers now trying to extract every last penny from clothes they're selling for good reasons. Clothes are sold because they're perceived as out of style, or because owners have gained or lost weight, changed lifestyles, made mistakes. Most women say that no matter how careful they are, one out of every four or five purchases of clothing is a mistake. Yet, only after they've worn a new garment a few times do the mists of self-deception lift and they see that the color makes them look terminally ill, or that those gathers add thirty pounds. Happily, one woman's bad judgment is a resale customer's good luck.

Particularly Good to Buy in Resale Shops

Classic trenchcoats and raincoats that tend to look much the same year after year; cashmere sweaters; A-line and modified dirndl skirts. Fashions in skirt shapes and lengths change with whirlwind speed, and a lot of women have the uncanny habit of hanging onto a skirt until just a split second before the style comes back, then selling. Since good-quality wools and cottons last forever, it's almost silly to spend $60 for the latest-length skirt in a department store when you can get one for $20 in a resale shop. Also, with a used skirt you won't hesitate as much at surgery such as raising a hem or taking in a waistband.

To find resale stores, consult local *"Guide to . . ."* books, or look in the Yellow Pages under *Clothes Bought and Sold.* Here are some good ones around the country:

LOS ANGELES, CAL.
Stars & Debs
1251½ Vine
469-0282
(Specializes in fashions by famous Hollywood designers or worn by famous movie stars.)

Fashions Anonymous
9859 Santa Monica Boulevard
277-5337
(Open Tues., Sat. 10:30–4:00)
(Clothing from socialites.)

Patina
511 South Glendale Avenue Gin.
(1½ blocks south of Colorado)
246-7018

DENVER, COLO.
Second Look, Ltd.
2328 E. Exposition Avenue
(at University Boulevard)
777-2473

SAN FRANCISCO, CAL.
Abbe's Nearly New Apparel
1420 Clement
751-4567

PORTLAND, ORE.
Act Two
1139 Southwest Morrison
277-7969

DALLAS, TEX.
My Sister's Closet
2522 Oak Lawn
521-1675

Clotheshorse Anonymous
1413 Preston Forest Square
233-6082

WASHINGTON, D.C.
Encore of Washington
3715 Macomb NW
966-8122

CHICAGO, ILL.
Fashion Exchange Center
67 E. Oak
664-1657

LAKE FOREST, ILL.
Mais Encore
(Five cluttered rooms
bulging with designer labels)

ATLANTA, GA.
Play It Again
(Buckhead Section)

NEW YORK, N.Y.
Encore
1132 Madison (at 84th Street)
879-2850

Michael's
1041 Madison (near 78th Street)
737-7273

Reprise
14 Fifth Avenue (just above
Washington Square Park)
260-0896

Rhodes, Zandra

English designer who makes wild, colorful, playful clothes. She handscreens her own prints on soft fabrics such as silk and chiffon, but there the resemblance to most other designers ends: her clothes have made news for their pinking-shear edges, sleeves held on by chains, holes fastened with jeweled safety pins. She loves to adorn her squiggly-patterned silks with pearls and pompoms. Somehow, all this whimsicality hangs together, and stores such as Bloomingdale's and Bendel's sell Rhodes dresses for $1,500 apiece.

Rib Knit

A stretchy fabric of wool, cotton, or synthetics, with small but pronounced vertical ridges. Very comfortable, because, like all stretch clothes, it moves with the body.

Ricci, Nina

(Ree-chee) French designer, born in Turin, Italy. She came to Paris in 1896, at age thirteen, to work as a seamstress. A rags-to-riches success, by 1932 she had opened a couture house, making quiet, graceful clothes known for exquisite workmanship. She died in 1970, and the business is now run by her son Robert; the head designer is Gerard Pipart. Nina Ricci is best known in America for its famous perfumes, such as "L'Air du Temps," sold in all good department stores.

Rubber

is obtained by heating the milky juices of tropical rubber plants, and is the most waterproof substance in the world. However, except for fisherman's boots, most "rubber" footgear is vinyl. See RAINWEAR.

Ruching

(roosh-ing) An edging of finely gathered or pleated lace for collars or cuffs. In his recent fall collection, Gerard Pipart of Nina Ricci put rows and rows of ruching—160 yards—on a taffeta dress.

Running Clothes

One of the nicest things about running is how comfortably people dress when they're doing it. Designers such as Adri and Liz Claiborne have even been copying the look for their fashion collections. Here's what to wear:

Summer Pull-on shorts with an elastic waistband, over a 100-percent cotton T-shirt. You may have to shop determinedly to find a T-shirt that's not a polyester blend, but on a 90-degree day, when you're sweating profusely, you'll be glad you took the extra trouble. Cotton has "moisture transport." Its little spongelike cells absorb sweat and allow it to evaporate; some athletes think they're cooler running in a light cotton T-shirt than in nothing at all, because cotton transports perspiration, whereas with nothing, it just lies there. Be sure to wear cotton panties (Dixie Bell, sold in ten-cent stores and shopping malls, is a terrific brand). Nylon lingerie, no matter how beautiful, is nonabsorbent and will stick to you. Low-cut cotton socks are considered most comfortable by many runners; others want the more fleecy, cushiony synthetic-fiber socks. Resist those luscious, dark-colored Fruit-of-the-Loom T-shirts for summertime running—dark blue, purple, brown, black, even gray absorb heat; white and light pastels reflect the sun's rays. If you're running after sundown, color doesn't matter, unless, of course, you're trotting alongside one of those sidewalkless suburban roads at twilight, in which case you'd best wear white so you'll be seen by bleary-eyed commuters on their way home. Better yet, wear large, lightweight, bicycle-type reflectors over your shirt. These are now generally available at sporting-goods stores.

Fall and Spring A 100-percent cotton velour running suit is ideal (and though scarce, they do exist). Geoffrey Beene makes such suits, as does Holmes, James, for from $80 to $100—expensive, but worth every penny. *Important:* get either straight-leg pants or the kind with zippers at bottom, and a zipped cardigan top rather than a pullover, so that you can get them off without stopping to pull and tug. If your pants have elasticized cuffs, you'll have to take your *shoes* off to get them off. The whole point of fall and spring gear is to be able to easily add or subtract layers, to account for variable temperatures and conditions. Wear shorts as much as you can, since the sun on your bare legs will help your body produce Vitamin D.

Winter What's important is to keep head and torso warm, as your body sends these areas extra heat, should they need it, at the expense of fingers and toes. Wear a wool pullover hat on your head, layers elsewhere. One heavy thick jacket would be *awful*—cumbersome and not nearly as warm as layers of light fabrics, which trap dead air between them. Wear absorbent cotton T-shirts on the inside to prevent sweat from accumulating; soft, chafeless merino wool on the outside. Protogs (55 Ludy Street, Hicksville, New York 11805 [516] 935-8830) makes a gorgeous wool warm-up pant and top for $86. However, if you're not financially solvent enough for a running suit for each season, next best thing is your cotton velour suit with light thermal pants and several cotton T-shirts underneath, with a heavy wool sweater, such as Ragg wool, on top. Old stained or damaged cashmere sweaters—warm, light, ventilated, and nonabrasive—make terrific winter running gear. Ditto—for an insulating underlayer—an old silk blouse with the sleeves cut off. For your fingers, try cotton garden gloves for mild winter days. For really cold weather, wool gloves are better than leather or acrylic, mittens warmer than gloves because you can curl up your fingers and keep them together. If you don't want to buy mittens just for running, wear heavy woolen socks over your hands.

Care

One-hundred-percent cotton suits will shrink a little when you first wash them in lukewarm water; should you wash them in hot water, they'll shrink a lot. *Don't* wash them in hot water. Never leave sweat-dampened cotton running gear wadded up somewhere—it will mildew, and nasty black and yellow spots will form a few days or even a week or so later. If you don't have time to wash immediately, hang the clothes over a shower rod to dry out.

Rykiel, Sonia

(ri-kel′) French ready-to-wear designer, known for her knits, interestingly stark yet soft, geometric yet feminine. "My clothes are for women like me, who have an androgynous sexuality and who like to stride in pants, hands deep in their pockets," she has said. Her pants, skirts, and famous long, long cardigan sweaters cost $400–$600 for an outfit.

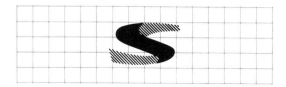

Sachs, Gloria

American designer. An artist who worked as a painter, sculptor, and handweaver before getting into fashion, she's been getting a lot of attention for her romantic wool suits with velvet trimming, which cost around $400.

Saddle Oxford

A white buckskin shoe with a saddle of black or brown leather across the top and a three-eyelet lacing down the center. Very comfortable, it has a low broad heel and large round toe, and has been worn by both adults and children since about 1910. Adorable with A-line woolen skirts and tweedy brown stockings. Looks a little mannish with slacks, but is a terrific walking shoe.

Sonia Rykiel is famous for her long cardigans and angular designs. (Photo: Dominique Isserman)

Safari Jacket

(also called a bush jacket) One of the first unisex items, the safari jacket has been a stock item in nearly everybody's wardrobe ever since Jacqueline Kennedy was photographed in one for the cover of *Life* magazine in the mid-1960s, when she was in Africa riding an elephant. These tailored jackets evolved in the late nineteenth century to fulfill the sartorial needs of African adventurers—a light, water-repellent corduroy or cotton in case of a sudden tropical thunderstorm, always furnished with four deep pockets to be used for shells or camera equipment. "They're the most useful garment ever made for safaris," says one anthropologist who regularly treks into the bush. "Unfortunately, now that all the tourists on buses are wearing them, nobody going on a real safari wants to be caught in one." Abercrombie and Fitch (P.O. Box 18211, Houston, Texas 77023; toll-free 800 228-5585) has sold the same bush jacket since the turn of the century, outfitting hunters going everywhere from the Australian Outback to Kenyan elephant preserves. Their jacket ($80) is the most authentic in the country. Army-navy stores and oriental import stores sell imitations for $20 or $30, and all hunting stores have a rack of them somewhere among their stuffed animal heads and photos of charging rhinos.

If you're going to bother buying one, better to spend more and get a good, sturdy cotton such as the one in Abercrombie's. The lighter, inexpensive ones wrinkle badly and curl around the edges, losing the crisp tailoring that makes the jacket distinctive.

Sailcloth

A strong, firmly woven cotton canvas. When it's used for clothes, such as jackets or pants, it's usually called duck (see p. 69).

The original American safari jacket was (and still is) made by Abercrombie & Fitch.®

Sales

Not all sale merchandise has something mysteriously wrong with it. All stores have new clothes coming in constantly, and limited space in which to put them; items that haven't yet been sold have to go, and the store's desperation is the customer's gain. Winter clothes are first marked down around Thanksgiving, with best bargains coming hot and fast between Christmas and New Year's, just when nobody has any money. Summer merchandise goes on sale around the end of June, and by July 4 is down to half price. *Why* don't things sell? Sometimes they've gone out of fashion with lightning speed, but other times they're ahead of the trend and the average customer isn't ready for them yet. Often, the most exciting clothes don't sell well at first, then catch on. Probably the most common reason for things to go on sale is simply that the stores overestimated and

Fernando Sanchez, known for sexy nightgowns, creates a lovely toga gown.

bought too much of one style. A few tips for sale shopping:

- Sale stuff marked "store-wide clearance" or simply "sale" is usually the best merchandise. "Special purchase" tends to mean the clothes were bought especially to be sold at a discount.

- Boutiques are usually about a month behind department stores on starting their sales. About the time all the good stuff has vanished from the big stores, you can find wonderful things in small ones.

- If you make a terrible mistake on something marked "final sale," you can usually take it back anyway if you're determined enough. Say you didn't realize that it was a final sale—somebody should have informed you—and don't budge.

Salt and Pepper Tweed

A tweed woven entirely of black and white yarns.

Sanchez, Fernando

is considered an American designer, though he was born in Spain and worked for years for Christian Dior in Paris. He's most celebrated for his lingerie. He is credited with having rescued lingerie from the doldrums and made it fashion; for years his was the only exciting name in the field. "I design for the woman who dresses to celebrate her femininity," he says. "Women's liberation has served to negate our erotic sides. The customer I design for would never want to deny her sensual nature." He made his lingerie from lace, maribou feathers, and satin, and won two Coty awards for it. (He's also won one for his furs.) Look for his glamorous, flowing wrap bathrobes ($120) and for his unique lounging clothes, so versatile that some garments can be worn for sleeping or hostessing or as underwear.

Sanforized

This trademark on a label is a guarantee that a cotton fabric won't shrink more than 1 percent. The cotton is pre-shrunk by a machine licensed by the Sanforized Company.

Sant'Angelo, Giorgio

American designer, though he started life in Italy as a count. In 1962 he came to the United States to work as an animator for Walt Disney. Trained as a graphic artist, he got into designing fabrics and jewelry and finally dresses. He's definitely on the side of the romantics in the eternal classicist/romantic conflict: he won a Coty Award for his swingy dresses lavished with Indian beadwork, another for his gypsy clothes of the early 1970s. Today he's doing stretchknits with a Victorian look and, saying he wants to dress the working woman in the 1980s, has lowered his prices. One best-selling chemise dress sells for only $120. Look for his beaded evening sweaters and lacy evening leotards.

Santora

Trade name for a soft polyester jersey by Klopman that doesn't pill or fuzz.

Santos Watch

This futuristic-looking watch is not only the most contemporary of status symbols, it's the oldest wristwatch. The Santos watch was fashioned in 1904 by jeweler Louis Cartier for his pioneer aviator friend, Alberto Santos-Dumont, who complained that while he was up in his balloon,

Giorgio Sant'Angelo likes to do stretchy leotards with matching skirts and embroider them with American Indian beadwork. (Courtesy of Giorgio Sant'Angelo)

he couldn't divert attention from flying to dig into his pocket for his watch. Cartier made him a small watch with an easy-to-read face and put a harness strap on it to fit Dumont's wrist—the first wristwatch. Except for a more modernistic strap, the watch is designed exactly the same today—at least on its exterior. Inside, of course, hums the very latest in watch interiors, and, besides impressing people, the Santos is shockproof, waterproof, and fully automatic, and you can buy one for from $1,050 (steel) to $9,950 (gold) in any good department store. It's a sportswatch and will look terrific with anything except evening clothes.

Tank

Santos

The first wristwatch was the Santos watch. This Cartier watch, along with the Cartier tank and the Rolex, are the great status-symbol sport watches.

Rolex

Sarape

A large, fringed shawl worn by Indian women of South America and Mexico for centuries—the colorful printed patterns are clearly Aztec designs. Find in import shops, and wear them for summer wraps.

Sarong

A rectangular piece of brightly printed cloth tucked in or tied on one hip and worn as a skirt. Sarongs were worn by both sexes on the Malay peninsula, and caught on here in the 1930s when Dorothy Lamour wore them in *The Jungle Princess*. A nice look for the beach with a matching swimsuit. Looks good on slender figures only.

Satin

has probably suffered the worst reversal of fortune of any fabric. Used for thick, quilted baseball jackets as well as for thin, filmy lingerie today, in former years it was worn exclusively at balls given by queens, to dinner at the Ritz, and for every candle-lit evening by the most beautiful actresses of the 1930s—a period considered the most

fabulous for clothes in all of motion pictures. Satin is a type of weave (the weave has more warps than fillings on the surface, which accounts for the shine), and can be woven from silk, rayon, cotton, or synthetics such as polyester into different thicknesses. It has a glossy front and a dull back. Different types of satin are:

Crêpe-backed satin The dull side is crêpe, and this reversible fabric can be used on either side.

Double-faced satin is glossy and light-reflecting on both sides instead of just one.

Duchess satin The rich, heavy satin used in wedding gowns.

Slipper satin Lightweight evening-shoe satin.

Sateen A satin made from cotton, durable and heavy.

The most expensive satin is made from silk, with rayon the next most desirable fiber. Synthetics can also be lovely. One of the most beautiful silk satins being sold today is Eve Stillman's peach-colored nightgown ($110).

Who can wear it The thin, as usual. Because it reflects light, satin makes you look larger than you are.

Care
Usually dry clean silk or rayon; synthetic satin is often machine washable. If you press between wearings, iron on the wrong side. Use a dry iron—satin watermarks easily, and steam irons drip.

Sarongs were launched by Dorothy Lamour in **The Jungle Princess**. (Courtesy of The Museum of Modern Art/Film Stills Archive)

Saxony Wool

A heavy, napped, fine-quality merino wool used for coats. The weave comes from Saxony, Germany.

Scaasi, Arnold

American couture designer named Arnold Isaacs, who has always spelled his last name backward. He won a Coty Award in 1958, when he was only twenty-seven, and is known for both his custom-made tailored suits and his made-to-order evening clothes. He's a big pet of actresses past the first bloom of youth, such as Zsa Zsa Gabor and Lauren Bacall.

Scarves

can draw attention to your face and away from out-of-control poundage below, can make you look thinner, and will add color where badly needed. A full-length suit of glorious red can be somewhat overwhelming, but a tan suit with a red scarf will be subdued and elegant, yet add color to your face. An oblong is the most versatile

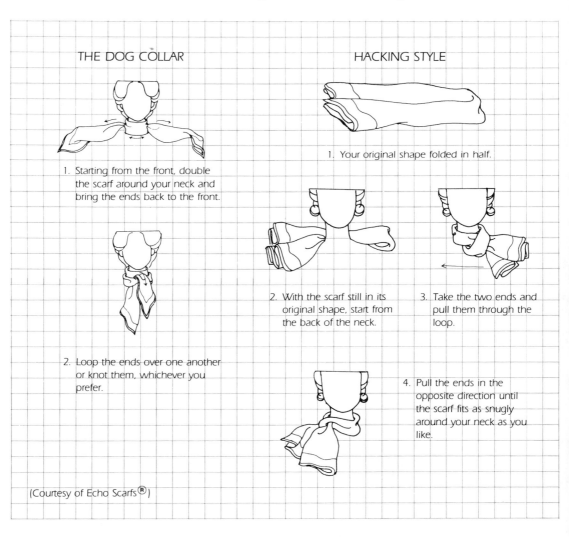

THE DOG COLLAR

1. Starting from the front, double the scarf around your neck and bring the ends back to the front.

2. Loop the ends over one another or knot them, whichever you prefer.

HACKING STYLE

1. Your original shape folded in half.

2. With the scarf still in its original shape, start from the back of the neck.

3. Take the two ends and pull them through the loop.

4. Pull the ends in the opposite direction until the scarf fits as snugly around your neck as you like.

(Courtesy of Echo Scarfs®)

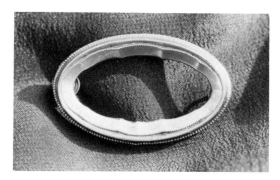

Old circle pins from the 1950s, a few dollars in antique stores, are terrific to pull scarves through.

shape; "handrolled" scarves (hand-hemmed) hang best. Here are some ways to wear them:

- Tie one in a big, droopy bow at your throat.
- Let one hang loose down the sides of your blazer or coat.
- Use as a sash at your waist, providing you have the sort of waist that merits attention.

- Wear cowboy style, folding a smallish square scarf into a triangle, then tying the ends in back with the point of the triangle hanging in front. Looks good with V-neck or scoop-neck sweaters.
- Tie high on your neck like a choker, a nice horizontal effect for long thin necks or faces.
- Tie loosely about six inches below the neck, which makes an oval that has, like a long strand of beads, slimming vertical lines.
- Tie an ascot (see p. 12).
- Do a "double dog-collar" (good for long, thin necks).
- Wear the scarf hacking style.

Scholl's Exercise Sandals

Probably every teenager in the country has Scholl's sandals with the sculptured beechwood sole. No shoe—but *no* shoe—looks better on a pair of good legs in shorts. First available in Sweden, home

Millions have become addicted to the muscle toning given feet and legs merely by walking in a Scholls Exercise Sandal.®

country of the now-international Scholl company, the shoe was introduced here fourteen years ago. Referred to as "My Scholl's" by millions, the sandal has a single adjustable strap on top in shades such as Chicken Bone, Blue, and Chocolate Brown, and the wooden sole has a raised toe-gripper bar that lets you work out while you walk. Here's the way Scholl's advises walking in your sandals:

1. Raise your heel as you step forward.
2. Grip crest with your toes, bringing sandal up against the foot with a gentle slap.
3. Relax toes as you step down and rest your weight on the sandal.

Walking in these shoes flexes the toes and anterior and posterior muscles of the calf and arches the foot, all of which tones all sorts of muscles without effort. Don't expect to step into a new pair and wear them on a long walk—you'll get blisters. Scholl's sandals have to be lovingly broken in by wearing a little longer every day. Once the sandals have been broken in, people don't like to take them off. "I love walking on just plain wood," is the comment one hears the most.

Scholl's sandals cost $17, and can be found in chain drugstores from April through July. Buy early—they tend to vanish by late summer. To find the purveyor of Scholl's nearest you, write Scholl, Inc., 213 West Schiller Street, Chicago, Illinois 60610.

Scoop Neck

Because of its lengthening effect and gentle vertical lines, this neckline is probably the most flattering of all to anyone who has a wide face and/or a short neck and/or a large bust. It's probably the most disastrous of all styles to someone with a long, somewhat horsey face and/or long neck and/or no bust. It's a simple, elegant sweater neckline for those who can wear the style.

Scroop

The pleasant rustle made by skirt fabrics such as taffetas or satins. For centuries men have been charmed by the sound of rustling skirts.

Sea Island Cotton

A lustrous, fine cotton considered the world's best for shirts. See COTTON.

Seersucker

A cotton or rayon fabric that you don't have to iron because the pucker is woven in. Loose warp yarns are alternated with

Scoop neck

tight warp yarns; when filling thread is woven in, loose yarns pucker. Seersucker was the most popular fabric for summer suits in the 1930s. Anyone who grew up in the South will forever connect the fabric with country lawyers. Brooks Brothers sells classic seersucker suits for both sexes, as it has for fifty years.

Sequin

Small, sparkly plastic disc sewed on for decoration. "Sequin" is a Venetian word derived from zequin, the gold coin of pre-Renaissance Italy. Whereas bugle beads are usually glass, both washable and dry-cleanable, washing or dry cleaning clothes with sequins should be approached with much caution. See BEADED CLOTHES.

Serge

Detectives of the 1930s and 1940s all wore serge suits. Serge is a sturdy woolen woven with a diagonal rib on both sides, still used for suits and coats.

Sharkskin

Unless specifically called sharkskin *leather*, which is rare, sharkskin is the unlikely name for a lustrous, medium-weight summer fabric made of rayon, acetate, or triacetate. Permanently pleated white skirts are traditionally made of sharkskin.

Shawl

A large rectangular or triangular scarf, made from a soft, crushable fabric such as cashmere, silk, or wool challis, and often bordered in fringe. Paying $25 to $60 for a luscious challis, paisley, or plaid shawl by YSL, Kenzo, or Anne Klein isn't such a terrible extravagance because you can do so much with them. Here are a few suggestions:

- Throw one over your coat. Ever since *Annie Hall*, everyone has been wearing large wool shawls over coats, a sensible idea because an extra layer of fabric provides a thermal effect and keeps you warmer. A light wool coat with a sweater or two underneath and a shawl on top is as warm as a heavy, single-layer coat of fur or down.

- Out-of-style suits can be revived with shawls. If lapels are too wide or otherwise funny-looking, you can often turn the collar up, mandarin style, button it all the way to the top, and throw a shawl over it. Or you can simply tie the shawl in a big graceful knot in front, hiding the lapel. Even on suits perfectly in style, a wool shawl can add an extra layer of warmth, which means you can avoid wearing a coat.

- A white wool shawl is indispensable for summer evenings—so much more graceful than a collegiate-looking sweater. You never know when air conditioners in restaurants or movie theaters will be laboring overtime.

- Women who are too thin to wear sweaters prettily can get away with them if a shawl is tied over the sweater. Since shawls add bulk, thin women look better in them in general than top-heavy women.

- Tie them around your waist, as Bette Midler does, for a dashing gypsy look. Of course, you'd need narrow hips, as Bette Midler has.

Shawl Collar

should really be called a "bathrobe" collar, as it was inspired by the common chenille bathrobe of the 1940s. What's important about this collar, so commonly found on wraparound dresses and tie-coats, is that

Shawl collar

you get vertical lines all the way from neck to waist and a deep elongating V-neck on top—on top-heavy or overweight women, this is flattering. Thin, small-bosomed women tend to look like children dressing up in their mother's clothes when wearing this style.

Shearling

A lambskin, tanned with the downy wool left on. The leather side is sueded and worn outside, while the wool side is usually sheared and is as soft and plush as sheared beaver; other times the wool is left curly. Because there's no synthetic lining and the coat is natural through-and-through,

shearling breathes more than almost any other kind of coat. (That's one reason shearlings and sheepskins have been favored by hard-working cowboys and ranchers ever since the days of Old Dodge City.) A sheepskin and a shearling differ from each other only in that a shearling pelt is always from a lamb that's never been sheared, while a sheepskin is from an older animal and isn't as soft. Shearlings are made into coats, vests, slippers, gloves.

The most celebrated shearlings are made by the French Creek Sheep and Wool Company (Elverson, Pennsylvania 19520). Owned by rugged-looking, bearded Eric Flaxenburg and his wife, Jean, the business is run mostly by mail from an eighteenth-century farm deep in Pennsylvania Dutch country. One seamstress sews an entire coat and signs it, a job taking eight hours. Prices are high (around $700 for a full-length coat) but few of the annual production of 3,000 coats go unsold. "I could earn a lot more money making cheaper coats," says Flaxenburg. "But I don't want to. I keep telling myself 'psychological income' is worth a great deal."

When shopping for a shearling, look for: soft, soft leather; even shearing; matching pelts; a guarantee that the coat won't waterspot. Not all dry cleaners can deal with shearlings, so get the address of somebody who can. Expect to pay $25 to get one cleaned; darker shades stay clean longer than the lovely dapple colors. To get out spots or dinginess, rub with fine sandpaper or flint, and then brush lightly with a suede brush.

Shetland Wool

was originally wool from sheep raised on the Shetland Islands off the coast of Scotland. Shetland sweaters were woven in peasant homes, where they'd pick up domestic odors such as smoked herring and

American ranchers have always worn shearlings while they were corralling horses. For urbanites, a vest allows arms freedom of movement on cool, busy days or while riding or skiing. (Courtesy of French Creek Sheep and Wool Co.)

corned beef and cabbage; on rainy days sweaters would have a faint odor of the same substances. These problems were solved and Shetland sweaters were then introduced in the U.S. in 1904 by Brooks Brothers, whose Shetlands are still knitted in Scotland. Today, any wool yarn that looks like Shetland is called Shetland. Crew-neck sweaters, worn outside shirts, are traditionally made from Shetland wool. Since it's not the softest of wools, is even somewhat scratchy, better to buy your turtlenecks in angora and lambswool and your crew necks in Shetlands. You can find them for $15 in the boy's department of department stores.

Shevelva

A polyester fabric that looks and feels like velvet but is machine washable and wrinkle-resistant. Vanity Fair uses it for robes.

Shirring

Decorative gathering, a "dressmaker's detail." Most tailored blouses are softly shirred in front, just below the shoulders; smock dresses are shirred at the yoke.

Shirtwaist

Besides being one of the most slimming styles around, a shirtwaist should be worn out of pure patriotism. The style evolved not from nineteenth-century Paris, which was busy designing elaborate dresses with bustles, but on the American frontier, where women found that you simply couldn't do a day's work in a woman's dress. In order to cut wood or hoe potatoes, pioneer women tucked men's shirts into the waistbands of their skirts. The style gradually evolved into a women's blouse and separate skirt, and from there into the shirtmaker blouse and separate skirt worn by the secretaries and typists who first flocked into offices after the typewriter was invented. Gradually, the shirtwaist blouse and separate skirt merged into the one-piece dress still considered ideal office wear.

Since a shirtwaist provides one continuous line, it's a good style for the plump or hippy woman. A belt covered in the dress material is best so as not to break the vertical line with a horizontal one at the waist; buttons all the way down front are also slenderizing. An A-line is a flattering skirt cut, or a modified dirndl—nothing baggy around the hips. Shirtwaists with elasticized waists aren't as flattering (or as well-made) as dresses with a waistband or seam. Since a waistband fits only one size, while a stretchy elasticized waist fits three sizes, manufacturers like to sacrifice quality for a better chance to sell dresses.

Shoes

Besides keeping our feet warm and protected from hard rocks, shoes relay all sorts of nonverbal messages. The way we dress our feet proclaims whether we want to be thought of as sexual or sensible, young-minded or sober, elegant or the sort of person who values comfort. Before looking at how to buy and take care of shoes, let's take a quick look at the three main shoe styles most of us wear, and consider what those shoes are saying.

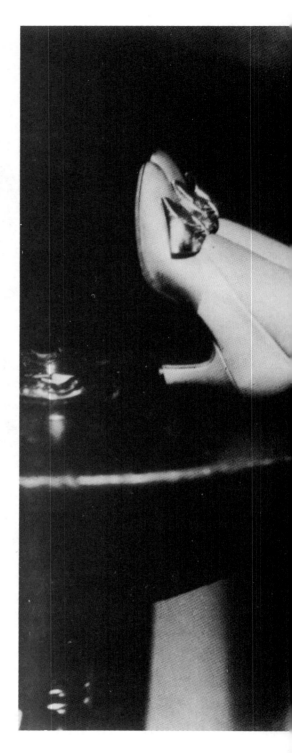

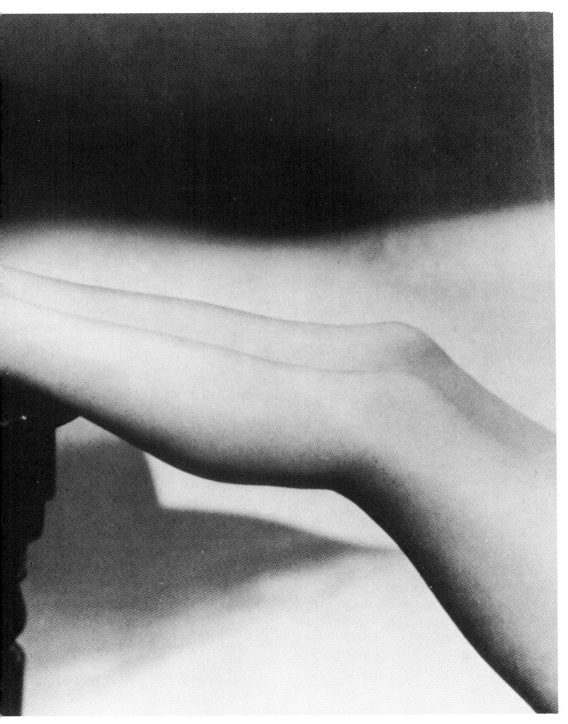

Somehow, a pair of new shoes makes any woman feel pampered, feminine, and sexy. (Courtesy of Manolo Blahnik)

SEXY SHOES. Do you have a closetful of impossible, perilously high heels consisting of little else but heel, sole, and a tiny strap or two? When you wear this kind of shoe you're saying that being noticed as a sexy woman is more important to you than health and comfort. Women have worn heels for 2,000 years, even though they cause bunions, muscle aches, impaired circulation, calluses on the ball of the foot, corns, and other ills, because few items of clothing have more clout in the business of attracting the male eye than do high-heeled shoes. The secret of this awful fashion is that heels make the female *walk* sexier. Heels set the lower torso, which happens to contain most female erogenous zones, into gently rolling motion, at the same time throwing the spine into an "S" shape emphasizing breasts and buttocks. (Men can't reciprocate this sort of erotic walk in heels—in cowboy boots, for example—because the male pelvis doesn't have the same sort of joints. Their roll is in the shoulders, a nonerogenous zone.) High heels also make thick ankles look thinner, skinny calves swell, bulging calves more slender, wide hips more narrow. If you prefer vanity to health, and want to buy the sexiest possible shoes, look for:

- *Bareness* Since most male feet are large, stubby, and hairy, when a man wants to look his best he makes sure his feet are deeply encased in leather. Since women's feet tend to be long, slender, and have high graceful arches, *our* feet are appealing enough to bare—a basic difference often serving to remind a man, at just the right moment, that he's male and you're female.

- *Delicate design* The shoe should give a *light* effect. Heavy stacked wooden heels and broad, round toes are far more comfortable but are associated with dowagers and problem feet. Heels don't have to tower or be thin as knitting needles, but they must blend into the shoe gracefully. If the shoe is of a covered-up design, such as a T-strap or slingback, long pointed toes mean the prettiest foot—round or square toes make feet and legs look chunkier.

- *Sensuous materials* The softer a shoe, the sexier. A supple kid is sexier than patent leather or vinyl; calfskin, a soft suede, satin are all materials people like to touch and stroke. A sturdy mocha brown is fine for daytime walking shoes, but for evening, *color* is more titillating to the senses—gold lamé, pale pink, amethyst, the gleaming metallic hues based on automobile colors. Whatever shoes are made of, they must fit perfectly—the merest suggestion of a gap or flapping heel detracts from the second-skin look necessary for sex appeal.

RESPECT-ME SHOES. If your closet brims with low-heeled shoes having covered-up semirounded toes, your interest is probably in saying, "I want esteem and respect." A pump would deliver such a message, and certain types of loafers, such as the classic Gucci loafer with the single gold tassel. These shoes are neither sexy nor sexless, often having simple lines that can be elegant and attractive. They're definitely right for officewear, when you do *not* want your shoes to detract from your authority as a businesswoman. Just as a man may view a woman in a tight skirt or décolletage neckline as more of a sex kitten than someone to be taken seriously, he is likely to see a woman in high lavender mules the same way.

ANTI-FASHION SHOES. The fastest-growing category of women's shoes today is neither high strappy sandals nor sedate pumps, but unsexy, mannish shoes with roomy, rounded toes. Running shoes, Timberland boots, lace-up oxfords, clogs, Top-Sider deck sneakers—all are being gobbled up and worn with enthusiasm, not only on hiking trails and jogging tracks but on city streets with pants and sweaters, even with *skirts* and sweaters. This type of shoe has no sex appeal whatever, and formerly was worn only by athletes, hardworking farmwives, or women of no-nonsense religious organizations such as the Amish or Mennonites. So why are so many women happily flouting fashion right now? "We've gotten smarter," says Clara Pierre, author of a book on the psychology of clothes called *Looking Good.* "We used to know only that high heels hurt, and suspected it was because our own problem feet were letting us down. Today we know so many more devastating facts about what heels do to our health that women are refusing to wear them any more than they have to. They're opting for the healthiest shoes, the ones doctors and podiatrists have been helping design, invariably the more roomy ones." Sociologist Anne Weber agrees. "The trend toward saner shoes reflects a new confidence that we can attract and hold men by other means than crippling ourselves to look provocative," she says.

Obviously, every kind of shoe has its assets and liabilities, and most of us want some of all three categories. Some desire shoes—any kind of shoes—so badly that they become shoe *addicts.* "We occasionally treat women who spend compulsively on shoes," says Dr. Barry Lubetkin of New York's Institute for Behavior Therapy. "Most of the true shoe addicts I've seen

were women who were ashamed of their bodies and faces, but who had nice legs. That way they could preen before a mirror without having to confront the parts of themselves they hated."

Most of us are not shoe addicts but slightly wistful consumers who'd like to buy only as many shoes as we can afford. Many of us are convinced, like former *Vogue* editor Diana Vreeland, that the first place to put clothes money is into shoes. You can tell a woman is well dressed more by her shoes than by her clothes. If you want to have well-dressed feet but are on a budget, you want to make no mistakes. Here's how to buy a pair of shoes.

- Never be complacent about knowing your size. Many customers think they wear a smaller shoe than they actually do, a misconception arising not out of vanity but out of the little-realized fact that most people's shoe size gets larger as they grow older. "The whole body gets larger," says Dr. Charles Glazer, president of the Podiatry Society of the State of New York. "The woman who can wear a size eight when she's twenty years old isn't too surprised when she's moved up to a ten by age thirty, but it never occurs to her that her shoe size may change too." Also, runners report that lots of pounding the track makes your feet "spread." Most doctors say it's not your feet that change, but your idea of what makes a comfortable shoe—at any rate, people who take up running often find themselves buying regular shoes a size larger.

- To buy the most healthful possible shoe, advises Dr. Myles J. Schneider, co-author of the book *How to Doctor Your Feet Without the Doctor* (Running Times, 1980), look for the softest, lightest shoe with a low heel. Leather, which is the material most like human skin, is the best choice. Synthetics, often labeled "upper of man-made materials," are the worst. Don't buy heels higher than one and a half inches, and make sure soles are flat. Some high-heeled women's shoes have soles rounded on the bottom, which makes your foot roll in and out. As for fit, you should have a finger's width of space between the end of your longest toe and end of the shoe, and shoes should be wide enough so that you can pinch the leather on the sides. The back of the shoe should fit and not slip when you walk.

- Shop for shoes after you've been on your feet awhile. Any shoe is likely to feel okay while your feet are fresh—the test is how they feel to slightly battered feet.

- Ask your salespeople what their most comfortable shoe is—they always know. Often one or two styles are so superior that customers come back raving and want to buy them in other colors.

- If one size is just faintly too small and the next is just a little too large, and you're determined to buy the shoes, always choose the slightly larger pair. Contrary to what salesmen say, shoes do *not* "give" as you walk in them—your feet "give" first.

- Try to shop in stores that display some measure of generosity in letting you return shoes, as it's amazing how different new shoes can feel once you get home. Certainly shoe stores are pleasant places to linger and ponder in these days—gone are drafty hole-in-the-wall shops with their wooden-slatted chairs;

today's purveyors of shoes try to outdo one another in opulence. While making your choice, you can sink into goose-down settees surrounded by palms and twenty-foot mirrors, as in Hollywood's Right Bank Shoe Co., or wander among French country antiques and a fully equipped bar, as in The Shoe Connection, Woodland Hills, California, or you can enjoy Italian sensuality while trying on silver-trimmed lizard slingbacks under a florid fifteen-foot-high mural of cherubs, satyrs, and nude angels at LaMarca in New York.

- Once you've bought your shoes, wear them madly. You can hang onto many clothes for years, but shoe silhouettes change subtly about every two years, and the heel or toe shape so chic (and so expensive) today will make you look dowdy tomorrow.

Snob labels in shoes Maude Frizon, Pasquali, Mario Valentino, Salvatore Ferragamo, Manolo Blahnik, Charles Jourdan, Bruno Magli. The Italians are considered the world's most skillful shoemakers. Though a few American designers, such as Susan Bennis and Warren Edwards, David Evins, and Joan and David, turn out shoes as elegant as the Italians', American shoes in general tend to be clunkier, wider, and much cheaper. Beene Bag, Bass, Gallen-Kamp are inexpensive but less chic.

Health shoes An entirely new kind of shoe is beginning to sell alongside the narrow and murderous shoe fashions we all love to look at but hate to wear. These shoes are shaped more as feet are shaped, tending to be as much as a half inch wider than department-store shoes of the same size, and made of leathers that are softer and more pliable. Many of these "health" shoe merchants do a mail-order business, and supply measurement instructions that will reveal your shoe size more accurately than regular store measuring techniques. A few addresses are:

The Cordwainer Shop
Wild Orchard Farms
Deerfield, N.H. 03037
(603) 463-7742

(Handmade shoes custom-designed around the individual foot; fit is guaranteed, there's a warranty on service, and the shoes can be rebuilt when they wear out. $110–$185.)

Birkenstock Shoes
c/o Impressionistic
462 Avenue of the Americas
New York, N.Y. 10011
(212) 243-7918

(Futuristic-looking German sandals and clogs designed to recreate the experience of walking barefoot, cost around $50. Birkenstock dealers can often be found near big college campuses.)

Shakti Corporation
1743 Whitewood Lane
Herndon, Va. 22070
(703) 437-0404

(These flat, custom-designed shoes have a cork-and-latex footbed that molds to your foot, and roomy leather tops guaranteed not to cramp toes. Boots and lace-up walking shoes are $40–$65, sandals $30–$40.)

Care

To spend three times as much money as you should on a pair of shoes wouldn't be so frightening if you knew how to make them last long enough for the investment to pay off. Here, professionals tell how to take care of shoes. (Special thanks to George Kourakos of Chris Shoe Repair, Riverdale, New York.)

- To protect brand-new shoes, the best product is Meltonian's Water and Stain Protector, which will keep shoes from getting salt-water marks should you get caught in light rain or snow. You have to wipe the salt off with a damp rag as soon as you get home; otherwise it will eat through the light coat of protection. Also, you must reapply it every couple of weeks, because any product will dry out after a time. As for a way to protect shoes from scuffs, no such miracle product exists.

- When shoes get drenched in the rain, take a sponge and wet the entire shoe when you get home. If only half is wet, you're going to get a water line. Rub on a little Lexol, if you like, and then allow the shoes to dry naturally, well away from fires, stoves, or radiators. Drying leather too fast causes it to stiffen and crack. When the shoes are just about dry, apply another thin coat of Lexol.

- If you get salt stains on your shoes, you can remove the curvy white lines but not the water stain—part of the shoe will always be irreversibly discolored and puckered. To take out the white lines, buy a bottle of Salt Stain Remover from the shoe store, or you can wipe the shoes with a mixture of vinegar and water (about a tablespoon of vinegar to a fourth of a cup of water) to neutralize the salt. Either way, several applications will probably be needed.

- You can do as good a job polishing your shoes as a shoeshine man, and can buy the same products he uses in the shop. Don't use saddle soap on fine leather—it was developed for rugged leather such as saddles and heavy work boots. Use a cream cleaner for spots, or try rubbing a little harder with your polish. Finish off with Lexol.

What a shoe-repair shop *can* do that you can't is "redress" shoes, which means the leather is stripped of all old polish and tanning glazes, and recolored. While this sort of reconditioning may not get rid of dark stains or scuffs entirely, especially on lighter shoes, it makes them less noticeable. Dyeing is the only way to cover scuffs; you can dye from light to dark, which costs around $10 in a neighborhood shoe-repair shop.

- Don't throw shoes out just because the heel seems wrong. Shoe repairmen can shorten a heel from a quarter inch to an inch (more makes the toes curl upward), and when a heel is too wide or too thin, can put on a new stacked heel of the preferred width. They can stretch shoes that don't fit to make them wider, but when a shoe is too short, not much can be done. They can also cut off or add straps.

Shoulder Pads

are standard in well-tailored clothes to soften the shoulder line and help maintain the shape of dresses, jackets, and coats. They look terrific on women with round, narrow, or thin shoulders, and on women with wide hips—shoulder pads somehow balance the hips. Broad-shouldered and large-busted women don't look good in them; small but slender women look good in small ones. Some of the most beautiful tailored effects in jackets are found in clothes from the 1940s—jackets sell for $35 to $45 in antique-clothing stores. Adding a pair of shoulder pads yourself is easy and will revive all sorts of droopy-looking clothes—find them in fabric stores and the notions section of department stores.

Silk

is considered the most desirable and sensuous natural fabric in existence. It is also expensive, mostly because it takes so much effort to farm the finicky silkworm. Read on to find out why silk is to be appreciated, how to get the best buys, and how to care for yours.

Why have those who can afford the very best so often worn silk? Here's a look at the qualities that make this fabric so desirable:

Lightness Silk is the lightest of all fabrics, including natural ones such as wool and cotton, and can be woven into a more gossamer dress/scarf/negligee than any other fabric.

Superb insulation Because of the silkworm's liking for comfort in all kinds of weather, silk is warm in winter and cool in summer (though not so warm as wool or cool as cotton or linen). Also, silk—like all natural fibers—"breathes" better than synthetics because it's more hydroscopic, meaning it easily absorbs moisture. Nylon can absorb approximately 4 percent of its own weight in perspiration without feeling damp and clammy, while silk will absorb up to 12 percent.

Beauty No other fabric has the luster of good silk, compared by poets only to pearls and the hair of beautiful ladies. Also, no other fabric can be dyed quite so gloriously as silk. A good silk and a good dye seem to enhance each other. Further, if you want to print a pattern or even handpaint it, silks can be drawn or printed on with the most clarity of all fabrics. Not surprisingly, silk printing has become a thriving industry, dominated by the Italians, who have produced superb textile artists ever since the Renaissance. Their colors are rich and vi-

Where Silk Comes From

The sole source of the material we call silk is a small gray worm called the Bombyx Mori, which looks like something out of a Looney Tunes cartoon: The worm's head is so small it's absurdly out of proportion to its body, and to move about, the creature must laboriously hunch up its back, drawing forward its rear end, and then, while holding on by its pads, extend its front section full length. This worm, which is really a species of caterpillar, eventually metamorphoses into a moth, and the cocoon it spins for protection during the changeover is pure silk.

What's *hard* about raising silkworms (and the reason none have been raised commercially in the U.S. for nearly a hundred years—most of our raw silk comes from China) is that silkworms demand an inordinate amount of attention. They must have chopped-up mulberry leaves five or six times a day and two or three times each night, and the mulberry leaves have to be the same age as themselves! Growth of mulberry trees must be timed along with growth of the worms, so that young worms can be fed on young leaves, older worms on more mature leaves. The leaves can't be wet, and neither can they be too dry, or the worms will consume too much sap and die. When they start spinning their cocoons, they must be in just the right temperature and undisturbed by noise, dirt, smoke, dampness, or pungent odors, or they may simply stop work. Once the cocoon is spun, the worm, if nature were allowed to take its course, would emerge after twelve days as a vivid moth. Instead, the industrious insect will quickly be gassed or baked in an oven for its labors, for should it be allowed to turn into a moth, it would tear its way out of the cocoon, ruining the silk. Two thousand cocoons produce about a pound of raw silk, enough silk for one dress. Silk stockings take about 350 cocoons, while a voluminous blouse takes a thousand.

There are two different kinds of raw silk. The worms described above, fed entirely on mulberry leaves, are "cultivated silkworms" and produce the finest, most lustrous silks. A more coarse variety is Tussah silk, often mistakenly called "raw" silk. Tussah comes from *wild* silkworms raised out in the open by villagers all over Asia, who simply cultivate the trees and plants the worms like, turn the newly hatched worms loose, and hope they'll stick around. They usually do, feeding on leaves such as oak, fig, and juniper. Salts and tannins in these leaves impart brownish colors of various shades to their cocoons, making wild silk difficult to dye; and, because the caterpillar absent-mindedly plaits in leaves and tender twigs as he spins, the wild cocoons are uneven and rough. Tussah silk is usually woven into lovely, tweedy tans and beiges and used to make blazers and suits. Silkworms, incidentally, often spin cocoons together, producing a wild silk—*duppion*—which has been advertised over the years with much sentimental copy written about cocoon-spinning *au deux*.

brant, and they add a special finish which makes the tones seem even deeper. Most of the dresses you see with patterns, such as perfectly even garlands of flowers at the hem that get progressively smaller toward the waist, are Italian silks. Many American designers, such as Albert Nipon and Charlotte Ford, look at silk samples in the offices of New York's Seventh Avenue merchants, order their silk from China, and have it shipped directly to Italy for printing. Of course, Italian printed silks cost considerably more than Oriental ones.

Durability   Silk is the strongest of natural fibers. Raw silk filament is finer than the finest human hair, yet a cable of silk threads will sustain heavier weights than will a metal cable of the same diameter. Even more important, since silk fiber doesn't break easily, the tiny threads can be woven to have the smoothest surface of any fabric. Its strength also gives silk a great resistance to aging. Chinese tombs from as far back as 400 B.C. have been opened to show the bodies turned to dust but swatches of colored silk still retaining their luster, and many European museums exhibit handsome silk garments over a thousand years old. (At St. Peter's in Rome, you can see Charlemagne's silken coronation robe from the year 800 A.D.— still a blaze of color—and the Cathedral Treasury in Bamburg, Germany, has silk court robes dating from 1000 A.D.) All this means that your silk blouse won't tear as easily as you might think, and neither will it get that frayed and faded look so common with aging synthetic-fiber blouses. When silk does fall apart, it's because the garment is too small and it pulls apart at the seams, or you've bought badly woven silk. Indian or Thai silk is more likely to disintegrate because much of the fabric's woven on old-fashioned hand looms, with poor quality control.

So who wants to live another minute without silk? No one who's inclined to pamper herself, that's for sure. Here, before we get on into shopping, are some terms you should know:

Broadcloth   The least expensive and most common of the good silks, also called China silk; a lightweight plain cloth, soft and caressing and with a subtle luster. When a blouse or dress isn't crêpe de Chine it's usually broadcloth.

Crêpe de Chine   Silk woven with a specially twisted yarn resulting in a lightly crinkled, lustrous surface. More expensive than plain silk.

Chiffon   Weightless, very transparent silk in a plain weave.

Georgette   A weightless, semitransparent crêpe with a faintly grainy surface. Resists wrinkles beautifully.

Noille   Silk from the parts of the cocoon left over after good silk fiber is reeled off. These shorter fibers are chopped up and spun into an inferior silk with such poor luster that you'd be better off buying a fine cotton.

Pongee   A lightweight silk woven with a mixture of thick and thin yarns of Tussah (wild) silk, resulting in a lightly textured surface; usually in its lovely natural cream or tan color. Great for light summer blazers.

Shantung   The nubbly-surfaced wild silks woven from heavy yarns with distinctive slubs running across the fabric; often used for suits.

Silk linen   One of the most popular spring fabrics, to call this fabric "linen" is a misnomer. It's simply a "linen-look" silk, with no real linen involved. (Linen, along with cotton, is vegetable cellulose derived from plants; silk and wool are protein.)

From Imperial China to Bloomingdale's in Only 4,622 Years

Considering that the silkworm is so nervous and hard to get along with, you might think that the discovery of silk was a miracle of modern scientific thinking. What actually happened, according to Chinese chroniclers of ancient times, is that silk was officially discovered in 2640 B.C. The Empress Hsi-ling-shi, on a walk through some mulberry groves, gathered a handful of the soft white cocoons clinging to the branches and carried them inside, where by accident she dropped one in her hot bathwater. Hot water is what softens the gum surrounding cocoon fibers so that the gossamer silk strands will unravel, and the empress was impressed by the tiny fiber's strength and luster. She called in the imperial weavers and set about devising a way to weave cloth from the strands, thus establishing China's most historic industry.

For the next few thousand years, Chinese silks were carried to the West over the Silk Road—hundreds of miles of deserts and mountains inhabited by murderous Huns. During all this time, though China was busily exporting silk goods, the Chinese were so secretive about the *source* of silk that most early Western naturalists thought silk was woven from the cobwebs of giant Oriental spiders. Finally, in 560 A.D., two monks risked death by torture to smuggle silkworm eggs and mulberry seeds out of China in their walking sticks, and sericulture was begun in Constantinople. A small sampling of the sort of women who launched silk fashions in the West: Cleopatra, who went to meet her future lover Marc Antony clad in a red silk robe woven in China and embroidered in Egypt; Byzantine Empress Theodora, who wore silks "finer than a cobweb" and in the colors of "a meadow sown over with flowers"; Tudor England's Queen Elizabeth, who had three thousand silk dresses in her wardrobe when she died (she never threw out anything).

Silk taffetas, velvets, and brocades These heavier silks can cost $100 a yard wholesale and are mostly seen in super-expensive couture dresses. However, manufacturers are busily working on new weaving processes to bring down costs.

Now, here's how to emerge from a store with the best of all possible silk blouses:

- *Comparison shop* First, go look at the best French and Italian designer silks—St. Laurent, Valentino, Ungaro are tops—then go to the basement and finger the $17 specials, which will now seem papery and dull. The idea is then to look for a medium-priced blouse that resembles St. Laurent's more than the bargain basement's.

- *Keep the right priorities* Though Italian prints are best, Oriental silk can be exceedingly lovely. Indeed, because Italy has gotten so expensive, many top American designers are now buying all their silks in Hong Kong or Korea. And since most silk is quite decent these days, what makes the difference between a good and a bad silk blouse is usually workmanship and design. *Don't buy a blouse that's skimpy.* A few years ago blouses were more fitted

Living with Your Silks

Shopping for silk is the *easy* part, you may be thinking . . . now, I'll be indebted to the dry cleaners for life. Not true. In spite of manufacturers who seek to protect themselves with Dry Clean Only labels, many silks can be washed. First, what *not* to wash: Be cautious with silks in dark colors or in vibrant patterns, as they tend to fade and streak. Don't wash chiffon or georgette, and head for the dry cleaners if you get a nasty spot on *any* silk. "Put cold water on a spot immediately," advises Art Carol Inc. Cleaners in New York, experts on silk. "Cold water dilutes the stain." If you take the garment in immediately and keep the spot damp with cold water until you get there, even such lethal substances as tea, coffee, red wine, and hot grease can be removed. Always point out exactly where and what a spot is—if you don't, and the cleaner misses it and puts it through heat, the spot will be doubly hard to remove. Also, the longer a garment sits in your closet with a spot on it, the more likely the spot is to "set." Always look at your silk clothes before putting them away. After they've come back from the cleaners, take them out of the plastic bags, as natural fiber needs to breathe.

When your silks have gotten dingy, you can wash them yourself if they're broadcloth, crêpe de Chine, pongee, or shantung. Indeed, says Bill Brandt of American Silk Mills, silks that are handwashed often look better than when dry cleaned, because dry-cleaning fluid sometimes makes them less lustrous. Wash in tepid water with Woolite or Ivory Snow, and don't rub—silk fibers are weakened by rough handling while wet. If you have a ring around the collar, apply a little Woolite only slightly diluted with water directly on the dingy spot, and let it stand a few minutes before washing. Rinse in cool water, and then in water with a little distilled white vinegar added. (Since soap is alkaline and vinegar is acidic, vinegar neutralizes soap residue and restores shine to silks.) Rinse some more, until all vinegar smell is gone. Do *not* squeeze or wring silk, but press dry in a towel, and hang on a padded hanger to dry. You must iron silk while it's slightly damp, or you won't be able to get out the wrinkles. As soon as the back dries, start ironing. If you can't watch the drying blouse like a hawk, wrap it in a large towel to dry, as it will dry more uniformly this way. Iron at about 300 degrees; if the silk dries, dampen it with a wet rag. To avoid wrinkles in the collar, start at point of collar and iron halfway back, then turn blouse and iron back from the other direction.

Most of the better silks today have finishes protecting them against waterspotting, but if your silk spots, these spots should disappear during washing or dry cleaning. If you have a Tussah silk blazer, little fiber balls may form on the surface, which can be carefully cut off with scissors.

If you perspire heavily, either wear a guard or stick to cottons. Excessive perspiration will fade colored silk. Most women prefer cotton—which is slightly cooler and more absorbent than silk—for really hot days.

If you want to hem a silk dress, go to a fabric store and buy silk or cotton thread. The "dual duty" thread sold in ten-cent stores is polyester and too heavy for silk, which may pucker. Also, since silk is so fine, a hem put in with polyester thread can

---

Living with Your Silks

end up with big dents running around the bottom as though you put in the hem with a staple gun.

Dare you wear a pin on your silk dress? Preferably not, since pinholes don't just disappear as with wools. If you must use a pin, try to put it where the fabric is reinforced by being doubled or with interfacing, or put a tiny piece of some heavier fabric behind the silk where you've pinned it.

Don't be afraid to wear your silks. *Enjoy,* as all those queens, empresses, and duchesses have for centuries.

---

and shirtlike than now, and you often see these passé styles on sale. Today a blouse should look like a blouse and not a shirt. What gives that expensive look is the graceful drape of the fabric, stitching detail around collars and cuffs, tucks, pleating, topstitching. Such dressmaker details make a blouse higher in quality, but also add labor costs.

Good-quality Oriental silk dresses are more challenging to find at moderate prices than are blouses. Manufacturers figure they can sell the dress just because it's silk, and skimp shamelessly on workmanship—some have crooked seams or tacky elastic waists. Even worse, a thin silk that will look passable in a blouse will look, in a dress, as though it needs to be lined, and the dress will seem flimsy.

- The less money you have to spend on silk blouses, the simpler you'll want the blouse, because the more versatile it will be. Advises Emily Cho, author of *Looking Terrific,* "If you can afford only one silk blouse, a cream-colored one seems to do more for most wardrobes than a color. I wear mine with garnet or jade jewelry, or under sweater vests or crocheted T-shirts. Be sure

to choose one long enough to wear belted over a skirt, or as a jacket over another blouse. Don't buy one with a bow—the classic open-collar is more versatile."

Silver

is the most lustrous of metals used for jewelry, and all civilizations have valued it highly. Ancient people spoke of the Milky Way as the "silver river" and thought silver was a remnant of a star that had fallen to earth. Silver jewelry is considered as beautiful as gold by many, but scratches more easily and demands a lot of care.

You can buy silver either as sterling or as silverplate. Like gold, silver is too soft to be useful in its pure state, so it's usually mixed with copper. In order to be called sterling silver, an object has to be 925 parts of pure silver to 75 parts of copper. Silverplate is made by electroplating a layer of pure silver onto a base metal. The more heavily coated with silver, the higher the quality silverplate is considered.

Care

If you buy silver jewelry, you should also buy a jar of Wright's Silver Cream to clean off the tarnish. *All* silver tarnishes, caused by a deposit of sulphide from sulphur in

Adele Simpson's clothes are soft and ladylike. (Courtesy of Garfinckels, Creative Director Wendy Bedenbough. Photo: Alen Macweeney)

the air. Still, nothing is more lustrous and beautiful than newly polished silver. To polish, the Sterling Silversmiths of America recommend rubbing with a natural polish such as Wright's rather than dipping the silver into a chemical cleaning dip. Use a clean, soft cloth, or disposable paper towels. An old soft-bristle toothbrush is good for hard-to-reach spots, though sometimes the shading created by leaving crevices dark is part of the design. Silver scratches easily, so keep it wrapped in a piece of cotton or a plastic bag; a wrap will also slow down tarnishing.

Simpson, Adele

American designer, conservative yet still soft and feminine. Married and the devoted mother of two grown children, she's always been more interested in clothes for "nice women" rather than in designing trendy, outré styles for the disco set. In 1947, she was one of the earliest winners of the Coty Award. A lot of distinguished older women such as Lady Bird Johnson and Margot Fonteyn are Simpson fans, but so are women of other ages. Her ladylike dinner dresses and evening clothes (around $325 for a dress) can always be counted on to be in good taste.

Slicker

Coats that used to be treated with oil or rubber to be made waterproof were called mackintoshes in Britain, slickers in the United States.

Smith, Willi

American designer, young, black, and fun. His clothes are not big favorites with Nancy Reagan's set, but women who are looking for affordable, young-at-heart clothes in natural fibers love him. He has a factory in Bombay, India, and is the only top American designer who spends several months a year there working with fabrics. His clothes are designed to be trans-seasonal—the most superb Indian cottons of every weight, silks, lightweight wools. Two hundred dollars will buy you several Willi Wear sportswear items, which can be mixed and matched with other clothes.

Smock Dress

A voluminous dress flowing downward from a square or round Victorian-type yoke often rimmed in ruffles. Smock dresses tend to be made in romantic fabrics such as cotton calico or challis, or flowery cotton prints. They often have high ruffled collars, crochet edging, and white collars or cuffs. A very comfy dress. Buy them ample enough to be cool but not so voluminous as to look sloppy. Wear with low-cut shoes such as Mary Janes, and opaque stockings—oxfords or moccasins would be too heavy, high heels too dressy. Bare sandals are fine.

Smocking

Multiple rows of shirring (gathering) used to elasticize a fabric. Sundress tops are often made this way; sometimes waists or hips of dresses are smocked. Avoid elasticized smocking anywhere that your figure is less than perfection.

Snakeskin

is one of the most beautiful but delicate leathers—after a few months of heavy wear, scales often begin to peel off. Since snakeskin isn't a practical leather, it's a tragedy that this product is now so popular for shoes, bags, and belts that ecosystems in several countries are endangered. Contrary to what many people would like to think, snakes can't be farmed because they refuse to lay eggs in captivity. All snakeskins come from the wild, from snakes with skins big enough to work with—boas, pythons, anacondas. According to the International Institute for Environment and Development, nearly all snakeskins come from Asia and South America and most are imported into countries such as Italy and Japan, which have virtually no import controls on endangered species, to be tanned and made into handbags and belts.

Though the U.S., Britain, West Germany, and Switzerland now have import controls on reptile skins, limited numbers are allowed to be imported and sold in stores. Still, anyone with an ecological conscience usually resists $300 snakeskin boots and handbags.

Smocking emphasizes any part of the body you want to show off: here, the hips.

Socks

One of the biggest-selling items in the booming outdoorwear business has been socks. Thin socks, fat socks, warm socks, wildly colored socks, and fashion socks by Anne Klein, Ralph Lauren, Geoffrey Beene; every imaginable kind of sock. Here are a few particularly distinguished socks to know about.

Heavy wool socks   Not only do thick woolen socks keep your feet warm inside boots and shoes, but you can wear them as house slippers indoors. College girls love to pad around in the dorm in them. Look for the Wigwam Ragg Wool sock, the Klondike Boot sock, the Elliot Gant wool boot sock, Irish-wool socks. Eastern Mountain Sports, Vose Farm Road, Peterborough, New Hampshire 03458 has a big selection of heavy wool socks in its catalogue. You can find them in any outdoorwear or army-navy store and the Army itself issues inexpensive wool socks in a wonderful olive color. Most heavy wool socks are $6 to $8.

Light wool socks   When you don't need the thickest and heaviest of socks to stay warm, but still want a natural-fiber sock, an excellent choice is the 70-percent wool, 30-percent nylon Summit Sock in the Early Winters catalogue (110 Prefontaine Place South, Seattle, Washington 98104). Made of fine worsted wool, this cream-colored, $3 sock absorbs up to 30 percent of its weight in moisture, which means your feet stay dry. Since wool cushions better and stays soft longer than synthetics or cotton, it's a comfortable sock for running or playing tennis.

Thermal silk socks   Wigwam makes a light, white sock to slip on under another sock. Since silk is such a fabulous insulating material, a thermal silk sock under a pair of light knee-highs will go a long way toward keeping your feet warm in beautiful but chilly high-fashion boots. They're even more help when wearing rubber boots, which do little to keep out cold. Usually $6.25 in outdoorwear stores.

Lectra Sox These "electric socks" are battery-heated and great for wearing at football games or other places where you're outside but not moving much. They run on alkaline D-cell batteries (not supplied with the socks) which are placed in a small pouch at top of the sock; Eveready E-95 is recommended. A pair of batteries costs $1.50 and provides four to five hours of heat, which can be switched on and off. Though these socks are commonly sold in Scandinavian countries and Canada, here you can get them only by mail. The socks are $14.95 plus $1 postage from: Big 3 International, 150 Nassau Street, New York, New York 10038 (212 964-1630). Sizes run small (6–9), medium (10–11), large (12–13); you can exchange or ask for a refund if they don't fit.

Soutache Trim

A rich braided edging on a suit jacket, reminiscent of costumes from Czarist Russia or military uniforms from the Hapsburg era. Adolpho edges his cardigan jackets in soutache, as does Chanel (see illustration on p. 44).

Spandex

is certainly one of the most useful synthetic fibers ever; as little as 5 percent spandex added to a fabric such as cotton, polyester, wool, even cashmere, makes it stretchable. Developed by Du Pont during World War

II to take the place of rubber, which was expensive and scarce, the fiber soon became a special blessing to women: spandex-elasticized waistbands on panties can be counted on never to snap. Today rubber is used mostly for tires—spandex is what makes bras, girdles, swimming suits, and leotards.

Trade names: Lycra, Elura, Glospan, Numa, Spandelle, Vyrene.

Care
Not harmed by perspiration or body oils, or by washing in detergent. But chlorine bleach will ruin spandex, especially the fiber in panties and bras. Machine wash in warm, not hot, water. Dry at lowest heat, shortest cycle.

Spectator Dress

An outfit somewhere between casual sportswear and officewear. A term with preppy WASP overtones, spectator clothes were worn by those watching the football or soccer game rather than participating in it. In the 1950s, appropriate attire for women college alumni at sports events leaned toward tweed or cotton suits, or maybe a shirtwaist dress and cardigan.

Spectator Shoe

A medium-heeled white leather pump with a strip of black, brown, or navy leather covering the toe and sometimes the heel, often in a perforated wing-tip design.

Spencer Jacket

A tailored jacket cut off at the waist, usually with a velvet collar. St. Laurent is famous for his Spencer jackets (see p. 197).

Yves St. Laurent accomplishes the feat of making his clothes both tailored and romantic at once. (Courtesy of Bloomingdale's)

St. Laurent, Yves

The Frenchman with an international reputation as the world's most talented designer. The breadth of his designs is what impresses people: he's as adept designing rich, gypsylike Ballet Russe evening gowns in lavishly embroidered velvets as he is at being the first to see possibilities in street clothes such as pea jackets, gaucho pants, and flannel slacks. He revived crêpe de Chine in the early 1960s, brought back blazers and 1930s high-platform shoes, knocked off military jackets from army-navy stores, designed see-through dresses to be worn over nude body stockings. At age nineteen, in 1958, he designed his first collection, which was a huge success; he's been a smash every year since except for 1960, the year he was drafted into the French Army. (He promptly had a nervous breakdown.) Back in Paris, his reputation as a highstrung genius untarnished by his confrontation with the military, he opened his own couture house. Within ten years or so he was making millions.

You'll find his predictably expensive ready-to-wear in good department stores in "Saint Laurent Rive Gauche" boutiques, and he has a New York store at 855 Madison Avenue. YSL designs manage to be both tailored and romantic at the same time, and often (but not always) have a timeless quality that transcends fashion. Look for his wool gabardine pants and silk blouses, considered the finest in the business, and his velvet-collared coats and jackets. Be prepared to spend $300 for a blouse, $500 for a skirt, over $1,000 for a coat. Of course, Rive Gauche has sales just as do all the rest of American department stores, and those prices can be cut in half. After Christmas, New York's Bloomingdale's reduced his silk blouses to $138, his trousers from $365 to $183.

Stadium Jacket

Because they're so comfortable to drive in, stadium jackets are favorite cold-weather coats in places such as Montana and Colorado. A stadium jacket is usually hip-length, lightly quilted with down or polyester, and has knit cuffs to keep the wind from whistling up your sleeves. A detachable hood, huge snap pockets, and a drawstring bottom are other distinguishing characteristics. Around $75.

Stains

Most women who like to wash their own clothes seem to follow these general rules:

1. Almost any fresh stain will come out if you douse it immediately in plenty of cool water, or water with a little bar soap or lightweight detergent such as Lux, Ivory, or Joy. Don't put water on lipstick or ink, however, as water may release the dyes and stain the fabric even worse. Delicate fabrics such as satins, taffetas, velvets, crêpes, or rayon moirés, particularly nasty-looking stains, or stains on expensive clothes, should be rushed to the dry cleaners. Tell the cleaner what the stain is and make sure he writes it on the ticket. Never rub vigorously at a stain or you'll damage the fibers—on silks and printed cottons, you could easily end up with a faded spot. Infinitely better to let an experienced dry cleaner's spotter dispatch the spot in seconds with his chemicals.

2. Haste is of the essence in vanquishing a stain. Whether you attack it yourself or turn it over to your cleaners, the longer a spot is left on a fabric, the more time it has to oxidize and be difficult. Never put away clothes for the season with spots on them.

3. For do-it-yourself spot removal, the best weapon against *grease*-based stains such as mayonnaise, butter, body oils causing ring-around-the-collar, hand lotion, gravy, or salad dressing, is an inexpensive prewash chemical spot remover such as Spray 'n Wash or Shout. These aerosol sprays contain solvents that are terrific for vanquishing grease. For *nongreasy* stains on washable fabrics—fruit, eggs, wine, underarm perspiration, blood, grass—an enzyme presoak such as Biz or Axion is more effective than cleaning-fluid chemicals in breaking down the proteins in these substances. Never use enzyme products on wool or silk, which are also proteins and will be "digested."

Here are some specific procedures that U.S. government publications, the Good Housekeeping Institute, detergent manufacturers, and the American Apparel Manufacturers Association all more or less agree upon:

BALLPOINT INK

Put paper towels under the stain, then sponge with a piece of cotton soaked in rubbing alcohol. When you can't get out any more ink, saturate the spot with Ivory or Lux, and wash. If the ink is blue or black, alcohol makes it an easy stain to dispatch, even on silk. Red ink is awful, and should be rushed to the cleaners. Alcohol is surprisingly harmless for most fabrics, but if you're worried about color fading, dab at a seam first and see if any color comes off.

BLOOD

Soak immediately in cold water until the stain turns light brown, then launder with plenty of suds. For old stains, let garment soak overnight in an enzyme presoak, and wash.

BUTTER

Spray with a prewash chemical spotter such as Spray 'n Wash, then wash in heavy suds. Not a difficult stain.

CANDLE WAX

What not to do: Don't follow old wives' advice about placing blotters over and under candle wax and pressing with a hot iron. Heat from the iron could turn candle dye into a permanent stain. Scrape off as much as you can, and soak in cleaning fluid such as Carbona or Afta. Dry naturally, then wash in heavy suds. (Always let cleaning fluid or soap and water dry completely before applying the other—the two don't work well together at all.)

CATSUP	If you sponge immediately with water and soap, catsup will come out. Laundering in lots of suds can also work. Otherwise soak in lukewarm water in an enzyme presoak such as Biz or Axion, one tablespoon Biz to one quart water for thirty minutes to overnight.
CHEWING GUM	Dab rubbing alcohol on all sides of the blob of gum, including underneath (from the wrong side). Gum should harden, and you can pull it off in one piece. Scrape any residue off with fingers. Rubbing the gum all around with an ice cube also sometimes works. If a stain remains, let fabric dry, spray with Spray 'n Wash, and wash again.
CHOCOLATE	Spray with prewash aerosol spotter, wash in heavy suds.
COFFEE	Plenty of lukewarm water and soap should get rid of fresh spills. Otherwise, rub detergent straight on stains, and launder. If coffee was *au lait,* making it greasy, spray with prewash spotter, wash in heavy suds.
IRON RUST	Do *not* soak in chlorine bleach—chlorine sets a rust stain. Buy a commercial rust-stain remover from the hardware store, or use a 5-percent or 10-percent oxalic acid solution (that's what's in the rust-stain remover) from the drugstore. A good dry cleaner can easily get out rust.
LIPSTICK, MASCARA, LIQUID MAKEUP	Applying water first does no good. Apply a prewash chemical spotter, then launder in heavy suds—no problem.
MILDEW	Chlorine bleach kills mildew fungus and bleaches color out of stains. For delicate fabrics, use an all-fabric bleach such as Clorox 2. Probably nothing will work perfectly, not even a professional dry cleaning.

MUD	Let mud dry, brush off, then launder. If greaselike stains remain, spray with a prewash treatment, wash again.
MUSTARD	Soak overnight in an enzyme presoak, one tablespoon presoak to one quart of water. Launder using a chlorine or all-fabric bleach.
NAIL POLISH	Don't follow advice saying to use nail-polish remover, which usually smears the stain horribly. Incredibly, dry cleaners can remove nail polish with relative ease.
PENCIL MARKS	Should come out easily in normal washing.
PERSPIRATION STAINS	Soak in a strong salt-water solution for an hour or so. Or sponge the spots with a solution of half a cup white vinegar to one cup of water before washing.
SCORCH	Tsk tsk! You've burned the fibers. A light scorch on cotton, linen, or rayon will usually come out with washing, but scorched silk or wool is probably ruined. Soak washable fabrics in a mixture of two tablespoons of chlorine bleach to a quart of water for thirty minutes; try soaking silks or wools overnight in all-fabric bleach.
WINE AND OTHER ALCOHOLIC BEVERAGES	Sponge spills, even white wine and colorless drinks, with cold water immediately, as heat can cause colorless stains to yellow weeks later. For fresh stains, soak garment in cold water before laundering. For older stains, soak thirty minutes to overnight in a solution of three tablespoons of an enzyme presoak to one gallon of water; wash.

In judging whether to labor over a stain yourself, to throw the garment out, or to take it to the cleaners, it's helpful to know whether stains are regarded as being easy or difficult for professional cleaners. The accompanying chart classifies stains by how hard it is for dry cleaners to remove them.

	Protein Fibers: Silk, Wool, Cashmere, etc.	Cellulose Fibers: Cotton, Linen, Rayon, etc.	Plastic Fibers: Acetate, Nylon, Acrylics, Polyesters, etc.
Alcoholic beverages	M	E	E
Beer	M	E	E
Blood	D	M	E
Candy	M	M	E
Carmelized sugar (fruit juices, soft drinks, previously set by heat)	D	D	M
Chewing gum	M	M	M
Coffee	D	E	E
Crayons	M	M	E
Dyes	D	M	E
Egg whites or yolks	M	M	M
Fish slime	D	D	M
Foundation make-up	M	M	E
Fruit juices	M	E	E
Grass stains	M	M	E
Gutter splash	M	M	E
Household cement	M	M	M
Ice cream	M	M	E
Ink, ball point	M	D	M
Ink, fountain pen	D	M	E
Ink, India	D	D	M
Ink, marking	D	D	M
Ink, printers	D	D	M
Ink, typewriter ribbon	E	E	E
Iodine	M	E	E
Lacquer	D	D	M
Lipstick	M	M	E
Mascara, eye makeup	E	E	E
Mercurochrome	D	M	E
Milk	M	M	E
Milk, chocolate	D	D	M
Mimeo correction fluid	M	M	E
Mustard	D	M	E
Nail polish	M	M	E
Oil, vegetable (two weeks old)	M	D	D
Oil, vegetable (fresh)	E	E	E
Oil, petroleum	E	E	E
Oil, animal	E	E	E
Paint			
Latex	D	D	D
Oil base or acrylic	D	D	D
Perspiration	M	M	E
Photo development fluid	M	M	E
Soft drinks	M	E	E
Soot	E	M	E
Tea	D	M	E
Varnish	D	D	D

KEY: D=Difficult; E=Easy; M=Medium.   (Courtesy of the International Fabricare Institute.)

Stole

A long, narrow scarf, usually with fringed ends. The ultimate stole is silver fox. Stoles are more popular in Europe than in America. St. Laurent likes jersey stoles with his sweaters and knitted dresses, Jean Louis Scherrer puts thick knotted stoles in jacquard patterns over his dinner dresses, Ungaro's outfits have challis stoles thrown carelessly over the shoulder.

Suits

Everyone should have a well-cut suit, even if one doesn't go to an office every day; if you do work, you should have *several* suits. Even if you're a housewife with children, or most people in your office wear jeans, you'll encounter times when only a suit will do—a job interview, a funeral, a lunchtime date in a really smart restaurant. The no-nonsense quality of a good suit can be a secret weapon when you're bent on returning a Final Sale item to a department store, or you're taking Aunt Betty's silver teapot to Sotheby Parke Bernet to sell. Any time you're doing business with men, always all too ready to dissolve into macho yahoos at the sight of someone inappropriately and sexily dressed, a suit is sophisticated and protective. Any time you're going directly from work to a dinner-and-theater type of evening, you can take a ruffly, romantic blouse to work and maybe some evening sandals and end up neither overdressed during the day nor drab and mannish for evening.

Harvé Benard does nifty medium-priced suits. Evan Picone and Jones of New York aren't as up-to-date on the latest lapel shapes or skirt cuts, but their fabrics and workmanship are impeccable. Among designers, Calvin Klein is probably the favorite of upwardly mobile career women. His suits stay carefully priced just out of reach of most of us but not so exorbitantly out of reach that they remain prizes everyone can easily resist. In summer suits, Geoffrey Beene's lightweight cottons have a timeless quality. A few guidelines to keep in mind when buying a suit:

- A nicely cut dark suit with jewelry or an interesting collar calling attention to the face is probably the most flattering possible outfit for anyone who's overweight. Thin women will look most elegant and classic in double-breasted suits; heavy women should buy them single-breasted, and always leave the suit jacket unbuttoned so as to get two vertical lines down the front. Top-heavy women look best in blouses with a deep V neckline, while thin, finely chiseled women look good in bows, ascots, or simple jabots—any style bringing the blouse top to throat level.

- Jackets should be easily buttonable, even if you don't intend ever to button them. Sleeves should just cover the wristbone. The back should lie flat—wrinkles or puckers are signals of underlying malaise. Waists, cuff lengths, too much roominess at hips can be easily fixed.

- If you can afford only one or two suits, stick to light wool gabardines or silk blends which will fit under coats, be bearable in overheated offices, and can be worn eight or nine months a year. The suit should have a *supple* feeling— you don't want to look stiff and you want to be comfortable.

Surplice Wrap

A dress in which one side of the front closure overlaps the other at the waistline, forming a deep V. *The* classic dinner dress for buxom women, not so flattering on slender ones.

Sweaters

were a British innovation but were named in America. "Knitted shirts" first appeared on various Irish and English islands such as Jersey and Guernsey, knitted for the fishermen by their wives. The knitted shirts were made of wool retaining its natural oils, so that they could absorb rain or salt water without feeling damp. By the 1800s, the "jersey" was being used by American college athletes, who called it a sweater, a word considered so inelegant that genteel people wouldn't mention it in polite company.

Today everyone has a wardrobe of sweaters. More bosomy women can look terrific in them; thinner women look better in blouses, as do the flat-chested, round-

Surplice wrap

shouldered, or swaybacked. Skinny women look best in bulky sweaters, while overweight or petite women look worst in them. Here's a rundown of who looks best in what.

Turtleneck The straight horizontal neckline and broad unbroken expanse across the shoulders make this style a face and body shortener, most flattering to long, thin faces and bodies, not good for broad, round ones. That is only your bare, unadorned turtleneck, however. A pendant, long necklace, or a scarf tied low add vertical lines, as does a suit jacket left unbuttoned. Or you can wear a V-necked blouse *over* the turtleneck. If your skin is at all sensitive, incidentally, buy turtlenecks only in soft fibers such as cashmere, acrylic, or lambswool; Shetlands are scratchy.

Cowlnecks provide a somewhat more elongating neckline than turtlenecks; if you want vertical lines, you pull the cowl into a low oval in front. If you'd like to add width to a thin neck or face, pull it as wide on the sides as it will go. Cowlnecks tend to be bulky around the throat when worn under a suit, not good if you're top-heavy.

V-neck If your head sits on your shoulders like a teapot on a table, this is the line for you. V-necks are most flattering for large bosoms, least flattering on the flat-chested. They're great for elongating a short, heavy neck, bad for thin, long ones. A versatile sweater, because you can wear it over blouses.

Scoop neck Everything that can be said about a V-neck applies to this style also.

Cardigan A nice shape for the plump or short because of the two vertical lines. Also an adaptable sweater—you can tie it around your neck by the arms, can button only the middle three buttons for a vestlike effect under a blazer, can belt, wear over a preppy boy's shirt, or put an antique crocheted collar around the neck.

Shopping

Sweaters can be found for less money in junior departments, crew-necks in boy's departments. In March and April you can find beautiful sweaters in thrift shops at giveaway prices.

Care

According to spokesmen for wool, cotton, mohair, angora, cashmere, lambswool, and man-made fiber associations, you should be able to handwash all sweaters, Dry Clean Only label or not. Angora and cotton-knit sweaters are least trustworthy, since a few unscrupulous manufacturers don't pre-shrink the yarn before knitting, as they're supposed to. If you have doubts, send a new sweater to the cleaners the first time—if it wasn't pre-shrunk or dyed correctly, this defect will be as likely to show up in dry cleaning as in handwashing.

What's hard about washing sweaters is not that they shrink but that they stretch. In a tiny apartment, home laundry can be a real nuisance, because you absolutely must dry sweaters flat—if you hang them over shower racks or side of the tub, you risk having them dry in an elongated shape. (They're not ruined—you simply have to douse them again and shape—"block"—into the shape you want.) To block a sweater, spread it out before you wash it on a large towel and put a few pins around the outline—just enough to show you how wide and long the sweater should be; when you lay the sweater out to dry on the towel, simply shape it to fit inside your pins. If the sweater isn't a heavy one, when

it's very nearly dry you can get away with hanging it over a towel rack.

Don't wash natural-fiber sweaters in detergent, even mild dish detergents, which are designed to cut dishwater grease and will strip fabrics of oils. Woolite is especially designed to protect wool fibers, and Ivory Snow is fine as well. *Never wash any sweater in hot water.*

Brush with a clothes brush or a dry sponge, or ever-so-lightly shave with an electric shaver to remove tiny fuzzballs.

Swimsuits

Never has more thought gone into scheming methods to make a few square inches of fabric help you look taller, wider, thinner, broader, bustier. Designing swimsuits to make the most (or least) of whatever you've got is now called "engineering." Here's how to pick out the swimsuit design most flattering to you.

Overweight Avoid suits of thin, stretchy fabric. Stick to one-piece suits in darker colors, with lots of lycra in them for support, as lycra acts like a feather-weight girdle and keeps midriff roll in check. Read labels: you want *more* lycra, *less* nylon. A print or a stripe down the side of a suit elongates the figure. Don't wear suits with tight elastic at bottoms of legs, a style calling attention to excess flesh there.

Topheavy Crisscrossed straps, though awful for tanning, provide the best support for large breasts (crisscrosses are also best for serious swimmers). You might look for a suit with the built-in support of a light underwire bra. Most flattering neckline is a V or scoop neck, a narrowing surplice wrap suit or a halter top.

Heavy thighs A French cut, meaning the suit is cut high up on the hip, can have an elongating, slimming effect on women with slightly heavy thighs. For a really serious bulge, try boylegs, a cut in which the suit bottom is cut like shorts, covering an extra inch of leg. Avoid tight knits with elastic cutting into your thighs.

Wide hips You need some balancing width on top. Look for a two-piece suit with top in horizontal stripes and widely spaced bra straps to draw the eye outward. (Halter necks would be the *worst* line.) Bottom of suit should be dark. For really wide hips, try a softly flowing, fluted skirt.

Small bosom Avoid deep V- or scoopnecks. Look for puckering, shirring under the bust, ruffled necklines, tucks, stripes or patterns that go horizontally across the bust. Avoid thin tubelike one-piece suits (maillots) which will flatten you, and stark, straight-across bandeau tops. A bikini with the top cut in two triangles with lots of shirring is good.

Too thin Follow the ancient wisdom: look for stripes or horizontal patterns. It really works.

Shortwaisted A one-piece suit will elongate a short waistline; a bikini or two-piece has too many horizontal lines. Try vertical stripes or patterns or an empire waistline. High-cut French legs may help by making your legs look longer.

Longwaisted A one-piece suit with a gathered, blouson-type waistline is a terrific style. Belts are for you, as are horizontal patterns and prints.

Wideshouldered Avoid camisole tops with straps widely placed. Keep the focus pulled in toward the neck with a halter, preferably straps running from center of the suit-top to tie in back of the neck. Neither is a straight-across bandeau for you, because of the horizontal line.

Ghostlike skin As white as a piece of typing paper after a long hard winter? Dark colors will look dramatic and interesting by contrast. Pale colors will make you look even more wan, and also add pounds.

Care
Rinse out your suit after each use—perspiration, salt water, and chlorine are all damaging to fabric. Hang to dry in a shady spot. Never put a swimsuit in the washer and dryer, and don't let one lie around in a damp heap. Synthetics won't mildew as much as natural fabrics, but they *will* mildew slightly.

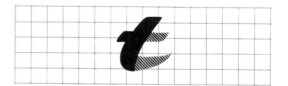

Taffeta
A plainly woven fabric with a smooth, shiny surface. Taffeta is one of the oldest luxury fabrics—the Persians were weaving it out of silk and calling it taftah as early as the time of Alexander the Great. A few silk taffeta clothes are being made outside of Paris couture houses—Bill Blass had a $200 white silk taffeta blouse in his line last fall—but usually it's made out of rayon, rayon or acetate for evening clothes, polyester for daytime blouses, nylon for parkas. St. Laurent brought the fabric back into fashion in his famous rich peasant collection of 1976, when he used it for billowing skirts and braid-embellished jackets. Princess Diana's wedding gown was silk taffeta.

Care

Dry clean unless care label specifies otherwise. Take care not to get caught in the rain or let a misting water glass drip on taffeta—often sizing, a special starch, is added for body, and spills leave water rings. Keep your sales slip in case you end up with permanent water rings, which are cause for a return.

Tailored Look

We don't always want to look soft, cuddly, sensuous, or casual ("easy," as fashion copywriters like to say). Sometimes we want a smooth, firm fit, with pockets, lapels, and other details perfectly stitched to look crisp, and that's when the tailored look is chosen. In tailored clothes, shape is permanently established by using a firm interfacing and stabilizing edges; the collar is firm, lapels lie flat against the jackets, and pockets, flaps, and other details are *perfectly* stitched. There is no fussiness—no buttoned pockets, epaulets, obvious buttons. Tailored clothes are traditionally made from woolens, worsted, tweed, doubleknits, corduroy, tightly woven flannels for winter; linen, seersucker, chino, poplin, piqué in summer. The quality of workmanship is more obvious in a solid-color suit.

Tap Pants

are a kind of underpants that have no elastic at the legs but are boxy and airy. They're made of silk, rayon, or silklike synthetics with lots of lace, and are exquisite but expensive. In the summer, when you're barelegged and want to wear the sexiest and most graceful lingerie, tap pants are perfect. They're adorable worn over a garter belt, not so great worn over pantyhose, and terrible under slacks—they push up and cause bulges.

Tartan

A woolen fabric with a plaid pattern distinctive to a Scotch Highland clan. Anybody can design a regular plaid, which will have no name; an authentic *tartan* plaid has to be approved by the Lyon Court in Edinburgh, Scotland, registered, and given a name. The lovely Royal Stewart tartan, with narrow stripes of blue, white, and yellow on a red ground, is the tartan of Britain's royal family. Black Watch represents the 42nd Royal Highland Regiment and has green stripes on a dark blue background. The tartan of the famous Campbell clan has green stripes on a blue background, while that of Barclay has wide stripes of black on yellow intercrossed by narrow white stripes. Anyone can copy a Scotch tartan, but few do the job accurately. To get a really accurate copy, your best bet is to buy an imported Scottish kilt skirt. (See KILTS.)

Tattersall Check

A small, rather gaudy check in two colors on a light background. The pattern was first used on horse blankets, and the name comes from Richard Tattersall, who owned a nineteenth-century horse auction house in London. Rodeo shirts of the Old West, fringed front and back, are usually made with a Tattersall pattern.

Teddy

A silky, lacy undergarment worn in lieu of panties and a bra. Yes, they do have snaps on the bottom so that you don't have to completely disrobe to go to the ladies'. You can wear pantyhose underneath if you wish.

A lacy silk teddy makes a sensuous substitute for bra, panties, and slip. And yes, teddies do have snaps on the bottom. (Teddy by Beth Goodman, Sabeth Row. Courtesy of Victoria's Secret.)

Tent Dress

A no-waistband dress that falls gracefully down the torso and flares out at hip level. A flattering style for the overweight.

Terry Cloth

A very absorbent cotton or cotton-blend fabric with uncut loops on one or both sides. Good for summer running clothes, beach dresses, bathrobes.

Thermal Underwear

is warmer for its weight than regular underwear. Today's styles are so light and nonbulky that you can wear thermal T-shirts under silk blouses and leggings under skirts or pants without adding unwanted bulges to your figure. There are three different kinds of thermal underwear:

Knitted These fabrics have been knitted in a wafflelike or honeycomb pattern, leaving tiny air pockets within the material. When the underwear is covered with another fabric, these air pockets provide extra warmth. Sears Roebuck and Montgomery Ward sell comfortable thermal separates of this sort in cotton for $5 or $6 apiece. Department stores have them in a mixture of 67 percent wool, 33 percent nylon, which is also stretchy and "breathes." Probably the most efficient knitted thermals are made by Damart, a mail-order company with an impeccable list of satisfied customers including Chris Bonnington, who conquered Annapurna and the southwest face of Mt. Everest and the Mt. McKinley Bicentennial Denali expedition members. Damart thermals are made largely from an acrylic but, though synthetic, are especially designed to let perspiration evaporate. They're nonallergenic and the warmest of all underwear fabrics. For a catalogue, write Damart Thermawear, 1811 Woodbury Avenue, Portsmouth, New Hampshire 03805, or call (800) 258-7300.

Insulated underwear has two layers of thermal knit, usually of different fibers, with an insulating layer between. Oldest brand name is Duofold (Mohawk, New York 13407), a company that's been making two-layer underwear since the turn of the century. Duofold puts 100-percent soft combed cotton next to your skin to absorb moisture and keep you dry; the outer layer is soft virgin wool, with air space between layers insulating like a storm window. People who own Duofold tops tend to get hooked on wearing them around the house as T-shirts, as well as for underwear. Most outdoorwear stores and army-navy stores sell Duofold. Ladies' sizes run small, so buy a size or two larger than you normally would.

Fishnet The least expensive of thermal underwear, fishnet T-shirts create air pockets in all the holes to keep you warm. L. L. Bean sells them.

Thrift Shops

One must overcome a feeling of dismay, of having come down in the world, when entering a thrift shop for the first time. A lot of people take one look at the stacks of ratty clothes mixed in with nonfunctioning toasters and chipped china, and quickly flee back to the tidiness and order of Saks. Others become ardent devotees of the *sport* of thrift shopping, the fun of picking through piles of dross until there—in the middle of mountains of faded polyester and dingy acrylic—is the treasure: a perfect pale blue crew-neck cashmere for $5. Sometimes you spot just what you need as you're coming in the door—the perfect parka, a pair of jodhpurs. Or you may be making a beeline for the half-buried blazer that looks like a Ralph Lauren when an arm—somebody else's arm—grabs first. Then, you follow strict self-discipline and pay no attention whatever to the other customer and her find, even though you can plainly see that what she's looking at with boredom *is* a Ralph Lauren blazer for $10. With marked enthusiasm, you grab another blazer, hold it this way and that admir-

---

Thrift-Shopping Tips

The best time to shop is late on Friday or Saturday afternoon, just before they close for the day and weekend. Lateness of hour and week seems to inspire generosity. Best time of year to buy is just before they close for the two-week summer vacation, or before the coming season. In late August, unpicked-over sweaters go for $2 or $3; in March, you'll find a winter's accumulation of summer cottons—dresses $7.50, blouses $4. January is also a good month because people donate merchandise before the New Year in order to get tax deductions, and sales abound. When thrifts get too high an inventory, they usually have half-price sales. Experienced thrift shoppers will buy *only* from stores having sales.

Try to visit a favorite thrift shop on a regular basis, and donate clothes there yourself. If the salesclerks grow fond of you as a "regular," you'll get better prices. Whether you know them or not, don't be afraid to bargain. Point out tears, stains, missing buttons. If the label says Halston, you've never heard of him; if the blouse is 100-percent Italian silk, complain because it's not drip-dry. Since most stains will come out with the right attack (see STAINS), don't be afraid of a little surface dirt, lipstick, or ballpoint ink. Tears can always be mended, and the ten-cent store has hundreds of button styles.

The main rule is: *Keep your head.* Don't be tempted to buy anything just because it's been reduced to $3 from $200. Once you learn not to be addled by the incredible bargains, and buy only what you'll really *use*, thrift shops are great places for such basics as belts, men's shirts, A-line skirts, caftans, and sweaters, especially those wonderful wools and cashmeres from the 1940s and 1950s. You may also spot great old alligator bags from those years, selling for $5 to $35.

ingly, and watch. If she puts the blazer down for even a moment, you scoop it up. Some people have developed such quickness at the sport of thrift shopping that if you put down your own coat for a split second, you may look up to see it across the room in the possession of another customer.

All thrift shops are charity-related stores to which people donate clothes for tax deductions (as opposed to resale shops, which pay donors half of the selling price of their goods). If you're lucky enough to find something you like, you can get it for the lowest prices going—an irresistible temptation to buy clothes you don't need. Hours in most stores are from 10:00 to 4:30; some are open from Tuesday through Saturday, others Monday to Friday—if in doubt, phone first. No, most stores don't dry clean everything they sell, but the better ones will only *accept* clean clothes (a few stains notwithstanding). Best shops are often, but not always, in wealthy parts of town. Stores operated by the Junior League (111 of them across the country) are usually good, especially San Francisco's Next-to-New shop. The Blue Bird Circle in Houston is outstanding, as is the Trading Post Rummage Shop in Lake Forest, Illinois; the Girls Club and Council thrift shops in New York are also worth a visit.

Timberland Boots

give you an unmistakable whiff of the Great Outdoors, undoubtedly one reason why they sell so well to city and college girls, both here and in Europe—even though they're hiking boots designed to keep your feet warm in temperatures as cold as 20 degrees below.

What's bad about them: Since they're lace-up boots, you can't just slip them off and on, you have to labor over them;

No longer do you see hiking boots only on the back trails of the Sierra Nevadas; Timberland® boots for women are worn to class, on icy city streets, and to the grocery store.

they're too hot to wear comfortably indoors for long; unlike regular boots, they can never be worn with skirts.

What's good: Timberlands are insulated and *guaranteed* to keep your feet warm when you're outside and it's horribly cold. Their silicone-impregnated leather is fully waterproof and they can be worn as rain boots as well as hiking boots; nonskid soles work equally well hiking over rocky terrain or on icy city streets.

Cost: Around $60. To find the dealer nearest you, write: The Timberland Company, P.O. Box 370, Newmarket, New Hampshire 03857.

Tippet

A small shoulder cape of fur, tying in front. You can get one for $30 in thrift or antique shops. They look especially good on white or ivory-colored coats with shoulder pads from the 1940s or 1950s.

You don't need a sailboat deck to appreciate your Top-Siders.®

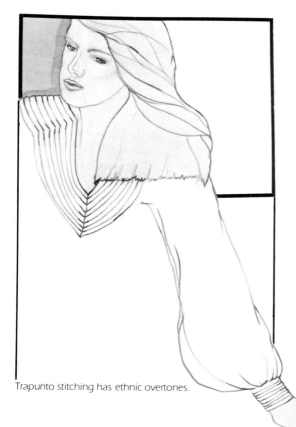

Trapunto stitching has ethnic overtones.

Top-Siders

These famous leather boating moccasins have been selling in exactly the same style for fifty years. Back in the 1930s they were bought mostly by people with yachts and sailboats; now they're considered cute American shoes in Europe, and all sorts of people who aren't boat owners buy them to wear with their cut-off jeans. The shoe's sole is so unusual that it was patented—it clings to the deck even when wet, and does the same to a slick or icy sidewalk. To find a dealer, write Sperry Top-Sider, 960 Harrison Avenue, Boston, Massachusetts 02118.

Toque

A small, brimless hat, *not* knitted.

Trapunto Stitching

Light quilting used as trim—bands are stitched around the neck, cuffs, hem of a garment.

Trenchcoat

Well-dressed anonymity is what trench-coats have to offer, which is why spies and detectives like them so much. Everyone should have one for spring and fall, and for rain. With a soft wool zip-out lining, they can also be worn on mild winter days. Unlike the case with most clothing classics, when buying a trenchcoat you do *not* look for the simplest style. The best ones have lots of military detail, as the style was first designed for British officers in the trenches in World War I. "Storm flaps," short ca-pelets sewn in just below the shoulders, front and back, are designed so that rain will drip off without drenching the bottom of the coat. Belts on cuffs are to be tight-ened to keep rain from running down your arm, while shoulder epaulets testify to the coat's military origins. Most important is that the coat not look *skimpy*—you want it to be full, having generous pleats up the back and lots of neat topstitching.

Burberry is the status name in trench-coats. Often department stores copy the Burberry and sell the coats under their own labels. While these coats aren't made with the perfection of Burberry's, they're a quarter the price and will often do quite nicely. Designer-quality resale shops are a gold mine for trenchcoats—they always have one or two good ones selling for $50 or $60.

Triacetate

A lustrous, silky fabric made, as are ace-tate and rayon, from wood pulp. Triacetate doesn't wrinkle, shrink, or fade, and is made from a renewable resource—trees that grow on lands unsuitable for farming. The fabric can be washed and ironed at a higher temperature than acetate, making it easier to launder. As with acetate, its ability to breathe is poor; if you wear it on a hot day and perspire, triacetate won't ab-sorb the moisture and will feel clammy. People who are concerned about harmful additives in clothes object to triacetate. "The fibers are made fire retardant and re-ceptive to dyes by impregnating them with an organic solution made with a polybro-minated phenol," say the Nussdorfs in *Dress for Health*. "A bromine is a corro-sive chemical element which burns and blisters the skin on contact."

Trade name: Arnel (by Celanese).

Care
Handwash or dry clean, unless label says you can machine wash.

Tricot

A thin, ribbed, knitted fabric, made from fine, soft yarn.

Trigère, Pauline

(tree-jair´, rhymes with hair) Born in Paris, this designer came to New York in 1932 and went on to become known for her loose, flowing coats with detachable scarves (Trigère for Abe Schrader coats can be found on sale for under $300 and are considered fashion classics), and for her capes, suits, and dresses in unusual tweeds. One of the first designers to be elected to the Coty Fashion Hall of Fame, she's now in her sixties and specializes in clothes flattering to older women. Her fashion signature is a turtle, found in her fabric designs, scarves, and jewelry; she even whimsically pins tiny gold turtles on skirt hems.

Tris

The most widely publicized of all flame-re-tardant additives put into fabrics. Studies have shown that Tris is absorbed through the skin and stored in vital organs. Because Tris was proven highly mutagenic and carcinogenic in studies done on animals, the Consumer Products Safety Commission banned its use in children's sleepwear. The chemical is still added to adults' pyjamas and nightgowns, and to fabrics made from synthetic fibers.

Trompe L'Oeil

(tromp l'oy) Visual deception, such as a chemise with collar, pockets, and seamlines printed on rather than sewn.

Tuck

A tiny fold sewn into a garment. Pleats are large folds; tucks are small ones and are purely decorative. They tend to add softness and femininity, and are a "dressmaker's detail" adding to the quality of a blouse or dress.

Tulle

A fine net of the sort used for bridal veils. Silk tulle, the most beautiful kind, looks as fragile as a spider web but is surprisingly strong. Nylon tulle is also lovely. Besides wedding attire, the fabric is used mostly for ballgowns with lots of sequins sewn on.

Tunic

A long, loose, shirtlike top, with or without sleeves or belt, reaching anywhere from hips to knees. An ancient style favored by comfort buffs, because it doesn't bind or constrict. A great look for hiding problem hips, flat derrieres, pot tummies. What's fashionable in tunic lengths varies a lot from year to year, so check the fashion magazines for current status.

Turtleneck Sweater

See SWEATERS.

Tweed

A fabric, usually wool, with tiny colored slubs of yarn woven in everywhere. Look for suppleness; if a tweed is so hard and scratchy it hurts your hand, don't buy. Three famous tweeds are:

Donegal The real thing is a thick tweed woven by hand in County Donegal, Ireland. Irish walking hats are made of Donegal tweed, and are amazingly water resistant for an untreated fabric.

Harris See HARRIS TWEED.

Linton An especially soft tweed made from merino wool and admired for its beautiful colors. Linton is the trade name of Linton Tweed, Ltd., of Carlisle, England, a weaver that's been in business since the nineteenth century.

Care
Since tweeds are nearly always used on crisply tailored clothes with linings, it's best to dry clean them.

Twill

A type of weave with a diagonal rib so fine it can be hard to see. Most famous twill fabrics are gabardine, khaki, denim, serge. All are good for sportswear because twills don't get baggy. Calvin Klein's cotton twill jeans for $40 are a huge bestseller.

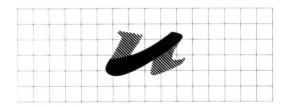

Ultrasuede

is a synthetic Japanese fabric, 60 percent polyester and 40 percent polyurethane, which is pressed, like felt. Making the fabric requires expensive equipment and high technological virtuosity, so Ultrasuede costs over twice as much as *real* suede. Europeans look down on the fabric as they do any synthetic, but it sells well in America because it can be tossed into a washing machine and tumble-dried. It can also be dry cleaned in the standard way, less expensive than cleaning real suede, which requires a special process. Ultrasuede doesn't wrinkle and travels well, can be worn year around, and is nice to touch.

Beware of cheap imitations from Southeast Asia, which tend to speedily disintegrate. They're often called ultrasuede too, but with a small "u" and no ™ symbol. The best American imitation is considered to be EnkaSuede, which is a little less expensive than the Japanese-imported original.

Umbrella

The word comes from the Latin *umbraculum*, which means a shady bower. Umbrellas have been around for several thousand years, made of silk or satin to keep out the sun, of leather to keep off rain. Everybody had one in the Orient and Middle East, but in the West only women used them until around 1860, when men began carrying them in the rain.

Umbrellas cost from $2 to $65. The $2 model is usually smaller than average and so flimsy that a breeze will bend its spokes, while the $65 model is handmade by Briggs of London, who have been in business since the early nineteenth century and are official umbrella makers for the British royal family. Briggs models are toothpick-thin and have a gold band carved with owner's initials around the handle, which is made of malacca, whangee, or ash, considered the most elegant woods for umbrella handles. One U.S. distributor of Briggs is Uncle Sam's in New York, a shop that has been selling umbrellas since 1866. They stock 1,000 different styles of umbrellas and as many walking canes, and also do custom work. John F. Kennedy's silver-handled walking sticks were from Uncle Sam, as were Teddy Roosevelt's rhino-hide umbrella handles and walking sticks, and Fred Astaire's ivory-tipped canes. For reasonable prices, you can buy canes that convert into umbrellas at the push of a button, telescopic umbrellas, and umbrellas for two—one handle but two covers. You can also buy beautiful tailored windproof umbrellas with natural wood handles for $20 to $30. For a free catalogue, write Uncle Sam, 161 West 57th Street, New York, New York 10019 (212 247-7163).

Best name in umbrellas are: Briggs of London, Fox of London, Turnbull and Asser, London Fog, Vera, and Knirps or Totes for folding umbrellas. The British have the edge in quality umbrellas. Umbrellas usually are made of nylon, which is most waterproof. Cotton, cotton/polyester, and silk are slightly less waterproof, but a lot of people are seduced by their handsome natural-fiber good looks. Most umbrellas are made with eight steel ribs, but some have up to sixteen, and the more ribs, the stronger an umbrella. A few terms to understand are:

Windproof All good umbrellas should have hangtags proclaiming that they're windproof; no other kind is worth paying over $3 for. Windproof means that in a high wind, the umbrella will still turn inside out but will quickly flip *back*—cheap, flimsy umbrellas will break and turn into mangled carcasses. If an umbrella didn't turn inside out in a strong wind, enough energy could be generated to make it into a sail—you'd either be propelled along by your umbrella, or have to let go and watch it disappear over the rooftops.

Self-opener   This means that all you have to do is press the release catch, and the umbrella top will glide open automatically. You don't have to push the top up the umbrella stick by hand.

Magic fold   Refers to the fold in a folding umbrella. The smallest folding umbrella sold is the Knirps Mini-Flat, which folds into a flat zipper case that's only eight inches long, yet opens into a normal-size umbrella. It costs $45; a similar eight-and-a-half-inch model is only $22.

Bubble   These are the umbrellas that curve way down over your face and shoulders—they're made of clear plastic so that you can see through them. Since the quality of the plastic wouldn't pass muster at any optician's, and since water tends to run down onto your back unless you hold the umbrella just so, bubbles aren't seen nearly as much as when they were a novelty a few years ago.

Golfer   An oversized umbrella. You can buy them plain or in loud stripes.

Care
Always leave a good umbrella open to dry, especially if it's cotton. Don't throw an umbrella away just because things have gone wrong—umbrella shops can easily repair broken ribs or springs, remove rust from the frame, re-cover, or replace handles. If you have a ratty-looking antique umbrella with a lovely wooden handle, you can re-cover in silk for a lot less money than you'd have to spend to buy a new silk umbrella.

Ungaro, Emanuel
(ung´-ah-row) An Italian who's become one of the biggest names in French couture and is a favorite designer of Jacqueline Kennedy Onassis. He regards de-

signing clothes as fine art, using color, prints, and texture as if he were making a collage. His combinations are daring but successful—at his last show, he got raves for a tailored plaid jacket which he combined with a red, white, and black flowered skirt and black lace top. His couture dresses cost thousands, but you can find his simply cut ready-to-wear on the designer floor of U.S. department stores such as Saks. Though you'd pay $600 or $700 for a wool-and-silk-blend dress, if you want to understand the fuss over European fabrics, this is a good place to look. He has a shop in New York at 803 Madison Avenue at 68th Street.

Union Suit
A warm, stretchy, one-piece outfit with buttons up the front and a buttoned flap on

This cherry red thermal union suit is as warm in underheated city apartments as in drafty farmhouses. (Union suit by Duofold.® Courtesy of Kreeger & Sons, New York)

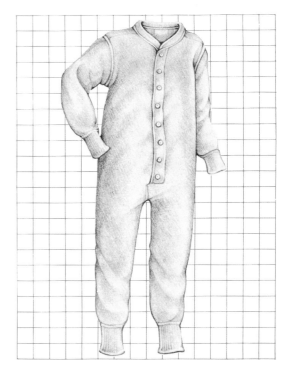

bottom, first designed as underwear for Union soldiers during the Civil War. Stores such as Sears Roebuck and Montgomery Ward's have put cotton union suits in their catalogues for a hundred years; the latest incarnation, a runaway bestseller to women, is Duofold's $26 fire-engine-red union suit. "We sell thousands of them in a season," says New York's Kreeger & Sons (catalogue available from 387 Main Street, Armonk, New York 10504). "Besides being thermal underwear, they cling in all the right places and are perfect for women to wear lounging in front of fireplaces. City folks love the poetry of these old farm clothes." Duofold's red union suit has a soft layer of cotton inside; the outer layer is a blend of cotton, wool, and nylon, and there's a microscopic air space, for insulation, between these two layers.

Care
Fully washable.

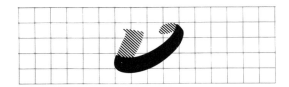

Valentino
Rome's leading couture designer, who shows in Paris and sells to every possible international socialite. Judging from the society pages, his specialty is a black strapless evening gown forming the perfect backdrop for one's jewels. American department stores carry his ready-to-wear in the usual beautiful Italian fabrics. Just after Christmas, Bloomingdale's had some of his silk blouses marked down from $480 to $119, a V-necked cardigan jacket from $680 to $169. A few Valentino classics, on sale or not, will guarantee that you'll be well-dressed in absolutely any circle in the world.

Valentino, Mario
A different Valentino, Mario is an Italian leather manufacturer known for his shoes in glove leather and his expensive but beautiful skirts, pants, and coats in suede and calfskin.

Van den Akker, Koos
An enterprising Dutch designer who came to New York in 1968 with only a portable sewing machine. He set up shop beside the fountain at Lincoln Center and took orders from passers-by, who certainly got a good deal, as now Koos clothes are collector's items and you can easily pay hundreds of dollars for an outfit. He's famous for quilt-like insets of lace and colorful prints, so delicately done that he's the only commercially successful designer whose work has been displayed at the Museum of Contemporary Crafts. You can find Koos clothes on the designer floor of many department stores, but the best selection is in his second-floor boutique at 795 Madison Avenue in New York.

Vanderbilt, Gloria
She said, "You're never fully dressed without a smile." Besides smiles, she sells jeans. Vanderbilt jeans are reputed to have the best fit on curvy women of all designer jeans; they cost up to $56 and were the first jeans to come in bright colors. That swan logo on her jeans is from a play, *The Swan*, in which Gloria made her debut as an actress at age thirty-one.

Vass, Joan
The big name in American sweaters. The quiet but exquisite $200 to $600 sweaters

that quickly won her a special Coty Award are handknit in beautiful yarns made from angora, alpaca, chenille, and the best wools. She runs her business out of a loft in New York's Chelsea area, with her forty-six knitters—ranging in age from twenty to seventy—coming to her office only to pick up yarn and a blueprint pattern and later to drop off the finished product. Vass herself has no fashion background: she graduated from the University of Wisconsin in philosophy and ended up as an assistant curator at the Museum of Modern Art. She founded her knitting business in 1972, at age forty-seven, to make a little money on the side and utilize the knitting talents of unemployed women friends.

Because they're often made from soft, fluffy yarns, Vass sweaters tend to pill and get tiny fuzzballs. These can be brushed off with a soft-bristled clothes brush.

Velour

(val-lure) A plushy, velvety knit or woven fabric that may be made from cotton or rayon (most comfortable) or from synthetics such as triacetate. Thick, short, cut loops of fiber produce the plushiness. Velours are machine washable and are being used for everything from evening skirts to running suits. Unfortunately, all velvety fabrics reflect the light and make the wearer look larger than she is.

Velvet

A soft, heavenly smooth fabric with a short, dense plush on one side (softer and smoother than velour). Silk velvet is an ancient luxury imported from the Orient, and was the favorite fabric of Renaissance Italy. Silk velvet is still the most beautiful variety, though today you find it mostly in antique shops or couture clothes. Most velvets are made from rayon (Ralph Lauren's choice for his black Victorian dresses)

and from cotton, nylon, triacetate, and polyester. According to the Neighborhood Cleaners Association, acetate is least serviceable.

Care
Dry clean. Velvets, especially acetate velvets, should never be dabbed at with water or a stain remover that contains water—even the slightest rubbing can cause matting. However, for the first time in several decades, American cotton mills are making velvet, and cotton velvet is washable.

Velveteen

is a lightweight velvet, traditionally made from cotton. Velvet is worn only in fall and winter, velveteen all year. Most velvety collars on suits and coats are made from velveteen. The fabric launders well.

Versace, Gianni

(ver-sash) Milanese designer, somewhat more daring than the other Italians. "You can't have really marvelous fashion by playing it safe," he says. He's best known for his exotic layered clothes—he might have a dress with a pantleg covered by a long skirt on one side, while the other leg will be bare.

Vest

A terrific look for the broad-shouldered because of all the up-and-down lines. Boxy vests—not fitted, body-hugging vests—are also flattering to those who are short, heavy, or thick-waisted. Vests are unconstricting and comfortable, providing a removable layer when you're unsure what temperature is awaiting you.

Victoria's Secret

is probably the most successful lingerie boutique in the world. "I'm not out just to sell merchandise," says proprietor Roy Raymond, thirty-two. "I offer a romantic atmosphere where both women *and* men can buy women's lingerie and consider the experience a pleasurable one." The idea for the business came to Raymond, who has a master's degree in marketing from Stanford, when he wanted to buy his wife some pretty lingerie for a present, and was humiliated and intimidated by the saleswomen in a regular department store. He opened the first boutique in 1977 in Palo Alto in a store with plenty of friendly salesclerks, lots of stained glass, and Victorian moldings, and with his satin peignoirs, silk teddys, bias-cut nightgowns, and can-can-style ruffled garter belts strewn around antique armoires rather than hung on stainless steel racks. He also designed a titillating, romantic twenty-four-page color catalogue featuring his lingerie, for which he charges $3. "I thought it would be easier for men to buy these things for their girlfriends if they could first actually see the clothes on another woman," says Raymond. As to the unapologetic sensuality of the catalogue, "I wanted to put fantasy back into lingerie." Today he prints over 90,000 copies of his catalogue, featuring work of the world's best lingerie designers. Prices range from $9 for LeBourget seamed stockings to $12 for a silk G-string with hand-cut lace to $280 for a silk robe with hand-painted designs copied from an antique Chinese screen. Though the boutique specializes in silk and satin, you can also get soft, pure cotton lingerie imported from Italy and Germany, and the Queen Anne's Lace white cotton gown with its tiny tucks and pink drawstring ($40) has to be one of the most irresistible gowns ever.

Stop in at the San Francisco, Palo Alto, or Cupertino stores or send $3 for a catalogue to: Victoria's Secret, Dept. PF-80, P.O. Box 31442, San Francisco, California 94131.

Vicuña

(vi-koon´-ya) is the aristocrat of animal-hair fibers—its fleece is twice as fine as the finest merino wool fiber and makes a deep, rich, faun-colored cloth used for jackets and coats selling for around $2,000. To buy a vicuña product is to perpetrate an ecological outrage—because vicuñas refuse to be domesticated, they have to be killed to get their fleece. A dozen animals to make a single yard of cloth, forty to make a coat. As late as the 1940s, vicuñas, which are a form of camel and live only in the mountain peaks of southern Peru, numbered approximately 400,000. During the 1950s and 1960s people discovered how soft and luxurious the animal's fleece and skin was, and by 1970 its population had dropped to less than 15,000. Moral: If you see vicuña cloth being sold, don't buy.

Viscose

Another name for rayon. See RAYON.

Viyella

A 55-percent wool, 45-percent cotton blend with the warmth of wool and softness of cotton. The fabric isn't at all scratchy, as wool sometimes tends to be; it has a lovely feel and texture, and can be washed. Shirts, lightweight suits, dresses, jackets, and bathrobes are made from viyella, which isn't expensive—a viyella shirt costs around $35. When "Viyella" has a capital V and a TM after it, that's the original, authentic Viyella made by William Hollins & Co. of England.

Voile

(voyl-ul) A thin, plainly woven, semitransparent fabric made from cotton, wool, silk, or synthetics. Indian drawstring blouses are often made from voile, but it can also be a luxury fabric: Christian Dior makes a beautiful flower-printed robe of pale blue cotton voile for $125.

Vollbracht, Michaele

(vol´-brack) American designer known for his bold, handscreened silk evening outfits which are big favorites among actresses and other women who aren't afraid of a little drama. There's something deliciously evil about a Vollbracht dress ... *dangerous*, definitely not understated, simple, sweet, tastefully refined, or soft. His dramatic dresses and flowing separates can be found at Saks and other stores for $1,000 to $5,000. Vollbracht, thirty-two, won the 1980 Coty Award.

Von Furstenberg, Diane

Many people who are vague about designers associate her with haute couture, but actually Princess von Furstenberg markets moderately priced dresses (as low as $40 on sale). She made an overnight $30 million in the early 1970s on her soft cotton-knit wrap dress with a provocatively cut neckline; the genius of this dress was that it clung suggestively to the body, somehow making women who were distinctly overweight look buxom and sexy.

Diane's specialty is still the sexy, slinky dress. "Women want to feel sensuous things against their skin—a silk dress, a soft nightgown," she says. Her silk dresses are especially handsome—the silk is lustrous and liquid, they fall gracefully and are designed to be worn year-round.

If you're thin, low-cut DVF dresses aren't becoming—you may look as though you're dressing up in your mother's clothes. If you're bosomy, von Furstenberg dresses are particularly effective for

One of the most clever designs of all time, Diane Von Furstenberg's wrap dress manages to make women who are fifteen pounds too heavy look buxom instead of overweight.

dinner dates with men—the neckline is ladylike but low.

As might be expected, the designer of slinky *femme fatale* dresses is a slinky *femme fatale* herself. A pale thirty-four-year-old beauty with dark, burning eyes and wild gypsy hair, she's actually a nice, middle-class Belgian girl who happened to captivate a genuine German prince, Egon von Furstenberg. For six years, the beautiful, rich von Furstenbergs were the darlings of the jet set's Beautiful People. Then their marriage broke up. Now, he designs men's clothes, and she works ten to twelve hours a day for her company.

Vuitton, Louis

(vwee-ton) French designer. Vuitton luggage is the most status-ridden luggage in the world, and some of the *cachet* has seeped over into Vuitton handbags. In spite of the vogue for natural fibers—Vuitton uses vinyl-covered canvas—the "satchel bag" is a true classic, as it has sold

This Vuitton "Satchel bag" has probably been the best-selling, most status-laden vinyl handbag in history. (Courtesy of Saks Fifth Avenue)

phenomenally for twenty years. So prevalent is the bag and its imitators that the dark brown vinyl strewn with tiny flowers and the initials LV in yellow are instantly recognizable. Vuitton satchel bags come in ten-inch to six-inch sizes, and cost $235–$275.

The Vuitton family has been in business since the 1850s, when they were appointed to make luggage for the Empress Eugénie, wife of Napoleon III.

Find them at Saks and other good stores or visit the Vuitton boutique in New York at 51 East 57th Street.

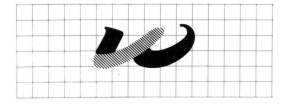

Wellington Boot

The military boot worn by Napoleon in the nineteenth century and by fashionable women in the twentieth, who tuck skinny pants into them. They're low-heeled, heavy black leather with a square cut out of the top in back.

Winter, Mrs. H.

An American designer, Harriet Winter got started in fashion when she and her husband opened a shop dealing in antique clothes, and she began experimenting with sewing new styles based on her 1930s and 1940s wares. Selling under the label "Yesterday's News," she's gone on to become one of New York's most original designers of feminine, romantic clothes. Mrs. H. Winter is known for disdaining hems, using pinking shears instead around skirt and jacket bottoms. She made her name doing clingy evening clothes, but lately she's been getting most attention for her unusual suits and coats, such as her fringed, ankle-length suits made from wool plaid blankets. You can find her lovely clothes for $200 or $300.

PURE WOOL ®

The sewn-in Woolmark label is your assurance of quality-tested fabrics made of the world's best...Pure Wool.

Wool

If a scientist had developed wool fiber in a test tube, she probably would have gotten a Nobel Prize and become rich and celebrated. In real life, nobody has even come close to duplicating the microscopic engineering genius of wool. Like human hair, wool grows from follicles in the skin of sheep and is basically a protein. Unlike human hair, sheep hairs grow with a pronounced crimp, like a coiled spring; this gives fibers incredible elasticity and resilience and is why wool yarn can be bent and twisted over and over without breaking. This crimp also creates millions of tiny air pockets throughout wool, providing warmth which works on the same principle as the best home insulation—up to 80 percent of the density of a wool fabric or sweater is entrapped air. Also unlike human hair, each wool fiber consists of a complex outer layer and an absorbent core. Cells of the outer layer act like tiny roof shingles, which is what causes liquid to bead and roll off the surface of wool. While this outer layer can repel moderate rains or a spilled glass of wine, wool absorbs moisture *vapor*, such as perspiration, *over*

the shinglelike cells. Because fiber cores are always "thirsty," wool can absorb up to 30 percent of its own weight in moisture, yet remain comfortable because its outer surface is releasing this moisture to evaporate into the air. These two characteristics, so cleverly given only to sheep hair by nature, are responsible for the many wonderful qualities of wool. In addition to its warmth, "breathing" ability, and rain-shedding, good qualities are:

- *Wool doesn't wrinkle*   at least not for long. Because of each fiber's built-in tendency to spring back to its original shape, most wrinkles in wool will disappear after the garment has been aired for a day or so.

- *It resists tearing*   Wool fiber can be stretched as much as 40 percent beyond normal length before it snaps. This durability also extends to snagging. When most fabrics catch on something sharp, the ensuing pucker is called a snag, and has arrived permanently. With wool, snags can be made to disappear simply by sponging and pressing. (Wool is the weakest fiber only when wet, which is why it is so prone to stretching at that time.)

- *It's flame retardant*   Because wool cells absorb water vapor from the air, each fiber contains enough moisture to make wool naturally flame resistant. This is why anybody whose clothes have caught on fire is wrapped in a wool blanket, and why blankets are used to beat out flames.

- *It resists dirt*   Since wool (like other natural fibers) absorbs moisture from the air, it has no dry friction to build up the static electricity that attracts greasy dust like a magnet. Also, that shinglelike structure of wool fiber keeps dirt on the surface, where it can be brushed off. When washed or dry cleaned, smudges come out without a struggle.

- *It is easily altered* If you put on ten pounds, stitchmarks from let-out seams steam right out, and new seams will lie flat. If you let a skirt down, you won't have a hemline mark.

In short, wool is a terrific fabric. If wool could be acquired only from some rare and exotic source, undoubtedly it would be more valuable and sought after than mink and gold. Fortunately sheep are docile, sturdy animals with an agreeable habit of flocking together so predictably that one shepherd and a few dogs can easily look after dozens of them. Unlike the kashmir goat, alpaca, vicuña, and mohair goat, sheep will reproduce in any reasonable circumstances. Wherever the Roman armies went, vast herds of sheep followed. Christopher Columbus had some on board on his second trip to the New World, and when Hannibal crossed the Alps, sheep were his walking food supply. The history of wool is inextricably tied to the history of Western civilization and, more than gold or jewels, the whereabouts of the cute, woolly creatures known as sheep have toppled empires and dethroned kings. . . .

How Sheep Got to Us

Nobody knows who first sheared sheep and figured out how to spin the fleece into wool, but archeologists do know that wool cloth was being used in the late Stone Age. Wool was worn in Babylon in 4000 B.C. and in England during the Bronze Age (3000 B.C.), and a pair of knitted wool socks was discovered perfectly preserved in an Egyptian tomb dating from the fourth century B.C. The Greeks, Persians, and Romans all experimented with cross-breeding sheep, and the Romans, who brought Western sheep to Spain for breeding with Asian sheep, succeeded in producing the merino, which has produced the softest and most desirable wool ever since. So important were merino sheep that the wealth of the Spanish empire was built on revenues from its fleece, and the penalty for illegal traffic in merinos was death. (The Spanish failed in keeping merinos to themselves—everyone had them by the seventeenth century, and the Spanish empire had no funds with which to recover from the Spanish Armada debacle at the hands of Sir Francis Drake.)

Meanwhile, England had not only developed many good, serviceable strains of sheep, but the English had also designed the world's most efficient machinery for manufacturing fabric from wool. To increase the supply of raw wool, England colonized South Africa, Australia, and New Zealand, and these countries, which turn out wool by the ton, became loyal members of the British Commonwealth. The American colonies, too, were raising sheep, but *they* were manufacturing wool in competition with England. When the British tried to suppress American wool production, this conflict of interest became one of the causes of the American Revolution. Today Australia is the giant of sheep-growing countries, producing 30 percent of the world's wool, most of it merino. New Zealand is next biggest, followed by South Africa, Uruguay, and Argentina. The U.S. produces less than 5 percent of the planet's wool.

Shopping for Wool

Labels give you few clues to quality of wool. You must rely on your own senses of sight and touch: better wools are soft and lustrous, and colors have depth to them. Inferior wool is scratchy, brittle, and dull, and colors aren't as pretty as those on acrylics. Skirts will wrinkle and *stay* wrinkled if you squeeze them with your hand. One guarantee of good quality is the Woolmark label, which is used by 11,500 manufacturers in thirty-seven countries. This logo assures you that the goods meet high standards for shrink and wrinkle resistance, colorfastness, and handsome appearance. If you're looking at wools by top designers such as St. Laurent or Valentino, however, you probably won't see a Woolmark label because these designers feel their name is a guarantee of the most superb fabrics. A few terms you may run into in connection with wool are:

Virgin wool   This is wool that has been manufactured into fabric for the first time.

Reprocessed wool   is wool that's been manufactured from fabric that was never used for clothes, such as cutting-table scraps, samples, and mill ends. A coarse but sturdy fabric.

Reused wool   is made from rags, old clothes, and other used wool products. It's cleaned and usually blended with some new wool to add strength. Inexpensive and a thick, warm wool for outdoorwear. Many Navy pea jackets are made from reused wool.

Botany Bay wool   is Australia's finest merino wool.

Icelandic wool   Icelandic sheep, roaming their damp volcanic island for 1,100 years, have evolved a fleece especially rich in lanolin, thus highly water repellent. While most countries concentrate on producing only white wool that's easily dyed, Icelandic wool comes in particularly lovely, natural earthtones of charcoal, gray, and white. For a catalogue of Icelandic wool products, write Landau, 114 Nassau Street, P.O. Box 671, Princeton, New Jersey 08540.

Laine   Means wool in French.

Melton   A dull and nonlustrous but long-wearing wool of English derivation.

Ohio wool   America's best merino wool.

Saxony wool   Germany's best merino wool.

Silesian wool   Austria's best merino wool.

Rambouillet   France's best merino wool.

Care

What's most important to remember about smoothly woven wools is that when you want to get wrinkles out fast, you should never iron with a dry iron because it will dry out the wool fibers and make them brittle. For the same reason, a wet wool coat or skirt should be hung to dry far away from radiators, fireplaces, or other direct heat. The best method of getting wrinkles out of wool, if you don't have time to let them fall out naturally, is to steam with a Wrinkles Away (see p. 40). Wool is rejuvenated by steam. Next best is to place the garment right side up on the ironing board, set the steam-iron control on "wool," and, holding the iron an inch above the fabric, steam back and forth over wrinkles. If wrinkles remain, repeat the process on the wrong side. If you only have a dry iron, put a

---

From the Outback to Macy's

Sheep are sheared once a year, in late spring. Professional shearers make a lot of money and can do up to 200 sheep a day, working with motor-driven shears that look like large barber's clippers. The animals are never killed for their wool. After shearing, the raw or "grease" wool is sorted, scoured, carded, spun, and woven into yarn. "Worsted" yarns (the process originated in Worstead, England) are made from combed, better-grade fibers destined for tightly woven, smooth fabrics such as gabardines, crêpes, challis, and serges. "Woolen" yarns are made from fibers that are softer, fluffier, and more loosely twisted than worsted. Knitted sweaters, tweeds, and meltons are examples of this bulkier type of yarn.

---

dampened press cloth, several thicknesses of dampened cheesecloth, or a damp linen napkin over the fabric and press by lowering and lifting the iron rather than sliding it across the fabric surface. The dampened press cloth will produce steam when heat is applied. For knife-edge pleats, fold damp pressing cloth over the creased edge, then steam press.

Tailored skirts, jackets, and pants are usually best dry cleaned, unless the label tells you washing is all right, in which case follow the care label. To remove lint, using Scotch tape is always effective. Lint rollers work well, but unless you have a drawer just for the lint roller, everything ends up glued on. A damp sponge works well, especially on fine wools, and brushing with a soft but firm clothes brush is marvelous: it fluffs the nap, gets rid of light lint.

When washing knitted wools, turn wrong side out. Dissolve Woolite or Ivory Snow in hot water first, and then add cold water to make it lukewarm. (Never, never wash wool in hot water; this and only this is what shrinks it.) Add clothes, submerge them completely, and let soak from five minutes to half an hour before kneading and squeezing gently through suds. Never rub hard at spots—you'll fray fibers. Rinse two or three times. Add about a third of a cup white distilled vinegar to rinse water, swish garment around, and then rinse again until all vinegar smell is gone (it disappears immediately, taking dulling soap with it). Compress garment against side of basin until excess moisture is removed, roll it in a towel, pat, and *dry flat*. If you hang it over the side of the tub, no matter how gently rounded, arms stretch and bodices end up longer and narrower than they were. (See SWEATERS, Care.)

Storing

As nearly everyone has been dismayed to discover, moths like to dine on woolens. For some reason, the cleaner your wool, the less likely moths are to attack, so if you're not going to wear wools for awhile, clean before you store. A cedar chest, a drawer with cedar chips, or a sealed garment bag is best. According to *Dress for Health*, mothproofing compounds should be avoided because they contain allergenic and carcinogenic substances such as benzene.

Woolworth Shoe

A lightweight cotton canvas sandal with a sponge-rubber sole, this shoe has been selling at Woolworth's since the 1930s. Also

The Woolworth shoe, which has been selling for nearly fifty years, **still** costs under $10. (Photo: Herb Dorfman)

called a "landlady shoe," the style is ensconced in the permanent costume collection of the Metropolitan Museum of Art in the company of clothes designed by Mainbocher and Erté. The sandal comes in navy, black, white, beige, red, or paisley, and can be worn bare in summer, with stockings in spring and fall. "We've easily sold thirty million," says Woolworth's shoe buyer.

Find these comfortable sandals, highly favored by models, in any Woolworth's store in spring and summer for $6.

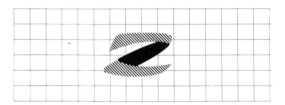

Zippers

tell you whether clothes are well-made or not. If a skirt even *has* a zipper, that adds quality, as sewing in a zipper these days means more money spent on the assembly-line process. Many manufacturers happily cut costs by using buttons or snaps. Zippers should always be entirely concealed in the seam, and be the same color as the skirt fabric. *If you can see the zipper, it's a poorly made skirt.*

Care
Always close zippers before laundering.

Selected Bibliography

Books:

Anspach, Karlyne Alice. *The Why of Fashion*. Ames, Iowa: Iowa State University Press, 1968.

Cho, Emily. *Looking Terrific*. New York: Ballantine Books, 1978.

Cudlipp, Edythe. *Furs: An Appreciation of Luxury, a Guide to Value*. New York: Hawthorn Books, 1978.

Editors of *American Fabrics and Fashions Magazine*. *New Encyclopedia of Textiles*. Englewood Cliffs, N.J.: Prentice-Hall, 1980.

Goday, Dale. *Dressing Thin*. New York: Simon and Schuster, 1979.

Kleeberg, Irene Cumming. *The Butterick Fabric Handbook*. New York: Butterick Publishing, 1975.

Lambert, Eleanor. *The World of Fashion: People, Places, Resources*. New York: R. R. Bowker, 1976.

Linton, George E. *The Modern Textile & Apparel Dictionary*. Plainfield, N.J.: Textile Book Service, 1973.

Louie, Elaine. *Manhattan Clothes Shopping Guide*. New York: Collier Books, 1978.

Molloy, John T. *The Woman's Dress for Success Book*. Chicago, Ill.: Follett Books, 1977.

Nussdorf, Maggie Rollo and Stephen B. *Dress for Health*. Harrisburg, Pa.: Stackpole Books, 1980.

Pierre, Clara. *Looking Good: The Liberation of Fashion*. New York: Reader's Digest Press, 1976.

Wilcox, R. Turner. *The Dictionary of Costume*. New York: Scribners, 1969.

Additional Sources:

The American Apparel Manufacturers Association, National Fabricare Institute, Neighborhood Cleaners Association, Man-Made Fiber Producers Association, National Handbag Association, Millinery Institute, Belgian Linen Association, Irish Import Board, British Trade Board, The Mohair Council, Fur Information and Fashion Council, Feather and Down Association, The Fashion Institute of Technology, and *The New York Times* fashion reporting of Bernadine Morris and Carrie Donovan.

Product Name Identifications and Permissions

The following listing serves to identify the various products, processes, and companies mentioned in this encyclo-pedia, and their trademark, registered trademark, copyright, and certification status. The author gratefully ac-knowledges the assistance of all those who helped to gather and check the following information, and regrets any possible errors or omissions.

CODE:

© =   Copyright.   ® = Registered Trademark.
™ = Trademark.   * = Certification Mark.

A-OK™ is a trademark of Flexnit® Company.
A & P® All Fabric Bleach is a product of The Great Atlantic and Pacific Tea Company, Inc. A & P® is a registered trademark.
Abercrombie & Fitch® is a registered trademark of Oshman's Sporting Goods Inc.
Acele® is a registered trademark of E.I. du Pont de Nemours and Co.
Acrilan® is a registered trademark of Monsanto Company.
Actionwear® is a registered trademark of Monsanto Company.
Afta® is a registered trademark of Afta Chemical Corp.
L'Air de Temps is a product of Nina Ricci Parfums.
Antron® and Antron III® are registered trademarks of E.I. du Pont de Nemours and Co.
Arnel® is a registered trademark of the Celanese Corporation.
Avril® is a registered trademark of FMC Corp.
Avron® is a registered trademark of FMC Corp.
Axion® is a registered trademark of Colgate-Palmolive Company.
Ballantyne® is a registered trademark of Ballantyne of Scotland.
Ban-Lon® is a registered trademark of Banlon Marketing Corp., a division of Garan, Inc.
Bass®; Bass Weejuns®; Bass Flying Boot®; Bass National Plow Shoe®; and Bass Sunjuns® are registered trademarks of G.H. Bass and Co., a division of Chesebrough-Pond's Inc.
Beene Bag® is a registered trademark of Geoffrey Beene Inc.
Betmar® is a registered trademark of Betmar Hats Inc.
Birkenstock is a product of Impressionistic Shoes Inc.
Biz® is a registered trademark of Procter & Gamble Co.
Black Orchid™ is a trademark of Christian Dior Lingerie.
Blackglama® is a registered trademark of the Great Lakes Mink Association (GLMA).
Blassport® is a registered trademark of Bill Blass, Inc.
Borateem Plus® is a registered trademark of the United States Borax and Chemical Corp.
Borg-Animal® is a registered trademark of Borg Textile Corporation.
Boston Traders® is a registered trademark of Boston Traders, a division of Boston Trading Ltd. Inc.
Brooks Brothers®, Brooksflannel® are registered trademarks of Brooks Brothers, a division of Garfinkel Brooks Brothers, Miller & Rhoads Inc.
Burberry's® is a registered trademark of Burberry's International Ltd.
Cacharel® is a registered trademark of Cacharel USA Inc.
Capezio® is a registered trademark of Capezio Ballet Makers, a division of United States Shoe Corp.
Carbona® is a registered trademark of Carbona Products Co.
Chanel No. 5® is a registered trademark of Chanel Inc.
Chinon® is a registered trademark of Toyobo Co., Ltd.
Chloé® by Karl Lagerfeld is a registered trademark of Goldin Feldman, Inc.
Ciao® is a registered trademark of Ciao Ltd.

Clorox®, Clorox 2® are registered trademarks of The Clorox Company.

Cloudhoppers is a product of Oomphies®, Inc., a division of U.S. Industries, Inc.

Coach® is a registered trademark of Coach Leatherware Company, Inc.

Coloray® is a registered trademark of Courtaulds North America Inc.

Cord-Set® is a registered trademark of The Sanforized Company, a division of Cluett, Peabody & Co., Inc.

Creslan® is a registered trademark of American Cynamid Company.

Cuddleskin® is a registered trademark of The Barbizon Corporation.

Cupioni® is a registered trademark of Beaunit Corp.

Cupro® is a registered trademark of Bemberg Industries.

Dacron® is a registered trademark of E.I. du Pont de Nemours and Co.

Danskin® is a registered trademark of Danskin, Inc., a division of Esmark Inc.

Dial® is a registered trademark of Armour-Dial, Inc., a division of Greyhound Corp.

Diminish® is a registered trademark of Carnival.

Dixie Bell® is a registered trademark of Dixie Bell Textiles, Inc.

dddominick® is a registered trademark of Dominick Avellino.

Duofold® is a registered trademark of Duofold, Inc., a division of Cluett, Peabody & Co. Inc.

Dynel® is a registered trademark of Union Carbide Corporation.

Echo Scarfs® is a registered trademark of Echo Scarfs Inc.

Elura® is a registered trademark of Monsanto Company.

EMBA®, EMBA Natural Lutetia® Mink, EMBA Lunaraine®, and EMBA Tourmaline® natural pale beige are registered trademarks of Emba Mink Breeders Association.

Encron®, Enka®, and EnkaSuede® are registered trademarks of American Enka Company.

Estron® is a registered trademark of Eastman Kodak Company.

Eveready® is a registered trademark of Union Carbide Consumer Products Co., a division of Union Carbide Corp.

Fendi® is a registered trademark of Fendi.

Fiberfill® is a registered trademark of E.I. du Pont de Nemours and Co.

Folkwear® is a registered trademark of Folkwear.

Fortrel® is a registered trademark of Fiber Industries, Inc., a subsidiary of Celanese Corporation.

Frankly Feminine® is a registered trademark of Vassarette Division of Munsingwear, Inc.

Fruit-of-the-Loom® is a registered trademark of Fruit-of-the-Loom, a subsidiary of Northwest Industries, Inc., a division of Gulf + Western Industries, Inc.

Frye® is a registered trademark of John A. Frye Shoe Company, a subsidiary of Alberto-Culver Co.

GallenKamp® is a registered trademark of SCOA Industries Inc.

Glossies® is a registered trademark of Lily of France, Incorporated. Lily of France® is a registered trademark.

Glospan is a trade name of Globe Manufacturing Co.

Gore-Tex® is a trademark of W.L. Gore & Associates, Inc.

Harris® Tweed is a registered trademark applicable only to Handwoven Harris tweed, spun, woven Outer Hebrides, Scot.

Haymaker® for Women is a registered trademark of David Crystal® Co., a division of General Mills Inc.

Helly-Hansens® is a registered trademark.

Herman Survivor is a product of Herman's World of Sporting Goods, a division of W.R. Grace & Co.

Hermès® is a registered trademark of Hermès.

Hot Sox® is a registered trademark of Hot Sox Co. Inc.

Impressions is a product of Oomphies®, Inc., a division of U.S. Industries, Inc.

Ivory Snow® is a registered trademark of Procter & Gamble Co.

Izod®, Izod for Men®, and Izod for Her® are registered trademarks of David Crystal® Co., a division of General Mills Inc.

Jaeger® of London is a registered trademark of Jaeger Sportswear Ltd.

Jordache® is a registered trademark of Jordache Enterprises, Inc.

Joy® is a registered trademark of Procter & Gamble Co.

Justin of Forth Worth® is a registered trademark of Justin of Forth Worth.

Jetspun® is a registered trademark of American Enka Company.

Anne Klein© is copyrighted by Anne Klein and Company.

Kleenex® is a registered trademark of Kimberly-Clark Corporation.

Knirps® is a registered trademark of Knirps International Ltd.

Kodel® is a registered trademark of Eastman Kodak Company.

Kreeger® is a registered trademark of Kreeger and Sons, Ltd.

Lacoste® is a registered trademark of David Crystal® Co., a division of General Mills Inc.

Lady Arrow® is a registered trademark of Arrow Company, a division of Cluett, Peabody and Co., Inc.

Lectra Sox is a product of Big 3 International.
Lee Riders® is a registered trademark of The Lee Company.
Les Must® de Cartier is a registered trademark of Cartier Inc.
Levi's® is a registered trademark of Levi Strauss & Co.
Lexol® is a registered trademark of Corona Products Co.
L.F. Petites is a product of Leslie Fay, Inc.
Light 'N Easy® is a registered trademark of General Electric Company.
Lirelle is a product of Courtaulds North America Inc.
L.L. Bean® is a registered trademark of L.L. Bean Inc.
London Fog® is a registered trademark of London Fog, a division of Interco Inc.
Loré is a trade name of Loré Lingerie, Inc.
Lucchese is a product of Blue Bell, Inc.
Lucite® is a registered trademark of E.I. du Pont de Nemours and Co.
Lurex® is a registered trademark of Dow Badische Co.
Lux® is a registered trademark of Lever Brothers Company.
Lycra® is a registered trademark of E.I. du Pont de Nemours and Co.
Majestic® is a registered trademark of Canadian Majestic.
Maine Hunting Shoe® is a registered trademark of L.L. Bean Inc.
Mark Cross® is a registered trademark of Mark Cross Inc.
Meltonian®, Meltonian Water and Stain Protector® are registered trademarks of Meltonian Wren Ltd.
Milliskin® is a registered trademark of E.I. du Pont de Nemours and Co.
Miracle White® is a registered trademark of Bristol Myers Co.
Misty Harbor® is a registered trademark of Jonathan Logan Inc.
Naked® is a registered trademark of Formfit Rogers, Inc.
Naturalizers ™ is a trademark of Brown Group Inc.
Albert Nipon® is a registered trademark of Albert Nipon, Inc.
No Exaggeration® is a registered trademark of Formfit Rogers, Inc.
Nocona® is a registered trademark of The Nocona Boot Co. Inc.
Nomelle* is a certification mark of E.I. du Pont de Nemours and Co.
Norka® is a registered trademark.
Numa is a product of American Cyanamid Co.
Old Maine Trotters ™ is a trademark of Penobscot Shoe Co.
Oomphies® is a registered trademark of Oomphies, Inc., a division of U.S. Industries, Inc.
Orlon® is a registered trademark of E.I. du Pont de Nemours and Co.
Outlander® is a registered trademark of Outlander Ltd., a division of Leslie Fay Inc.
Palladium ™ is a trademark.
Pendleton® is a registered trademark of Pendleton Woolen Mills.
Poly Tex® is a registered trademark of Purex Corporation.
Princess Sumi is a trade name of Don Sophisticates, Inc.
Q-Tips® is a registered trademark of Chesebrough-Pond's Inc.
Qiana* is a certification mark of E.I. du Pont de Nemours and Co.
Rawsilque® is a registered trademark of Collins & Aikman Corporation.
Rive Gauche and Saint Laurent Rive Gauche are trade names of Yves St. Laurent.
Rolex® is a registered trademark of Rolex Watch U.S.A., Inc.
Round-The-Clock® is a registered trademark of Esmark Inc.
Running Bra® is a registered trademark of Formfit Rogers, Inc.
SAGA® is a registered trademark of Saga Furs of Scandinavia, Inc.
Sanfor-Set®, Sanforized® are registered trademarks of The Sanforized Company, a division of Cluett, Peabody
    and Co., Inc.
Santora® is a registered trademark of Klopman Mills Division of Burlington Industries Inc.
The Santos Collection is a trade name of Cartier, Inc.
Sasson® is a registered trademark of Sasson Jeans Inc.
Scholl's Exercise Sandals® is a registered trademark of Scholl, Inc.
Scotchgard®, Scotchlite® are registered trademarks of 3M.
Shevelva is a product of Vanity Fair Mills, Inc., a division of VF Corporation.
Shout ™ is a trademark of S.C. Johnson & Son, Inc.
Sierra Designs® is a registered trademark of Sierra Designs, Inc.
Simplicity® is a registered trademark of Simplicity Pattern Co. Inc.
60/40 Mountain Parka® is a registered trademark of Sierra Designs, Inc.

Snowy® Liquid is a registered trademark of Gold Seal Company.
Spray 'n Wash® is a registered trademark of Texize, Division of Morton-Norwich Products Inc.
Sweet Nothings® is a registered trademark of Maidenform Inc.; Maidenform® is a registered trademark.
Spandelle® is a registered trademark.
Taslan™ is a trademark.
Thinsulate® is a registered trademark of 3M.
Timberland® is a registered trademark of The Timberland Company.
Tally-Ho™ is a trademark of Tally-Ho Division of Henry Pollak Inc.
Tony Lama of El Paso® is a registered trademark of Tony Lama Co. Inc.
Top-Siders® is a registered trademark of Sperry Top-Sider, a division of Stride Rite Corp.
Totes® is a registered trademark, ©Totes, Inc.
Trevira® is a registered trademark of Hoechst Fibers Inc.
Turnbull & Asser™ is a trademark.
Tuftees® is a registered trademark of Crowntuft Mfg. Corp.
Ultrasuede® is a registered trademark of Skinner Fabrics Division of Springs Mills Inc. Skinner® is a registered trademark.
Underglows® is a registered trademark of Vanity Fair Mills, Inc., a division of VF Corporation.
Vera is a trade name of Vera Industries Inc.
Verel® is a registered trademark of Eastman Chemical Products, Inc., a subsidiary of Eastman Kodak Company.
Viyella™ is a trademark of William Hollins and Co.
Vyrene™ is a trademark of Uniroyal Inc.
White King® is a registered trademark of White King Inc.
White Magic® is a registered trademark of Safeway Stores Inc.
Wigwam®, Wigwam Ragg Wool® are registered trademarks of Wigwam Mills Inc.
Williwear is a trade name of Willi Smith Ltd.
Woolite® is a registered trademark of Boyle-Midway, Inc., a division of American Home Products Corp.
Woolmark® is a registered trademark of The Wool Bureau, Inc., U.S. branch of the International Wool Secretariat.
Woolrich® is a registered trademark of Woolrich Inc.
Wrangler®, Lady Wrangler® are registered trademarks of Blue Bell, Inc.
Wrinkles Away® is a registered trademark of Franzus Co., Inc.
Wright's® Silver Cream is a registered trademark of J.A. Wright & Co.
YSL is a trade name of Yves St. Laurent.
Young Secret® is a registered trademark of Olga Company, Inc. Olga® is a registered trademark.
Zantrel® is a registered trademark of American Enka Company.
Zefran® is a registered trademark of Dow Chemical USA.
Zepel® is a registered trademark of E.I. du Pont de Nemours and Co.
Zest® is a registered trademark of Procter & Gamble Co.

INDEX